CASES AND MATERIALS ON NEGOTIATION

Second Edition

Unit Five
of
Labor Relations and Social Problems
A Course Book

LABOR RELATIONS AND SOCIAL PROBLEMS

UNIT ONE—Collective Bargaining in Private Employment

UNIT TWO—Social Legislation

UNIT THREE—Discrimination in Employment

UNIT FOUR—Collective Bargaining in Public Employment

UNIT FIVE—Cases and Materials on Negotiation

UNIT SIX—Arbitration and Conflict Resolution

UNIT R—Reference Supplement

UNIT R-2—Reference Supplement—Discrimination in Employment

CASES AND MATERIALS ON NEGOTIATION

Second Edition

Civil and Criminal Litigation
Business and Commercial Transactions
Labor Relations
Miscellaneous Disputes

Unit Five
of
Labor Relations and Social Problems
A Course Book

Prepared by

Cornelius J. Peck, Chairman, Unit Five
University of Washington

for

The Labor Law Group

The Bureau of National Affairs, Inc., Washington, D.C.

Library of Congress Cataloging in Publication Data

Peck, Cornelius J., 1923-
 Cases and materials on negotiation.

 (Labor relations and social problems; unit 5)
 Includes index.
 1. Collective bargaining—United States—Cases. I. Title. II. Series.
  KF3369.A1L26   Unit 5, 1980   344.73'01s   [344.73'018912]
 ISBN 0-87179-335-0   80-16908

Printed in the United States of America
International Standard Book Number: 0-87179-335-0

LABOR LAW GROUP

Foreword

Starting in 1971, the Labor Law Group made a sharp break from the traditional format and content of law school teaching materials in the area of labor relations and social problems.

The Group had its genesis in a paper delivered at the 1946 meeting of the Association of American Law Schools by Willard Wirtz, then a professor of law at Northwestern University. Inspired by the vision of this address, a group of law teachers obtained a grant from the Carnegie Corporation of New York. With the cooperation of the University of Michigan Law School, the group held, at Ann Arbor in June of 1947, a two-week "Conference on the Training of Law Students in Labor Relations."

After the conference, the law teachers began the preparation of teaching materials. Eventually, the materials were published in 1953 by Little, Brown and Co. under the title LABOR RELATIONS AND THE LAW. All of the preparation of the preliminary drafts and the first published edition were under the general editorship of Professor Robert E. Mathews.

The law teachers soon thereafter established a common law trust, obtained recognition of tax-exempt status, and assumed the name "Labor Law Group." The original membership was 31. Over the years some teachers have dropped out and others have become members. Altogether almost 70 persons, including some practitioners and government officials, have been members of the Group. Three of the original members—Benjamin Aaron, Donald H. Wollett, and Edwin R. Teple—are still active. All royalties from Group publications have gone into a trust fund to finance the Group's planning and editorial activities. No member of the Group has ever received personal financial remuneration.

In 1958 Professor Mathews, to whom we continue to pay honor as the foremost of our founding fathers, resigned as head of the group, and he was succeeded by Professors Benjamin Aaron and Donald H. Wollett as co-chairmen and co-editors of the second edition of LABOR RELATIONS AND THE LAW, which appeared in 1960. They in turn were succeeded by Professor Jerre Williams, who was general editor of the third edition in 1965 and Group chairman through 1967. The Group has also published EMPLOYMENT RELATIONS AND THE LAW (1957, Benjamin Aaron, Editor) and READINGS IN LABOR LAW (1955). From 1967 to 1972, Professor William P. Murphy served as chairman of the Group's Executive and Editorial Committees. He was succeeded by Professor Herbert L. Sherman, Jr., who was Group chairman from 1973 to 1977. Since January 1978, Professor James E. Jones, Jr., has served as chairman of these committees.

The Group reexamined the teaching of labor law at a one-week conference held at Boulder, Colo., in 1969. The conference was attended by law teachers, academic authorities from other disciplines, and management and labor spokesmen. As a result of this meeting and others, the Group decided to publish a series of books on LABOR RELATIONS AND SOCIAL PROBLEMS. Between 1971 and 1977 ten books, and subsequent editions of several of these books, were published by the Group.

In 1976 the Group decided to reorganize the materials for future books (starting in 1978), and to publish six books, including a substantial amount of nondoctrinal material, on the following subject matter: Collective Bargaining in Private Employment, Social Legislation, Discrimination in Employment, Collective Bargaining in Public Employment, Negotiation, and Arbitration and Conflict Resolution. Each of these books is designed so that it may be used by itself, but two or more of these books may be used in the same course or seminar.

The following characteristics distinguish this series of books from standard labor law casebooks:

1. The format of separate units (each dealing with a separate topic in the general field) in recognition of the fact that it is impossible to teach all of these subjects in one course.

2. For each subject a book which is shorter in length than a standard casebook, thus making it more practical to use in a typical course.

3. Frequent updating of units to keep abreast of a fast-changing field of law.

4. Inclusion of a separate unit on social legislation.

5. Coverage of matters not covered in standard casebooks, e.g., the art and techniques of negotiation and the myth of expertise.

6. Inclusion of material on professional responsibility and comparative law.

7. A blending of legal and nondoctrinal materials so that a greater appreciation of the "law" can be achieved.

8. Meeting of the need for materials for seminars and advanced courses.

9. Meeting of the need for legal materials in the labor-management area for use in undergraduate courses.

10. Greater flexibility for the law teacher in putting together a course or courses of the teacher's own liking.

It is our hope that these books will give students an idea of industrial relations law and practices, and also shed light on the variety of techniques which are available for the peaceful resolution of significant social disputes.

THE EDITORIAL POLICY COMMITTEE

Summary Table of Contents

Detailed Table of Contents

1. Introduction

One year of law school study should alter a student's expectation that the practice of law will consist of days spent in courtrooms subjecting adverse parties to devastating cross-examination or capturing juries with moving but carefully reasoned arguments. Nevertheless, because the study consists largely of examination of reported appellate decisions, a law student may retain the erroneous impression that the most frequently performed service of a lawyer is that of an advocate in a courtroom. The recent emphasis given to clinical education may have only reinforced the idea that litigation skills preempt all others required of an accomplished lawyer. Ability as an advocate is important, or even essential, in many aspects of the practice of law, but other important qualities of an effective lawyer have been given but slight attention in traditional legal education. It is almost as though, for purposes of comparison, an education for the practice of medicine consisted of only courses developing surgical techniques. But if attention is directed to what lawyers actually do in practice, it becomes apparent that great weight must be given to skill as a negotiator in determining what is required for the successful practice of law.

Recent empirical studies indicate that relatively few disputes are finally settled by litigation. To state the converse, most disputes are settled by negotiation. A study of automobile accident costs and payments conducted at the University of Michigan revealed the following: Lawyers were hired in 49 percent of the cases involving serious injuries. Suit was filed in 26 percent of the cases. Pretrial conferences were held in 12 percent of the cases. Trial was begun in only 5 percent of the cases. Negotiated settlements were agreed upon in a number of cases before judgment. Appeals were taken in only 2 percent of the suits filed, or less than one tenth of 1 percent of the total cases of economic loss. Nor did the 5 percent of the cases which went to trial have a much greater economic significance than those settled at an earlier stage. They involved only 6 percent of the aggregate payments made. Conard, Morgan, Pratt, Voltz, and Bombaugh, AUTOMOBILE ACCIDENT COSTS AND PAYMENTS 184, 241-242 (1967).

Studies of automobile accidents in New York City have produced comparable data, including that only 8 percent of the claims of automobile accident victims were processed to trial; that most of those cases were settled during trial; that less than 2 percent of the claims made were directly controlled by a court adjudication; and that those cases adjudicated accounted for only 3 percent of the money which changed hands

1

in the course of settlement. Franklin, Chanin, and Mark, *Accidents, Money, and the Law: A Study of the Economics of Personal Injury Litigation,* 61 Colum. L. Rev. 1, at 10 (1961); Rosenberg and Sovern, *Delay and the Dynamics of Personal Injury Litigation,* 59 Colum. L. Rev. 1115, at 1124 (1959).

According to the National Labor Relations Board's annual report for its 1978 fiscal year, the Board issued 1,146 decisions in unfair labor practice cases, whereas 95 percent of the 32,192 unfair labor practice charges were closed by the regional offices. Twenty-five percent were settled or adjusted before an administrative law judge had issued a decision. 43 NLRB ANN. REP. 9, 18 (1978).

In its 1976 fiscal year the Federal Trade Commission issued 21 complaints in consumer protection cases, and accepted 131 consent orders which had been negotiated by its Bureau of Consumer Protection. 1976 FTC ANN. REP. 18. The Internal Revenue Service encourages the resolution of tax disputes through an administrative appeals system rather than litigation, and in the 10 years prior to 1977, 97 percent of all disputed cases were closed without trial. Since 1974 the district conference staffs, which are the first level of the appeal procedure, have had authority to settle cases, giving consideration to the hazards of litigation, where the amount of tax in dispute is $2,500 or less. In 1977 the district conference staffs reached agreement with the taxpayer in 70.5 percent of the cases; more than 70 percent of the remaining cases were settled in the appellate division, which is the second level of the appeal procedure. 1977 ANN. REP. COMM'R. INT. REV. 26-27.

In the criminal law area, negotiation is used more frequently than trial to fix the guilt of an accused. One study published in 1964 indicated that over 75 percent of prosecutors definitely engaged in plea bargaining and that less than 15 percent said they refused to engage in the negotiation process to reach an agreed-upon disposition of a case. Note, *Guilty Plea Bargaining: Compromise by Prosecutors to Secure Guilty Pleas,* 112 U. of Pa. L. Rev. 865, at 897 (1964). As will be seen, the U.S. Supreme Court has since given judicial approval to the practice, and a more recent study indicates that 99.3 percent of the criminal cases disposed of in New York City were closed by guilty pleas. H. Miller, W. McDonald, J. Cramer, PLEA BARGAINING IN THE UNITED STATES, Appendix A 32 (1978).

Lawyers become involved in the negotiation process in matters other than the settlement of disputes. Frequently they serve as negotiators or advisors to negotiators in business transactions, collective bargaining between unions and management, or in inter- and intra-governmental agencies. It is strange, then, considering the importance of negotiation in the professional activities of a lawyer, that formal legal education has devoted so little attention to developing an understanding of the negotiation process and skill in its practice. Perhaps the ready availability of appellate decisions had an undue effect upon the selection of teaching materials for law schools. Analysis of judicial opinions to determine what the law is and how it was applied by courts in particular cases has perhaps diverted attention from how the law is much more frequently used by lawyers in the vastly greater number of instances which do not involve a litigation-controlled result. Perhaps even more important has been an assumption that negotiation is an unteachable subject—that ability as a negotiator involves innate qualities which cannot be developed in formal education.

These case histories and materials are presented with the belief that there are meaningful generalizations which can be made about the negotiation process, that limits of those generalizations can be identified and appreciated, and that the knowledge and experience thus gained can be later utilized by students of law. This is not to say that there will not remain much which is innate or unteachable. However, the same can be said about music, the appreciation or practice of which can be greatly improved by study.

At the outset, however, it is important to caution that negotiation is not a single and uniform process or procedure, with fixed rules of equal force and value in the many and varied contexts and relationships which present occasions for negotiation. Quite to the contrary, the important things to learn about negotiation are the limits which exist for almost any statement which can be made about the subject. It is inaccurate to think of negotiation as a single process because the factors which work to produce or prevent agreement—the force field of a negotiation—vary in as many ways as may the details of the relationship and the external events affecting the interests of the parties. Even with what might be identified as the same type of negotiation situation, the various processes encompassed in the term cannot be adequately understood unless consideration is given to other aspects of the practice of law.

Negotiation in legal dispute settlements differs from the negotiation of business transactions in a number of ways. In dispute settlements, judicial procedures exist by which one party usually can force a determination of rights if the other party does not agree. In business transactions, there is no established machinery of compulsion. Forces of the market and the other party's uncertainty that he will be able to find an equally attractive offer are the significant forces bringing about agreement. In legal dispute settlement, discovery processes available for preparation for trial make it possible to educate the other party as to the weakness of his case and the strength of the claim or defense asserted. In business transactions, a comparable education of the bargaining opposite may be impossible, helpful as it would be to one seeking agreement.

Negotiations in business transactions vary in many ways. Obviously there are significant differences between the sale of a car or house and the sale of a large, going business. There are important differences in the force field of a single-phase transaction or exchange and negotiation of the terms of a long-term relationship, such as a lease or employment contract. In the former, a party may appropriately decide to maximize gains in every way possible despite the adverse effects upon the bargaining opposite, whereas in the latter a party may sensibly make concessions to the bargaining opposite which will enhance their relationship with a consequent benefit to both. Indeed, some provisions of a long-term agreement may be designed to be advantageous to both.

Collective bargaining involves negotiation in a still different context. There is a permanence in the relationship, since the relationship probably will endure even if agreement is not reached and the parties resort to economic weapons available to them. In most situations compulsory arbitration does not exist and there is no forum to which either party may resort to force a resolution of their dispute in the absence of agreement. From the employer's viewpoint, the concern is not that the union will be able to obtain more favorable terms for its members from other employers, but instead that it will fail to do so. In a mature bargaining relationship, both sides know that animosities engendered by a lengthy strike or lockout will survive to create difficulties with their enduring relationship, but it frequently is the credibility of a threat of strike or lockout that is the primary force bringing about agreement.

The relationship of negotiation to other aspects of the practice of law likewise varies in different negotiation situations. The primary force operating to bring about agreement short of litigation and judgment in dispute settlement usually is the belief that the other side has such a substantial chance of obtaining more or giving less in a litigated determination that it is prudent to accept its proposed terms of settlement. One does not reach such a conclusion unless he believes that the other party is represented by a lawyer who is in fact ready to litigate and competent in doing so. But competence in the courtroom may not suffice in certain dispute-settlement situations unless the lawyer is sufficiently accomplished in counseling to maintain his client's morale and will to litigate, whether the case be a claim for personal injuries or defense of a claim for additional alimony. Indeed, unless the lawyer is competent in counseling, he may win for his client in court a victory which in personal terms becomes a disaster. Brilliance in understanding of the law and a creative imagination may serve well in developing fully all facets of a matter in dispute, but they also may create a paralysis of fear for a lawyer so gifted who undertakes litigation. The same qualities may go far to enable him to do an excellent job for a client in negotiating a complete and safe agreement for a business transaction in which he may use his creative imagination to shape the terms of the agreement and thus control future contingencies.

Personal integrity of the lawyers involved may also become a factor in negotiation. Crude as it may seem, it appears that with appreciable frequency, defense offers in personal injury cases are made at a time when it appears likely that the plaintiff's attorney will need money (e.g., quarterly estimated income tax payments are due) and defense counsel believes that that need might induce plaintiff's attorney to recommend acceptance of an offer he would otherwise consider inadequate. A less than perfect handling of a case may expose a lawyer to liability for malpractice, and this might be converted into a bargaining tool and be used against his client. On the other side, a lawyer's desire to obtain the publicity and notoriety associated with recovery of a large judgment may lead him to recommend rejection of an offer of settlement which, considered only on the basis of the client's interest, would seem to be a fair appraisal of the value of the claim.

Meaningful generalizations can be made about other aspects of the negotiation process. The problem of making or obtaining the first realistic offer is a persistent one for negotiators, and techniques for dealing with it deserve careful consideration. One may generalize about the adverse effects of publicity upon negotiation, as for example where parties engaged in collective bargaining for a labor agreement rigidify their postures by publicly declaring their "minimum demands." But publicity or the threat of it may become a major bargaining tool for one of the parties in negotiation for settlement of certain disputes. Personality clashes or difficulties of communication between particular negotiating pairs may be cured by involving additional parties. Upon occasion, adverse parties may be able to reach agreement by finding a third party as to whom, at least with respect to certain issues, the adverse parties have mutual interests. A common example is that of private parties who may, by their agreement, reduce the income tax liabilities of one or both. Psychodynamics of the negotiation process create situations in which pressures may be skillfully used to produce an unsophisticated and undesirable response.

Let us turn to some commentaries and case histories of negotiation to see what meaningful generalizations can be made about the process of negotiation as practiced by the lawyers involved. In doing so, it is necessary to note that the case histories are not presented as models of the best or most effective negotiation. Indeed, what was effective negotiation on one side may have been accomplished because of the other side's failure to negotiate expertly. The case histories provide an opportunity for observing how lawyers undertook to represent their clients, for noting what things they did well and what things they did poorly, and for considering what things they might have done to improve their performance.

2. Negotiation Models

A. Dispute Settlement Through Legal Procedures: The Forces Generated in Judicial Proceedings

(1) Tort Claims Settlement

MIRACLE AND BURCH, CONTEMPORARY TECHNIQUES IN PROCESSING SMALL PERSONAL INJURY CLAIMS [1962]*

We have all heard a great deal about large settlements and large jury verdicts in personal injury actions. Lawyers achieving these outstanding results are justly proud; how they were obtained is informative and interesting to all of us. However, most lawyers handling injured persons' claims have never seen a $200,000 verdict.

The personal injury claim that can be expected to result in small or medium monetary recovery occupies most of our working hours; it represents the bulk of our files; for most of us, it represents the majority of our fees. Yet, the unspectacular case has been generally overlooked in articles discussing the handling of injured persons' claims.

This article deals exclusively with those injuries that might be expected to bring anywhere from a few hundred dollars to about $15,000. What is said, however, is also generally true of those actions involving more seriously injured clients.

. . .

THE INITIAL CONTACT

Telephone information alone is unsatisfactory. We ask all new clients to make a personal appointment and to bring all available information. One lawyer then interviews the client, recording all relevant information on a dictating machine. Ordinarily, at this time we decide whether or not to undertake the case. If there is an unusual feature to the case or facts are unclear, this decision might be postponed.

At this first interview we have our new client sign two forms. One is our standard fee agreement, providing that our fee is to be one-third of the total recovery. After subtraction of the one-third fee, it is provided that costs, which we are to advance, are to be subtracted and the client is to receive the remainder of the recovery. There is no adjustment of the one-third percentage depending upon whether the case is settled, tried, or appealed to the supreme court. These adjustments can be construed to result in a conflict of interest and may result in client or attorney dissatisfaction.

The client is also asked to sign several copies of a standard "release of medical information" form. Not only do many treating doctors require such a form, but an extra copy can often be unexpectedly useful.

The secretary is then requested to open a new file and to type up the recorded information obtained from the client; at the same time she places our "personal injury check list" in the file, and she prepares an "action" card.

. . .

FILE THE ACTION?

Yes.

Although there are times when a case should be settled with the adjuster, these should be looked upon as exceptions. Only very exceptional or very minor actions should be settled at the adjuster level. When a case is valued at an amount exceeding $1,500, it is generally inept practice to fail to serve a complaint. Almost without exception, satisfactory results are impossible to obtain prior to formal commencement of the law suit. Many times, dissatisfied persons have entered law offices, complaining of a lawyer just severed. The severed lawyer, they say, has had the case for months, no action has been started, and his only accomplishment has been delay.

Filing the action as soon as a medical report has been received accomplishes two results: First, if the matter cannot be settled, no time has been lost bringing it to trial. Second, filing the action takes it out of the adjuster's hands and places it in the hands of those persons who are the only ones ordinarily capable of providing a satisfactory settlement—the defense lawyers.

Adjusters greatly prefer to retain control of cases, for they know that any settlement obtained by them will be at a discount.

Failure to start the law suit immediately is an indication to the defense that the plaintiff's lawyer is not experienced in handling personal injury cases.

. . .

DISCOVERY

Naturally, full use should be made of discovery tools—motions to produce, depositions, interrogatories, and admissions.

. . .

MEDICAL REPORTS AND EXAMINATIONS

It is of definite advantage to have a personal meeting with your treating doctors prior to trial, particularly if you do not know the doctor, or if the injury is at all unusual. It should be made clear to the doctor that he is to be paid for his time. The lawyer will be much better prepared for his direct examination of the doctor; and the doctor, unless he spends much time on the witness stand, will be more at ease as a result of the conference.

It is usually unwise to exchange medical reports with the defense attorneys. Although in some states the plaintiff's lawyer must surrender the reports, in Washington the plaintiff is compelled to exchange medicals only when he has first requested the defendant's report.

Doctors often make statements in medical reports that they would not make in a court room. Perhaps they have given a personal opinion not founded upon objective findings, or perhaps, since the time the report was written, the patient's condition has worsened.

. . .

Even where your doctor's reports emphasize the seriousness of the injury, it is not advisable to provide the report. Cross examination becomes much easier for your opponent if he has the findings and conclusions of the doctor in written form and has had, prior to trial, an opportunity to study them. Without these reports, the attorney would have to probe and most likely would not be nearly as direct and effective. He is also much more likely to miss important questions.

SETTLE OR TRY?

No generalization can be made. But one point should be emphasized: every case should at all times be treated *as if it were going to be tried,* even though a valid effort should be made to settle all cases. Too many lawyers assume that they will eventually settle a case; this results in improper procedure and preparation.

The plaintiff's lawyer should always open settlement negotiations. By providing the first figure, he takes the initiative and consequently gains an advantage. To ask the defendant to submit the first figure is to suggest that the defendant's attorneys are better qualified to evaluate the case.

Many offices settle their best cases because an "adequate" figure can be obtained, and try their weakest cases where the amount offerd has not been satisfactory. We believe in the reverse of this policy.

Courtrooms all over our country are clogged with personal injury cases, most of which should never be tried. Juries tire of listening to cases that have no business taking up their time. The trial of the weak case detracts from the truly important personal injury action; and the lawyer who is continually in the courthouse with "another dog" certainly adds no luster to his reputation. If a case is weak, a particular effort should be made toward settlement; and if a case is particularly strong on liability and the client is seriously injured, then the full worth of the case should be obtained at trial if, on consideration, it cannot be obtained beforehand.

. . .

McCONNELL, SETTLEMENT NEGOTIATIONS*

SHOULD SETTLEMENT BE DISCUSSED?

Perhaps one of the first ideas counsel for the defendant may remember with profit is that almost any case should be settled if the parties can agree on the amount. There is very rarely a case which the defendant ought not to settle for $1. There is very rarely a case which the plaintiff ought not to settle for a million dollars. There is rarely if ever, therefore, a valid reason for refusing to discuss settlement.

By refusing to discuss settlement counsel for the defendant risks making three different mistakes:

First, he may thereby quite possibly fail to obtain an obtainable token settlement.

Second, he thereby denies himself access to one of the best possible sources of information about the nature of the plaintiff's case. A conversation about the case with counsel for the plaintiff can be of serious importance in preparing the defendant's attorney to meet the claim he must defend in court.

Third, in refusing to discuss settlement counsel for the defendant runs the risk of generating in counsel for the plaintiff an understandable resentment which, by spurring him on to his maximum efforts, may very well enhance the cost and difficulty of obtaining for the defendant the anticipated victory.

On the other hand, by discussing settlement even in a case he regards as impregnable, counsel for the defendant gains the opportunity to impress counsel for the plaintiff with the weakness of the plaintiff's case and the futility of pressing it. At the same time he remains free to accept or reject as he sees fit the lowest offer counsel for the plaintiff may care to make.

With respect to this thought, as with respect to all of the general rules suggested here, there may of course be certain exceptions. Nevertheless, as an everyday working rule of thumb, it is probably helpful to defense counsel's thinking to accept the fact that almost any case should be settled if the parties can agree upon the price.

WHEN AND HOW SHOULD THE QUESTION OF SETTLEMENT RE RAISED?

Experienced defense counsel frequently will say that the better strategy

---

* Copyright 1955 by The American Law Institute. Reprinted with the permission of *The Practical Lawyer*. Subscription rates $18 a year; $3.75 a single issue. "Settlement Negotiations," by John R. McConnell, appeared in the February 1955 issue of *The Practical Lawyer*, Vol. 1, No. 2, pp. 33-42.

is invariably to refrain from opening settlement negotiations. Others, such as Mr. Hickam in the book cited, suggest that if the defendant's trial counsel knows the value of his case it costs him nothing to be the first to broach the subject of settlement.

Perhaps here more than in any other phase of this subject it is necessary to note that no single general rule can be valid in every case. This is apparent if we consider several diverse situations.

Assume first a liability case of serious personal injury which by virtue of the simplicity of the operative facts will be anything but difficult for the plaintiff to try. Under these circumstances it is all but axiomatic that the defendant must settle if a fair figure can be obtained. At the same time it is also clear that counsel for the plaintiff need not hesitate to try the case if no attractive offer from the defendant is forthcoming. Here, therefore, it will be difficult indeed for the defendant to escape the necessity of initiating settlement discussions.

On the other hand, in a contract action where a possible verdict in favor of the plaintiff cannot exceed a certain known sum and where trial of the plaintiff's case would be tedious, difficult and fraught with both practical and legal problems, compulsion to initiate settlement negotiations is normally upon the plaintiff and not the defendant.

Ultimately, of course, the test by which the defendant's counsel should decide whether or not to open settlement negotiations is the effect that action will have upon the price of the settlement. If the experience, outlook and background of counsel for the plaintiff or the circumstances of the case itself are such that the initiation of settlement talks by defense counsel will suggest to the plaintiff's counsel that the defendant is anxious to settle, the result will necessarily be an increase in the price of the plaintiff's case.

Since the above considerations are understood by most trial counsel and since they represent almost as much a problem to counsel for the plaintiff as to counsel for the defendant, experienced trial counsel on either side usually manage to broach the subject of settlement indirectly. This is usually done either in the course of a conference with one's opponent about some other phase of the coming trial or by inducing the trial judge to open the subject of settlement in a pre-trial conference. Thus the benefits of a settlement discussion may be obtained without the burden of being the first to ask the question.

WHEN SHOULD A CASE BE SETTLED?

Formerly defendants generally believed that a maximum postponement of settlement discussions was to a defendant's advantage. This attitude arose from a belief that with the passage of time the plaintiff's witnesses might become unavailable, some claims would be abandoned and the plaintiff's ability to try his case would be seriously impaired.

In recent years, however, defendants have been inclined to change this point of view, noting that the longer the case is on the docket the more expensive it seems to become. There is consequently a present tendency upon the part of many defendants to eliminate claims at a reasonably early date if possible for fear that the passage of time will better enable a dishonest plaintiff to exaggerate out-of-pocket expenses, loss of earnings, claims of protracted pain and suffering, and other forms of damage.

. . .

Experienced trial counsel are well aware of how completely the presence or absence of some one particular factor may completely change the settlement value of a case. Likewise, they are also aware of the fact that a thorough preparation of one's own case and a thorough study of the opponent's engenders a certain grasp of the over-all strength or weakness of the case which is all but indispensable in attempting to decide its value. This is the real reason why a large majority of cases are settled on the courthouse steps. It is usually not until then that each counsel believes himself as fully informed of the details of the case as he can ever hope to be.

. . .

THE ATMOSPHERE OF SETTLEMENT CONVERSATIONS

It may well be that an important factor bearing upon the ultimate figure to be arrived at in settlement is the atmosphere in which the conversations are conducted.

Many experienced defense counsel follow no particular practice in this respect. Some few others prefer that the negotiations be so conducted as to present defense counsel as the last stalwart on the crumbling ramparts of civilization defending organized society against the onslaught of the barbarian hordes. Others, perhaps involuntarily, cast themselves in the role of the lord of the manor dealing with inexplicable unrest among the peasantry. A third class creates an atmosphere in which the plaintiff appears as a thief and perjurer whose attorney is either his accomplice or his dupe.

Such attitudes are happily not only unjustified but also inexpedient.

Any dispassionate mind trained in the careful thinking required by our profession will concede that it is usually impossible for defense counsel to state with any reasonable degree of certainty that a given plaintiff is either a liar or an honest man. All of us can agree that it is difficult for the attorney of one of the parties in a lawsuit to pass objectively upon the credibility of the opposite party. We can also agree that there is no need for trial counsel to make such judgments. Trial counsel are advocates, not judges and not jurors. It is their function to present the evidence of their client in its best possible light within the confines of ethical conduct. It is not their function to pronounce legal, let alone moral, judgments upon the conduct of either the opposing party or his counsel. A fortiori we can all agree that the dispute in which our client is involved with a plaintiff is decidedly not a dispute between counsel for plaintiff and ourselves.

It follows that there is no valid reason to conduct settlement negotiations, or indeed any phase of a trial, in an atmosphere of bitterness, with the exchange of unconcealed or thinly veiled insult and recrimination. Such conduct is unnecessary and unprofessional.

From the client's point of view, the atmosphere created by such ill-conceived conduct is obviously not as conducive to settlement at the lowest possible figure as is an atmosphere of pleasant, objective, rational consideration of the main point at issue—that is, what a jury is likely to say under all the circumstances of the case.

As a matter of mathematical probability a plaintiff's attorney who has been ignored, snubbed, insulted and figuratively trodden upon in general will necessarily devote greater enthusiasm and energy to the prosecution of his client's case than the attorney who has been treated, as he deserves to be treated, as a brother member of a learned and honorable profession. Economic loss, not gain, results to the defendant whose attorney neglects this rule.

. . .

Were the plaintiff's opening figure no greater than say one and one half times the actual settlement value of the case, this system of matching offers would hold no perils for the defendant. For example, assume a case worth about $5,000. If the plaintiff opens at $7,000, the defendant can open at $3,000 and an ultimate settlement at about $5,000 is reasonably to be expected.

But suppose in the same example the plaintiff's opening figure was not $7,000 but $30,000. What can the defendant do then? Even were he to make a counteroffer of only one dollar, the system of matching offers would then impel him towards a settlement of $15,000.

Hence, the general rule that where the plaintiff's opening figure is in excess of say one and one half times the defendant's estimated settlement value, the defendant plays the game of matching offers at his peril.

At this stage of the negotiations, then, it is hazardous for defense counsel to make a counteroffer. Instead his best rejoinder is to induce counsel for the plaintiff to modify his initial demand—which is by no means as difficult as a layman might imagine.

. . .

It is inherent in the nature of advocacy that each attorney accept, within reason, his own client's version of what has occurred. Just as it was not his business to pass upon the truth or falsity of the opponent's story, so it is not his business, within reason, to prejudge his own client's veracity or accuracy. Hence, counsel for the defendant should never permit himself to become embroiled in an extended argument with his colleague as to the facts of the case. It is one thing to learn from counsel for the plaintiff what the plaintiff or his witnesses are going to testify and to tell counsel for the plaintiff why that evidence will be insufficient either to go to the jury or to impress the jury sufficiently to return a verdict commensurate with the plaintiff's demands. It is an entirely different thing to attempt to convince counsel for the plaintiff that the plaintiff is lying. There is no profit in a pointless argument between trial counsel as to what the actual facts may be.

. . .

Defense counsel can, therefore, take it as a good working rule that any figure which he may mention before the very last stages of negotiations will *not* be the figure at which the case will ultimately be settled. Hence, the wisdom of deferring the making of a counteroffer until it is impossible not to do so.

. . .

Finally, it is a good working rule for defense counsel to remember that if he has properly exercised his professional skill in estimating the probable range of verdict, then no matter what forces are brought to bear upon him to accept a settlement figure in excess of his maximum estimate, it will profit his client to try the case. Until the plaintiff expresses a willingness to settle the case for at least the maximum of defendant's predicted range, counsel for the defendant should prefer to try.

. . .

HERMANN, BETTER SETTLEMENTS THROUGH LEVERAGE *

Uncertainty is by far the most effective lever that one can use to increase or decrease the settlement value of a personal injury case. However, few lawyers or insurance company claims representatives take full advantage of its enormous power.

Most lawyers and insurer's representatives are keenly aware of the elements of uncertainty in their own personal injury cases. They allow uncertainty to affect adversely their own positions as respects settlement, but many do not adequately consider the powerful effect that uncertainty has on the opposing party. For example, an attorney for the plaintiff may so seriously concern himself with the prospects of a small or defense verdict that he may settle the claim for a small fraction of its value. He may fail to realize that the insurance company and/or defense counsel may be equally worried that the verdict may be extremely large, and, because of this uncertainty, may, if properly maneuvered, be willing to pay a sizable amount to effect a settlement rather than submit the case to a jury.

THE DANGER OF PROTECTING THE OPPOSITION FROM UNCERTAINTY

Perhaps the most serious mistake of all, and one that is made daily by many attorneys and insurer's representatives, is to insulate the opposing side from the effect of uncertainty. As ridiculous as it may sound, many attorneys and insurance companies, instead of enlisting uncertainty's

* Reprinted from Hermann, BETTER SETTLEMENTS THROUGH LEVERAGE (1965), pp. 9-10; 122-24; 130-32, by permission of the copyright holder, The Lawyer's Co-Operative Publishing Co., Rochester, N.Y.

enormous power, unwittingly make certain that the other side does not have to concern itself with the problems and depreciating influences of uncertainty.

To illustrate: assume that both the plaintiff's counsel and defense counsel privately evaluate a personal injury case as having a value of $5,000. In addition, both sides are of the opinion that, if the case is submitted to a jury, the verdict may range from zero to $15,000. The plaintiff's attorney, to allow ample spread for negotiation, makes a demand of $15,000. This effectively insulates the insurance company from uncertainty. The insurer calculates that if it is very unlucky, the jury will bring in a verdict of $15,000. Yet, the verdict is likely to be much less, and even zero. Accordingly, so long as the plaintiff's attorney adheres to his original demand, the insurance company has little to worry about in refusing to accede.

What is a typical response to such a demand? The insurance company may (and frequently does) take the position that a ridiculous demand merits a ridiculous offer. It may decide to offer $500, or perhaps nothing. The effect of this is to insulate the plaintiff and his attorney from the depreciating effects of uncertainty. If the offer is zero, the plaintiff (and his attorney) has nothing to worry about in not accepting it—if the jury brings in zero, he is not much worse off; even if the insurer's offer is $500, the possible loss involved in rejection is relatively nominal.

Thus, we see that each side has insulated the opposing side from the effects of uncertainty. The end result may be that although each made a similar evaluation, the case, because of the insulation, may have to be resolved by the expensive trial process.

EMPLOYING UNCERTAINTY PROPERLY

Now, let us consider what could have happened if, in the case assumed above, uncertainty had been taken advantage of. The plaintiff makes a *firm* demand of $7,500. The insurance company, concerned with the prospect that the verdict might be $15,000, must seriously consider a demand of this amount. In many instances, the insurance company may, as a prudent move, pay the $2,500 more than its own evaluation of the case to eliminate the possibility of a verdict far in excess of $7,500.

But what would happen if the insurance company decided to make a *firm* offer of $2,500? Again, many a plaintiff or his attorney, although believing the case to be worth $5,000, may be sufficiently concerned with the prospect of a defense verdict to accept the offer as a prudent means of eliminating the uncertainty of outcome at the hands of a jury.

. . .

The proper bargaining method for today's attorney for the personal injury claimant is to appraise the claim on the basis of verdict expectancy statistics, allowing for adjustments upward or downward to reflect whatever negotiation leverage may be brought into operation. He should then demand an amount closely approximating this appraisal. It is permissible to make a demand slightly higher than the appraisal in order to allow some room for adjustment, but, as a general rule, the asking price should either be adhered to or, at worst, not materially departed from, unless unforeseen events indicate serious error.

Barring change in valuation as a result of new information, the demand figure should be "Price As Marked."

It may be conceded that the principle of standing on "Price As Marked" may seem a revolutionary one. And it should be recognized that many insurer's representatives may refuse to honor a demand notwithstanding their belief that it is in line with the true value of the claim, basing their refusal on the thought that they themselves may be wrong in valuing the claim, or on the hope that somehow they may be able to obtain a bargain settlement.

But it will pay the plaintiff's counsel to stand firm; from his firmness his adversary will learn the costliness of an unjustified refusal to honor a sound demand. The recalcitrant adversary will be faced with investigation expenses, attorneys' fees, and out-of-pocket expenses, and, perhaps, the cost of trial. Of course, plaintiff's counsel whose sound demand has been refused will also be faced with increased expenses, but, in the long run, as insurers and defense lawyers understand that his practice is to make an initial demand that is a firm and fair one, their tendency will be to accept it, and at an early date. The ultimate result will be a method of negotiation far superior to haggling.

A firm, fair demand has obvious persuasive value that haggling lacks. The plaintiff's counsel who names a fair but firm figure and sticks to it is likely to exude confidence which the opposition will be quick to sense.

A word of caution: to the extent that there is a difference between a claimant's demand and the defense's offer, the difference may be explainable on the basis of information available to one side but not the other. To avoid this situation, the negotiations between the parties should be characterized by frank and open discussion, and clear communication from each side of the basis of its valuation of the claim. It is one thing—and a desirable thing—to change one's demand on the basis of newly discovered, relevant information; it is something else—an undesirable something else—to change one's demand purely as a result of haggling.

. . .

THE BENEFITS OF A YEAR-END LAWSUIT

Insurance companies typically operate on a calendar year basis, and their claim managers are ordinarily required to report lawsuits initiated against the insurer at the end of the year. In the insurance business, this year-end report is a very important document. It is this report that is compared with the reports for previous years, and it is on the basis of this report that the work of the insurer's claims personnel is judged. An insurance company may prefer a lawsuit to substantial overpayment in settlement negotiations, but most insurers are very sensitive to year-end increases in the number of lawsuits in which they are named as defendants.

Cognizant of their employers' lawsuit sensitivity, many insurance company claims managers begin, as each year draws to a close, to consider critically the number of lawsuits pending and if there are more than there were the previous year, these claims managers are likely to make every effort to settle as many of the pending suits as possible, and to settle pending claims short of the lawsuit stage.

. . .

The close of the year brings a good settlement climate not only to the claimant but also to the defense, whether a defense attorney or an insurer. The good feeling that accompanies the holiday season may be reflected in a more charitable attitude on the part of both claimant's and defendant's counsel. Similarly, the claimant who cursed the insurance company for offering so little may look at the situation with a more kindly eye. Not to be overlooked is a need for money for the Christmas season: the needy claimant or claimant's counsel is the kind of adversary in settlement negotiations that every defense counsel and insurer dreams of.

. . .

We have already seen how much settlement leverage one can gain if he can make it clear to his adversary that, unless a favorable settlement is agreed upon, the case will be tried. But this kind of leverage cannot possibly be exerted unless the attorney seeking to employ it impresses his adversary with his complete willingness to try the case in order to achieve a result compatible with his position during settlement negotiations. Regardless of how great a lawyer's trial skills may be, once his opponent discovers that, in this case, he is reluctant to enter the courtroom, his chances of exerting leverage disappear.

It follows that if, for any reason (whether ill health, a recent unfavorable verdict or series of unfavorable verdicts, personal problems, or whatever), you wish to avoid trial of a case, don't let your adversary at the settlement table know about it. Do your best to make whatever effort is necessary to give the appearance of eagerness to do battle before judge and jury.

But act with some caution, and some common sense. Development of maximum settlement leverage requires demonstration of eagerness to go to trial, *not* obstinate determination not to settle without a trial. If it seems that you will insist upon going to trial no matter how fair a settlement offer is made, the obvious result will be to make all of the settlement efforts futile, and to make you look foolish.

. . .

How can one determine whether his adversary is really willing to try the case rather than substantially alter the position he has taken in settlement negotiations? Probably the easiest way is to find out whether the adversary has, in fact, tried a great many cases. If, over a period of years, the adversary tried cases to verdict only rarely or not at all, it is reasonable to conclude that whatever trial eagerness he displays is feigned.

. . .

ELINOR K. BEAN'S WHIPLASH AND UNINSURED MOTORIST COVERAGE*

At 8:30 a.m. on November 14, 1962, the automobile owned by Elinor Bean and her husband was struck from behind by a station wagon while Elinor Bean was seated in the driver's seat. She had just crossed an intersection, and had come to a stop because the cars in front of her had also stopped, blocking the road. The force of the blow from behind was sufficient to throw the Bean auto forward into contact with the automobile in front of it, though no harm was done in that collision.

Mrs. Bean felt her head and shoulders go back as the front seat of the car came out of place, and then her head went forward, striking the steering wheel. She got out of the car by herself, but was immediately aware of pain and a sprain in her neck and shoulders. She was taken in a police car to Seattle General Hospital, where she was examined and treated by an orthopaedic physician. The examining physician suggested to her that she not settle any claim she might have until approximately six months had gone by so that they could be sure of the extent of her injuries and of whether there would be any permanent effects of the accident. She remained in the hospital under observation for two days before being released to her home, fitted with a cervical collar.

The driver of the station wagon which struck her was employed as a truck driver; he was 37 years of age; he earned $3.05 an hour; he was married with three children; and he carried no liability insurance and had no substantial assets.

On the next day, an accident report was filed by Russel Bean, Elinor's husband, with his insurer, Merchant's Insurance Co., informing them that his wife had suffered a neck injury in the accident. The insurance company immediately assigned an investigator to the case, who interviewed both Mr. and Mrs. Bean that day. He also prepared a report, designating it an Uninsured Motorists Investigation Report, in which he set a dollar evaluation of the claim at $1,500. He noted that Mr. Bean was 29 years old, employed as an engineer at United Corporation, and that he had a good appearance and would make a good witness. Mrs. Bean, aged 27, was reported to be employed as a secretary in a department store, and her qualities as a witness were likewise appraised as being good. His report further stated:

"This personal injury claim comes under our UM [uninsured motorist] coverage. Assured is still receiving treatment from Dr. Miggs, and the

* Reproduced by permission of the copyright holders, Robert L. Fletcher and Cornelius J. Peck.

husband states that he does not want to settle until her treatments have been concluded. Negotiations should be possible and underway in February 1963.

"Liability of the driver "B" is clear. He was cited for following too close, and forfeited $25.00. Mrs. Bean had a similar accident in 1958, and settled with Hartford at that time."

On November 19, 1962, Mrs. Bean visited Dr. Miggs at his office. Dr. Miggs prepared a memo for the case record, in which he recorded that in 1958 Mrs. Bean had been in an accident in which she was injured slightly. She then received therapy for about a month and a half; and had no residual effects. When a child of 15 she had injured her lower back in a fall from a swing, but this she believed had been cured by a chiropractor. The conclusion, based upon examination of the patient was stated as follow:

"X-rays taken at Seattle General Hospital of the skull, neck and dorsal spine on date of accident reveal no evidence of bone damage. Patient has complaint of right shoulder pain, radiating down to lower third of right arm. There is no clear-cut clinical evidence of cervical nerve root trauma. Patient advised to wear cervical collar intermittently and to report for therapy weekly. Patient may return to work as secretary next week."

Dr. Miggs examined Mrs. Bean again in December 1962 and January and March 1963. The memo for the case record following the March examination contained the following conclusion:

"The patient should continue on remedial routines. Her general posture is somewhat slumped and she is having some increased difficulty with work at her desk because of neck pain due to sedentary posture with neck posture. She has now received eight physical therapy treatments. 5 mg. Librium three times daily have given some relief from headache and neck pain, and will be continued. She will discard foam pillow for feather. Treatment to continue for at least another month."

In March 1963, the claims representative of Merchants Insurance Company, who was still dealing directly with Mr. Bean, filed a periodic report indicating that Mr. Bean would not discuss settlement until his wife was released from treatment by her doctor. The claims representative stated that he expected to close the file within six months, and recommended an increase in the reserve assigned the policy from $1,500 to $2,500, mentioning that treatment was continuing and specials increasing.

On May 9, 1963, Russell Bean retained George St. Paul as attorney to represent the Beans in their uninsured motorist claim, giving him the copy of the insurance policy which the Beans kept in the glove compartment of their automobile. Mr. St. Paul informed the insurers that he now represented the Beans, and stated that he would be in touch with them when the medical picture had become a bit clearer. Mr. St. Paul then advised Mrs. Bean that she should be examined by another physician other than Dr. Miggs, and suggested that he make such arrangements with Dr. Miggs. Mrs. Bean agreed, and in June 1963 she was examined by

Dr. Leslie Tankin. In his letter reporting his findings and conclusions, a copy of which was sent to Mr. St. Paul, Dr. Tankin stated:

"The right grip records at 220-240 and the left at 280. The patient is right-handed. There is hyperesthesia of the right upper quarter of the body compared to the left and spotty hyperesthesia of the right side of the body below this. Deep tendon reflexes are physiologic. There are no pathologic reflexes. Cerebellar tests are normally performed. There is a full range of painless movement of the lumbar spine.

"An electromyogram of the right arm demonstrates grade i denervation in the field of the sixth cervical nerve root on the right side.

"On the basis of this examination I believe the patient sustained an injury to the soft tissues of the cervical spine in the accident of November 1962. I believe her present complaints are valid and are due to this injury. She will require a continuation of her present conservative treatment. Her condition is not fixed."

In September 1963, Mrs. Bean was again examined by Dr. Miggs, whose memo to the case record indicated that the complaints continued, with the exception of pain at night, that she was advised to continue therapy, but to obtain a neck sling and, after instruction in its use, to gradually withdraw from physical therapy, continuing home routines only.

Upon receiving this report from Dr. Miggs, Mr. St. Paul wrote to Merchants Insurance Company, enclosing copies of all the examination reports made by Dr. Miggs and Dr. Tankin. In the concluding paragraph of his letter of transmittal he stated:

"If there be no change in Mrs. Bean's condition between now and her next visit to Dr. Miggs, I will ask the doctor whether or not he has an opinion as to any permanent disability in this case. When that report is received, I will send it on to you and perhaps we can begin serious negotiations to terminate this matter."

Early in November 1963, the claims manager of Merchants Insurance Company telephoned Mr. Charles Martin of the firm of West, Key, and Martin and discussed the Bean case with him. In particular he mentioned that under the provisions of the current insurance policy the company's liability under the uninsured motorist coverage was limited by a requirement that a demand for arbitration be filed within one year after the accident giving rise to the claim. He asked whether the company was under any obligation to Mrs. Bean or Mr. St. Paul to call this provision to their attention. Mr. Martin said he saw no reason why they had to call the provision to the attention of the insured or his attorney, but that they should break off negotiations with them if the company desired to preserve its position with respect to that defense.

In November 1963, Mrs. Bean was examined for the sixth time by Doctor Miggs. He then reached the conclusion that she had sustained multiple soft tissue injuries in the accident of November 1962, and that they constituted a permanent partial disability. He noted that there was no clear-cut clinical evidence of cervical nerve root trauma, but stated that the history was typical of the condition. She was instructed to return for further physical therapy treatments (of which she had then had 10) if there were exacerbations of pain not controlled by the home treatment remedies which she had learned.

Early in December 1963 Mr. St. Paul forwarded this report to Merchants Insurance Company, along with an itemization of bills indicating that Mrs. Bean had now incurred medical expenses of $737.45 and suffered a wage loss of $115. A few days later he telephoned the company's claims representatives and, while discussing the case, stated that he would favorably recommend to his client a settlement of $6,000. The claims representative responded that he thought this a gross overstatement of the claim, suggesting instead a settlement at $2,000. (In his file, however, the claims representative made a note of the offer and counteroffer, adding the comment that, "The claim is worth $3,500 if I can get the attorney to come down.") The claims representative closed the conversation by offering to send Mr. St. Paul proof of claim form to be filled out by Mrs. Bean, and in particular requested that they be given some proof of the loss of wages.

Holidays and other events intervened, and it was not until April 1964 that Mr. St. Paul returned the proof of claim with a letter requesting that he hear from the claims representative at his early convenience. The claims representative did call, but the conversation produced no change of position. Mr. St. Paul informed the representative that he would file a demand for arbitration under the provisions of the insurance policy. He did so on April 28, 1964.

Merchants Insurance Company then forwarded the demand and supporting papers to Charles Martin of West, Key, and Martin. The letter of transmittal directed attention to the fact that the claim arose under the 27th edition of the company's insurance policy, and quoted the following provision:

"Determination of the amount to which the insured is legally entitled shall be made by agreement between the insured and the Company, or in the event of disagreement, by arbitration, *provided the demand for such arbitration is made within one year from the date of the accident.*"

The claims manager of Merchants Insurance Company suggested that Mr. St. Paul had waited too long, directing attention to the fact that he had represented Mr. Bean since May 1963 and hence could not claim that the company was guilty of deception or misrepresentation on the time issue. He further stated that while he thought the demand for arbitration should be resisted, he was willing to make a reasonable settlement.

After several unsuccessful attempts to telephone Mr. St. Paul, Mr. Martin wrote him, directing his attention to the policy provision requiring that a demand for arbitration be made within one year after the accident. He requested a call from him before it became necessary to file a declaratory judgment proceeding for a determination that the claim was barred by the failure to make the demand. Mr. St. Paul thus telephoned Mr.

Martin, and the discussion soon revealed that the insurance policy which
Mr. Bean had given Mr. St. Paul was a 26th edition of the company's
policy and that it did not contain the requirement that the demand for
arbitration be made within one year.

Mr. Martin assured Mr. St. Paul that the policy in effect at the time of
the accident was a 27th edition of the policy, but offered to check further
with the company for confirmation. He further stated that this did not
foreclose the possibility of settlement and that in his opinion the $2,000
previously offered by the Company was a fair and adequate figure. Mr.
St. Paul replied that he had advised his client to reject that offer before
and that his advice would still be the same. Mr. Martin suggested that
the claim certainly was not worth what one might have assigned to it if
there were not the possibility of a time bar, apologizing that he had found
it necessary to raise a defense which might give rise to a malpractice
liability on the part of Mr. St. Paul. Mr. St. Paul responded forcefully
that he did not believe the time bar defense was valid or that it had any
effect upon the valuation of the claim. He again stated his willingness to
proceed to arbitration. Mr. Martin told him that instead the Company
would file a declaratory judgment action. In reporting this conversation
to Merchants Mr. Martin stated that he would value the claim at between
$2,500 and $3,000, and that he thought such a settlement might be
arranged.

The declaratory judgment proceeding was filed in August 1964, leading
the Regional Manager of the American Arbitration Association to hold
in abeyance any further administrative processing of the demand for
arbitration. The case did not, however, come to trial until May 1965,
when it was tried before Judge Ahern, sitting without a jury.

In April, about one month before trial, Charles Martin telephoned
Mr. St. Paul and informed him that Merchants had authorized a settlement at $3,000. Mr. St. Paul replied that he believed the case now had a
value of $7,500, but that he would accept a settlement at $4,500 and would
even discuss $4,000 with his clients, though he was not inclined to recom-
mend acceptance of such an offer. Mr. Martin thought Mr. St. Paul
might get in touch with him immediately before trial, but nothing further
developed.

In the course of the trial, Mr. Martin placed considerable reliance upon
a provision of the Washington Insurance Code, RCW 48.18.470, which
declares that investigating any loss or claim under any policy or engaging
in negotiations looking toward a possible settlement of the claim shall
not be deemed to constitute a waiver of any provision of the policy or of
any defense of the insurer under the policy. Company records were admitted showing that at the renewal immediately preceding the accident a
copy of the insurance policy was sent to the Beans and that it was on the
form designated as the 27th edition.

In June 1965, Judge Ahern wrote to counsel announcing that his decision was for the Beans. Although he found that they had in fact received

a copy of the 27th edition of the insurance policy, he found that they mistakenly believed the copy kept in the glove compartment was the current copy, and that Mr. St. Paul had been given that copy with the advice that it was the current copy and the only copy the Beans had. He further held that by continuing to negotiate with the Beans, the insurance company had led them and their attorney to believe the matter was still open for adjustment, and hence that it was estopped from raising the bar of the time limit found in the 27th edition of the policy. The formal findings of fact prepared by Mr. St. Paul, and approved by Judge Ahern, were filed in September 1965. They included the following statement:

"During this time plaintiff willfully conveyed the impression that continued negotiation would resolve the matter in an amicable settlement, but knew that the 27th edition contained the one-year limitation for demand for arbitration, and intended to rely on that, and in fact, sought legal advice regarding this limitation shortly before the one-year limitation date."

Upon receipt of the findings of fact, conclusions of law, and judgment, Charles Martin discussed with Merchants' claim manager the possibility of taking an appeal from the judgment, pointing out that by utilizing the concept of estoppel Judge Ahern appeared to have frustrated the purposes of RCW 48.18.470. However, the claims manager thought that enough time had now been spent in legal maneuvers and he was very reluctant to give publicity to the finding that the company had willfully misled an insured by taking an appeal. Accordingly, in December 1965 it was decided that no appeal would be taken.

Mr. Martin then telephoned Mr. St. Paul and told him that there would be no appeal. He inquired about what might be done to get this case settled. Mr. St. Paul replied that the only question seemed to be how permanent the injuries would be, and indicated his willingness to have an independent medical examination made. Arrangements for such an examination were made, and the report received by Messrs. Martin and St. Paul in January 1966. That report concluded with the following statement:

"It would appear that as a result of the accident in question the patient sustained sprains of the neck and upper back. As a result of treatment rendered and/or the passage of time she has made a good recovery. At the present time she describes non-disabling subjective residuals but on clinical examination there are no findings of disability. X-ray studies of the neck and upper back reveal no evidence of abnormality and no evidence of old or recent injury. The stress which patient is under supporting her husband as he pursues studies for a graduate degree and the tension which exists concerning her long standing unsettled claim may be a causative factor in prolonging her subjective residuals."

Following receipt of the report, Mr. St. Paul sent Mr. Martin a statement giving the details of the special items of damage which had accumulated as of January 18, 1966. It indicated that medical bills had now reached a total of $1,190, and that salary lost from work now amounted to $315.

On January 20, 1966, Mr. Martin wrote to Merchants informing them that the claim had been set for arbitration on February 24, 1966. He further advised that the attorney chosen as arbitrator by the American Arbitration Association was not, in his opinion, the best man they could have obtained, but that he was better than many others on the local panel and that objection to the designated arbitrator probably would not result in selection of a better man. He concluded his letter by recommending that he be authorized to settle the claim for the sum of $4,500. He did not believe the prospects for settlement within those limits were very good, but he thought it desirable to attempt settlement within those limits.

The claims manager of Merchants authorized settlement at $4,500, but before Mr. Martin could communicate this offer, he received a letter from Mr. St. Paul offering to settle for $4,500, contingent upon the offer being accepted within a ten-day period and before additional expenses were incurred in preparation for the arbitration hearing. Mr. Martin immediately accepted on behalf of Merchants, and the details of settlement were thereafter quickly accomplished.

QUESTIONS

1. Why did it take so long to settle this relatively simple case?

2. Why did Merchants Insurance continue to negotiate with Mr. St. Paul for more than one year after the accident without raising the question of whether the claim had become timebarred? Why did the claims manager wait until November 1963 before getting in touch with Martin? Would not Merchants have fared better if it had earlier received Martin's advice to break off negotiations?

3. Do you see a technique of negotiation in the claims manager's conversation-closing offer to send forms in the telephone interchange of December 1963?

4. Why did Martin try to phone St. Paul rather than write? Do you think he thought he could use this possibility of malpractice to better advantage by telephone than in writing?

5. Why did Mr. Martin file the declaratory judgment proceeding if he was willing to settle the case at $3,000?

6. Note how much Merchants Insurance Co wanted to avoid a reported appellate decision which probably would have publicized Judge Ahern's finding that it had willfully misled an insured. The practice followed at that time was to require prevailing counsel to prepare proposed findings of fact. Do you think St. Paul drafted the proposed finding with this consideration in mind?

7. Did the Beans receive any benefits from the delayed processing of the claim?

8. Do you think it possible or even likely that the pendency of the claim prolonged and aggravated the pain experienced by Elinor Bean? See C. Peck, W. Fordyce, and R. Black, *The Effect of the Pendency of Claims for Compensation Upon Behavior Indicative of Pain*, 53 Wash. L. Rev. 251 (1978), reporting the results of a detailed study that revealed no significant effect of either litigation or representation by attorneys upon the pain behavior of persons having worker's compensation claims with the Department of Labor and Industries of the State of Washington.

9. How well do you understand the medical reports? Aside from the doctors' conclusions about disability and prognosis, why are the reports important from the standpoint of negotiation?

    a. Where are the dorsal and cervical areas of the spine?

    b. What is a cervical nerve root trauma?

    c. What is Librium and how is it taken? Is it pleasant or unpleasant?

    d. What is hyperesthesia?

    e. What is the meaning of physiologic?

    f. What is denervation? Is it good or bad?

    g. What is an electromyogram? Is it painful?

You may obtain a better understanding of insurance company practices from J. S. Rosenbloom, AUTOMOBILE LIABILITY CLAIMS: INSURANCE COMPANY PHILOSOPHIES AND PRACTICES (1968).

NOTE

There is a high correlation between the size of a settlement and the frequency with which claims reach trial. A study of personal injury and wrongful death cases in New York indicates that only one out of 20 suits in which there was a recovery of $3,000 or less reached trial, whereas one out of five suits in which more than $3,000 was recovered went to trial. On the other hand, once the suits reached trial, there was no greater tendency for large suits to reach verdict than small suits. Rosenberg and Sovern, *Delay and the Dynamics of Personal Injury Litigation*, 59 Colum. L. Rev. 115 (1959). What factors about the process of negotiation would lead to these results? Does the wide range of possible verdicts make the parties more willing to undergo the expense of preparation for trial? Does the knowledge gained after preparation for trial make it possible for both sides to make a more realistic appraisal of the worth of a claim? Do defendants conclude that they have used delay to maximum bargaining capacity? Do plaintiffs believe they know more about the total extent of the harm suffered?

Recommended as additional readings on the negotiation of personal injury claims are Kelner, *Techniques of Settlement*, 38 Wis. Bar Bull. (Dec. 1965) 27, and Foutty, *The Evaluation and Settlement of Personal Injury Claims*, 1964 Ins. L.J. 5.

(2) *A Will Contest*

THE ESTATE OF ABIGAIL SCHNURE*

When Abigail Schnure died in 1964 at the age of 68, she left an estate valued at approximately $250,000. The estate consisted primarily of blue chip stock holdings in 26 different companies. About $30,000 was held in deposits in 12 different banks and savings and loan associations, and there was approximately $45,000 in cash in her safe deposit box at the Seattle First National Bank. She was renting an apartment at the time of her death, and the furniture which she had was appraised as having a value of $500. In addition, she owned ten pieces of jewelry, which were appraised at a total value of $240.

Her will, drafted in 1960 by the firm of Wall, Doomor, and Seth, was a simple two-page document. To her nephew Walter Pigor she left a moss agate stick pin, described in the bequest as having belonged to her father, Walter Schnure, plus one dollar. To her nephew Thomas Pigor she left a gold watch fob, likewise described as having belonged to her father, plus one dollar. To her niece Carolyn Firth she left pearl earrings, described as having belonged to her mother, Evelyn Schnure, plus one dollar. She did this, so she stated in her will, because her nephews and niece had already been well provided for by their mother and father, the late Mrs. and Doctor Pigor. All the rest and residue of the estate she left to Danish Hospital. She nominated David Burnham, manager of the Boylston Savings and Loan Association, to serve as her executor. The 1960 will revoked a prior will drafted in 1948 by Ernest Tutworthy of the firm of Lawson, Tutworthy, and Blinn, by which Abigail Schnure had left essentially all of the estate to her two nephews and her niece, share and share alike.

After Abigail Schnure's death David Burnham, to whom she had delivered a copy of the 1960 will, got in touch with Kenneth McFarland of the law firm of Newman, Byse, Jaffe, and McFarland, and retained them as counsel. (He and Kenneth McFarland had been roommates in college and had remained close friends thereafter.) McFarland prepared the petition for probate of the will, and David Burnham was appointed executor of the will on April 20, 1964. Burnham immediately sold the furniture to a secondhand furniture dealer for slightly less than $500, and undertook a program of sale of the various stocks held by the estate, purchasing certificates of deposit from the Seattle First National Bank with the proceeds. He likewise used the cash found in the safe deposit vault to purchase certificates of deposit.

On May 4, 1964, Walter Pigor, Thomas Pigor, and Carolyn Firth, acting through their attorney, Leslie Shell of Lewis, Carpenter, White, and Jones, filed a petition contesting probate of the 1960 will and asking

* Reproduced by permission of the copyright holders, Robert L. Fletcher and Cornelius J. Peck.

for probate of the 1948 will. The ground advanced for the action proposed was that Abigail Schnure lacked testamentary capacity at the time she executed the 1960 will. More specifically the petition alleged the following:

"Abigail Schnure was a maiden lady who lived until 1949 with her father in an old but fashionable part of Seattle. Her mother, Evelyn Schnure, died in an auto accident in 1935. Her father, Walter Schnure, had been a professional chemist and had so successfully devoted his talents to the development of detergent soap formulae that at his death in 1949 he left an estate in excess of $1,000,000. By his will he left property valued at $150,000 outright to each of his two daughters, placing the rest in a trust which was to terminate upon their deaths, with the proceeds going to such of their children as might then be living. Abigail Schnure was unable to make an emotional adjustment to her father's death, but became estranged, developing a second and fictitious personality. In that personality she believed that she was not the true daughter of her parents but instead an orphan child whom they had befriended, but to whom they had left no property. Pursuant to this delusion and in 1955, Abigail Schnure sold the house in which she had lived with her father, and moved to quarters which she rented at $80 per month.

"Since 1955 Abigail Schnure lived a frugal and impoverished life in the insane belief that she was a person of meager means. She persisted in this belief despite periodic receipt of substantial sums from the trust established by her father and despite the fact that she continued to exercise undiminished control over the property inherited from her father.

"Because she insanely believed she was an orphan, she did not recognize her niece and nephews, the children of her late sister Martha, as the natural objects of her bounty, but instead, believing herself to be of very limited means, attempted to give all her estate to the Danish Hospital. She so described her situation to Mr. Seth, who drafted her will for her and who, pursuant to the policy of the law firm, made no charge for drafting a will leaving modest sums for charitable purposes."

Soon after the filing of the petition contesting the probate of the 1960 will, Kenneth McFarland telephoned Leslie Shell to discuss the case. Mr. Shell willingly supplemented the allegations of the petition with information he had received from his clients.

According to his clients, for two years after her father's death, Abigail Schnure did not allow any of his personal belongings to be removed from the house in which they had lived, but instead kept them exactly as they had been at the time of his death, even to the detail of leaving his razor and razor strop in place in the bathroom. Until the time she sold the house in which they had lived, she would set a place for her father at Sunday dinner, insisting that he had returned in spirit and that she had been able to communicate with him in some manner. Upon occasion she even set an additional place at Sunday dinner for Leslie Yorth, a man who had paid her some attention before going with the American Expeditionary Forces to Europe in World War I, where he died.

During the period before the sale of the house other idiosyncrasies developed, including her growing belief that she was impoverished. For example, she concentrated her marketing in the Pike Street Market, where she could obtain damaged fruits and vegetables, day-old bread, and horse meat. For Christmas of 1953 she gave to the three children of Thomas Pigor a dime store checkerboard, making separate gifts of the board, the black checkers, and the red checkers, each of which was wrapped in paper saved from an earlier Christmas. It became more and more difficult for the Pigors and Mrs. Firth to visit their sister and aunt for lack of mutual interests. Nevertheless, Martha Pigor, Abigail's sister who was then still living, visited her in 1955 and learned that in her Sunday "dinners" with her father she had been informed that she really was an orphan child and hence not a true member of the Schnure family. It was shortly after this that she sold the house and moved into an apartment in what might be called a working-class neighborhood.

Thereafter her contacts with her niece and nephews became fewer and fewer, although she did attend the funeral of her sister Martha in 1958. The withdrawal became almost complete thereafter, broken only by the short and ritualistic visits made by her niece and nephews during subsequent Christmas holidays. She always thanked her niece and nephews for making the calls but had little to say to them and gave them Christmas presents quite clearly purchased in secondhand stores.

In June 1959, she registered to vote for the first time in the precinct to which she had moved in 1955, using the name Abigail Schnure Gibbons. She voted several times thereafter, using the name as registered rather than her real name. Her death from a heart attack on a Seattle transit bus was first reported as the death of Abigail Gibbons because a public library card and other identification found in her purse carried that name.

Because of her belief that she was impoverished, she kept very detailed records of her personal expenses. These, and other financial records contained no indication that she had made a contribution to a charity within the last 10 years. She had taken no interest in the Danish Hospital until 1960, when she was brought there for emergency treatment after having been struck by an automobile while crossing the street. The examination given her revealed no serious injuries, and while she had been dazed initially, she was allowed to leave without staying overnight.

McFarland received Shell's supplementary account with interest, but concluded the discussion by indicating that he thought such evidence, even if true, would not establish a lack of testamentary capacity. Moreover, he said that he was not inclined to believe that a woman who could increase her property holdings by over $100,000 in 14 years was of unsound mind. Shell requested McFarland to get in touch with him if his investigation of the information Shell had supplied produced any different appraisal of the case. Otherwise, Shell said they should attempt to agree upon a trial date.

McFarland relayed the information he had received from Shell to Burnham, the executor of the estate. He found the story incredible. Miss

Schnure was, in his opinion, a very intelligent and well-informed woman, even though somewhat eccentric in particular mannerisms and by no means a fashion plate. He had come to know her because they both used the same stockbroker and had made somewhat similar investments, which she discussed with Burnham as a check on the advice given her by the broker. Moreover, while he did not attend regularly, he frequently saw Miss Schnure at the luncheon meetings of the World Affairs Council, and short exchanges of conversation they occasionally had indicated to him that she had an excellent understanding of a wide range of topics discussed by the various speakers who appear before that group. He was inclined to consider the attempt at setting aside the will as nothing more than a holdup operation conducted in the tradition of very wealthy people who, unlike many less fortunate, live in constant fear that they will become impoverished.

On May 25, 1964, Mr. Shell served upon Mr. Burnham interrogatories in which he sought to explore the relationship which had existed between Mr. Burnham and Miss Schnure. The responses summarized the information given above. Shell also served notice that he would take the deposition of the director of the hospital as well as other persons on the hospital staff with whom Miss Schnure had discussed the making of the bequest. Preparation for the taking of the depositions put Mr. McFarland in touch with Charles Gregory of Holcombe, Hafer, Lutz and Gregory, Danish Hospital's attorneys.

The information obtained in the taking of the deposition indicated that in October or November 1960 Miss Schnure had made an appointment to see the director of the hospital. The director's secretary, who was the only other person to whom Miss Schnure had spoken, recalled that Miss Schnure had telephoned the hospital, saying that she wanted to talk to someone about the possibility of leaving some money to the hospital, and that she, the secretary, had fixed an appointment date. The director recalled that Miss Schnure did come to see him in his office. He did not know before she came what was the purpose of her visit, and was pleasantly surprised when she explained that she was thinking of leaving her estate to the hospital and wondered for what specific purposes a gift be most useful. He explained to her that they did have a need for an additional surgery room, but that it was generally better not to limit the use of gifts to specific purposes. She stated that she thought then that she would leave her property to the hospital without limitation. In the course of her conversation she did mention that the only relatives she had left were her two nephews and her niece; that they did not like her and had shown no interest in her since their mother's death; and that in any event they had already been well provided for by their father and mother. A month or two later Miss Schnure came to his office and left with him a copy of the will. He remembered that he had expressed his thanks to her, assuring her that the hospital had very good use for any gifts it received, but that he had no idea at the time of the size of the gift. He did know that her father had been successful financially, and that her sister and brother-in-law were quite wealthy, but he assumed that there had been financial reverses on the Schnure side of the family and that the wealth of the Pigor side came from Dr. Pigor himself.

In discussions between Kenneth McFarland and Charles Gregory it was agreed that the following constituted the major questions to be resolved in bringing about a settlement of the will contest:

(1) Would the contestants be able to prove by evidence which is clear, cogent, and convincing (whatever that means) that Abigail Schnure lacked testamentary capacity? (See *In re Measher's Estate,* 60 Wn.2d 691, 375 P.2d 143 (1962).)

(2) In this connection, will the contestants be barred by the Deadman's statute from testifying concerning their various conversations and meetings with Abigail Schnure?

(3) Will the contestants be allowed costs and attorneys' fees from the estate if they do not ultimately prevail?

It was further agreed that Mr. McFarland should address interrogatories to the contestants exploring (1) the amounts of money and property which they had inherited from their father and mother and (2) the lack of any close relationship between them and Miss Schnure. The response to the first part of these interrogatories was a refusal to answer upon the ground that the information concerning the money and property which the claimants had inherited from other sources was irrelevant and immaterial. The response to the second portion of the interrogatories indicated that the frequency of contacts between the claimants and Miss Schnure had been drastically reduced, as described above, for the reason that her insane delusion prevented any normal family relationship.

Nothing further developed in the case during the summer of 1964 except that early in August 1964 Mr. McFarland happened to meet Mr. Shell in court during the calling of the motion calendar, and conversation turned to the will contest. Mr. Shell said that they ought to get together to discuss settlement, and that, while he had not specifically discussed the subject with his clients, he believed it possible that they would accept a settlement giving them approximately 40 percent of the estate. McFarland made no counter offer, saying he was more inclined to try the case. Shell said that in that case they should get together to select a trial date.

On September 8, 1964, Mr. Gregory telephoned Mr. McFarland to inquire about the status of the case. When informed of the settlement feeler, Gregory commented that there probably would be a settlement sometime, but that the present was not the right time. McFarland responded that that might be the case, but he was reluctant to give in to what had the appearances of a holdup. Gregory suggested that depositions should be taken of those people with whom Miss Schnure had had business or other relations in the years immediately before her death and near the time of the making of her will. When he learned that McFarland had not yet taken any depositions, he volunteered to do so.

Harry Krug, the stockbroker who handled the accounts of Miss Schnure and Mr. Burnham, stated in his deposition that he considered Miss Schnure to be a very intelligent and alert woman; that she was not one of the helpless type who leave everything to their broker, but instead had some well-formulated views of her own; that upon some occasions she had failed to follow his advice and suffered losses, but that on other occasions she had made decisions which proved to be quite profitable; and that she probably had a better recollection of exactly what stocks and the number of shares she held than most of his customers. He did recall that upon one occasion when she had sold at a considerable gain he had asked what celebration she would have with her profits. She had responded to the effect that they certainly wouldn't go to her nephews and niece, who didn't like her and hardly ever came to see her. He thought she was somewhat eccentric, and did not understand why a woman with a portfolio such as she held dressed in such old and unfashionable clothing.

Roberta Piper, executive secretary of the World Affairs Council, stated in her deposition that Miss Schnure regularly attended World Affairs Council luncheon meetings, but that she usually reserved only a seat after the luncheon and did not pay for or eat the meal. She had briefly discussed the performance of speakers with Miss Schnure upon a number of occasions, and believed that Miss Schnure had shown considerable understanding of the issues discussed. She thought Miss Schnure was somewhat eccentric, but believed that she was no more so than a number of other older people.

Lawrence Seth, of the law firm of Wall, Doomer & Seth, deposed that he had drafted the 1960 will for Miss Schnure; that he would not have done so if he had not thought her to be of sound mind and of testamentary capacity; that she had discussed with him the reason for leaving only token gifts to her nephews and niece; that she had told him that her estate was a modest one, and that its size would depend upon how long she lived, but that even a few thousand dollars would be a help to the Danish Hospital, which had a real need for money.

Ernest Tutworthy, of the law firm of Lawson, Tutworthy and Blinn, testified that he had been a long-time friend of both the Schnure and the Pigor families; that he had drafted Miss Schnure's will in 1948, at which time she was of sound mind; that he had noticed eccentricities develop and grow in Miss Schnure following her father's death; that, though his wife detested every such occasion, he had prevailed upon her to invite Miss Schnure out to their house approximately twice a year for dinner because of his sympathy for her and his loyalty to the Schnure and Pigor families; that upon such occasions Miss Schnure had indicated that she communed with her father's spirit and learned that she might not in fact have been his daughter; and that in his opinion from and after 1958 or 1959 she was so deranged as to be lacking in testamentary capacity even though she was not dangerous to herself or society.

Thelma Porter, wife of a graduate student at the University of Washington, deposed that she and her husband lived in the same apartment house as had Miss Schnure at the time of her death; that Miss Schnure seemed to her to be a refined and gracious lady, who was quite well-informed about things—particularly about international affairs; that upon occasion she had borrowed sugar, flour, etc., from Miss Schnure, who had loaned it freely and seemed reluctant to accept the return. Mrs. Porter expressed the opinion that Miss Schnure was definitely sane, and that only a person who did not understand the process of aging, particularly among those who are lonely, could think otherwise. She did think it puzzling that she lived such a simple life having such a sizeable estate, but thought her no more peculiar than the many people who try to live so far above what they can afford.

Gregory prepared summaries of these depositions as well as of the information received from Shell, and consulted three psychiatrists. One of them said he could form no opinion concerning Miss Schnure's mental condition without having interviewed her and observed her. The other two said they could not affirmatively state that Miss Schnure was sound of mind and memory, but that even if accurate the evidence indicating that Miss Schnure had developed a dual personality did not affirmatively convince them that she could not or did not arrive upon her plan for disposing of her estate upon rational grounds.

Gregory forwarded the depositions along with the opinions of the latter two psychiatrists to Mr. McFarland, and suggested that McFarland get in touch with Shell, calling to his attention the rather consistent theme which appeared in the depositions to the effect that Abigail Schnure was quite eccentric, but certainly sane and of testamentary capacity when she executed the will in 1960. McFarland was very enthusiastic upon hearing this summary of the depositions, and expressed the hope that this would lead to a withdrawal of the contest. Gregory further suggested that McFarland attempt to establish a trial date in December 1964 or January 1965 with Mr. Shell. McFarland did so, and the case was set for trial on February 23, 1965.

On February 9, 1965, Mr. Shell wrote to Mr. McFarland, offering to settle the claim against the estate for $15,000 to be divided equally by the three claimants. McFarland conferred with Gregory, suggesting that an offer to settle for nuisance value deserved no more respect than an attempt to get a sizeable amount in a hold-up operation. Gregory insisted upon consulting his client, who, as he pointed out to McFarland, was really the only party in interest.

In that consultation Gregory urged the Danish Hospital Board to accept the offer. As he saw it, the claimants had started the will contest in the sincere and firm belief that Abigail Schnure was of unsound mind and lacked testamentary capacity. He believed that the original offer of settlement at 40 percent of the estate had been prompted by Mr. Shell's evaluation of the general difficulty of setting aside a will. He thought the rather sharp drop in the settlement price came as the contestants approached trial, and began to wonder whether they would be left with only a bill for attorney's fees. He thought they also became concerned that, as the depositions indicated, there would be a number of witnesses testifying that their aunt had been sane, putting them in the difficult and unpleasant position of attacking that conclusion by revealing a number of things which previously had been well-kept family jokes.

In any event, he saw no virtue in continuing the contest if the result were to be additional fees for the executor and his attorneys of as much as $15,000, which he believed likely if the matter were litigated and carried to the Supreme Court on appeal by either party. The one route offered the possibility of costing $15,000 or more with the added danger that the entire bequest might be lost; the other route offered the possibility of limiting additional expense to $15,000 with the certainty that the bequest would come to the hospital. The Danish Hospital Board accepted his recommendation, and approved a settlement at $15,000.

Gregory informed McFarland and Shell that his clients would approve a settlement at $15,000, and McFarland and Burnham, the executor, reluctantly went along. Shell then suggested that it would be preferable to designate a certain portion of the $15,000 as his attorney's fee, offering to have his clients enter into an agreement to reimburse or indemnify the estate should the Washington State Tax Commission declare that the money paid to him for his fee was subject to the state inheritance tax. McFarland and Gregory agreed to this variation. Shell then drew up an order approving the settlement of the will contest by which the executor was directed to pay to Shell the sum of $4,768 as attorney's fees and to pay to each of the three claimants the sum of $3,410.70.

At the same time, in separate discussions, Gregory agreed to McFarland's being paid $15,000 as attorney's fees for services rendered the estate, but he refused to agree that the executor receive a fee of $12,000. Gregory suggested that the executor be paid $7,500, but upon some remonstrances from McFarland, agreed to raise the figure to $8,500. Gregory's firm received a fee of $20,000 for its services.

QUESTIONS

1. Gregory took quite a charitable view of the motivating factors underlying the contest started by the two nephews and the niece of Abigail Schnure. Should he have conducted the negotiations on behalf of his client in any other way if he believed that the contest came from more base motives?

2. How do you account for the fact that Mr. McFarland and Mr. Burnham were more suspicious of the claimants' motives and were inclined to reject the offer of settlement as a matter of principle? Should Danish Hospital try all will contests as a matter of principle?

3. Were there any reasons other than those of the expense of litigation which would lead to the conclusion that it would be better to close the estate by accepting the offer of settlement? Would you have approved of the executor's action in converting the stock into cash and purchasing deposit certificates?

4. How much more complicated would the negotiations have been if the settlement figure had been high enough to result in a federal estate tax liability?

5. To what extent was the settlement of this case based upon legal considerations? How clearly were the issues that McFarland and Gregory had isolated resolved before the settlement agreement was reached?

6. Do you think Mr. Shell had any purpose other than that of obtaining information when he arranged to take the deposition of the director of Danish Hospital? Do you think he knew or could have found out who was counsel for Danish Hospital?

7. Do you think Mr. Shell arranged the meeting in court during the calling of the motion calendar? How did it happen that he was prepared to discuss settlement charges? It would have been possible for him to know from the calendar that McFarland would be in court that day, and such an "accidental" meeting would not signal concern for the weakness of the contestant's case.

8. Why did Mr. Gregory volunteer to take the deposition in the telephone conversation of September 8, 1964?

9. If you were Mr. Gregory, how much would you have been worried by the views expressed by Ernest Tutworthy in his deposition? Would you be troubled by the fact that Miss Schnure did not mention to anyone the trust established by her father?

10. Was the information sought by McFarland concerning the wealth which the contestants had inherited from their parents relevant to the will contest? If relevant and admissible, do you think the greatest purpose served by that testimony would be to support a conclusion of the type which made the evidence relevant and admissible?

11. Do you think that Mr. Shell failed to anticipate the difficulties which developed for his clients, or at least the difficulties which Mr. Gregory believed led to their decision to accept a nominal settlement? How else could Shell and his clients have obtained the information indicating that Miss Schnure had testamentary capacity?

12. Do you think that Mr. Shell ever intended to try the case? Did he create the impression that he was planning to do so? How important was the creation of such an impression to make an acceptable settlement offer?

(3) *A Property Settlement in a Divorce Proceeding*

WITH ALL MY WORLDLY GOODS . . .*

In January 1966, Thelma Jasper came to James Wallen of Richards, Nottlemann, Hawley, Wollett & Wallen to seek his assistance in getting

---

* Reproduced by permission of the copyright holders, Robert L. Fletcher and Cornelius J. Peck. The community property law of the State of Washington is substantially as summarized by the attorneys in this case history. A detailed description of the law may be found in Cross, *The Community Property Law in Washington*, 49 Wash. L. Rev. 729 (1974).

a divorce from her husband John. They had been married in 1946. John Jasper was now 45 years of age; Thelma was 43. She said she still loved John in some ways, but not enough to make it possible to live with him. He had always been a heavy drinker, but in recent years his drinking had become much worse. Three years earlier she had moved to a separate bedroom because she could not tolerate the smell of alcohol and tobacco and the noise of his snoring with which he filled the room every night while sleeping off what had been a substantial amount of liquor consumed the evening before. Moreover, his drinking had made conversations at home impossible and appearances in public a source of constant embarrassment. Wallen thought that in addition, at the age of 43 she had become convinced that there must be more of substance to life than she was able to find in her marriage. Her eldest child, a 20-year-old girl named Eunice, was about to finish college and would probably be married in the near future. The other child of the marriage, a boy named John and aged 17, had but one more year of high school before he would be ready for college.

Thelma knew very little about John's financial condition. They lived in a large house in a very fashionable area of Seattle with a maid, a cook, and a part-time gardener. When she had threatened John with divorce if he did not mend his ways, he had responded that she could get not a penny out of him and that he doubted that she wanted to live on the limited amounts she could earn by working. Nevertheless, she wanted the divorce.

Under Wallen's questioning Thelma was able to produce the following information. John Jasper was the president and general manager of Standard Meter and Gauge Co. of Seattle, a business which he had inherited from his father when his father died in 1952. She recalled hearing John say about six years ago something to the effect that his salary alone was more than $50,000 a year. She also remembered that it was in 1951 that they had purchased a waterfront summer place on Vashon Island, and that more recently, in 1960 or 1961, they had purchased a much larger but undeveloped piece of land on Cypress Island in the San Juan Islands. In addition, John had become interested in oil and gas leases and had traveled frequently to Colorado and New Mexico on business connected with such leases. She was not certain who were his attorneys, saying that he had so many attorneys and accountants she couldn't keep track of them.

Wallen prepared a complaint seeking a divorce upon the statutory ground of cruel treatment, rendering life burdensome, with an offer of a bill of particulars if requested. The complaint listed the Seattle home and the two parcels of island property as community property, and further alleged that there were undetermined amounts of real and personal property held by the community both in and outside of Washington. In addition, the complaint alleged that John had substantial amounts of separate property and that he currently earned in excess of $50,000 per year. The complaint ended with a prayer that Thelma be granted an absolute divorce; that she be given custody of the minor child, John, with reasonable rights of visitation reserved to the defendant, that provision be made for the education and medical protection of the children, that she be given $1,500 per month for support of the children, plus a reasonable amount of alimony. In addition, the complaint asked for an equitable distribution of the property of the community, giving due consideration to the value of the defendant-husband's separate property. An initial allowance of $1,500 as attorney's fees and other appropriate relief were also requested.

Wallen also prepared and had served a motion for a temporary restraining order, requiring that John Jasper remove himself from the family home during the pendency of the divorce proceedings, and that he make payments of $1,500 per month as temporary support for Thelma and the children.

The day after the complaint had been served, Wallen received a telephone call from George Mower of Edwin, Mower, Lewis and Turk, informing him that he would be representing John Jasper in the divorce proceeding. Wallen knew Mower from previous contacts, and knew that he was his firm's expert in the office practice aspect of advising business clients. Saying that he thought that determining what was separate and what was community property would probably be the biggest problem they faced, Wallen inquired as to whether Mower was well versed in the business affairs of John Jasper. Mower said that he had served Jasper with respect to the legal problems of Standard Meter and Gauge as well as those of his separate property, but that he knew as little about the community affairs as did Wallen. This was the case because from the time of his father's death Jasper had kept completely separate records for community affairs and for the affairs of the company and his separate property. This, it seemed to Mower, would be of great help in simplifying the problem of identifying which was community and which was separate property. He informed Wallen that Richard Adams of Adams, Hoffman, and Nickerson had handled the legal problems of the community.

Wallen briefly discussed with Mower the other aspects of the divorce proceeding and learned that there would probably be no difficulty with respect to the adequacy of the grounds for divorce or with respect to custody of the children. He then suggested that he get in touch with Mower after he had had an opportunity to go over the community affairs with Adams.

Adams gave confirmation to the thoroughness with which the affairs of the community had been kept separate from the business and separate property affairs. The principal items of community property were the family home, the two pieces of island property, life insurance policies, a retirement pension fund, checking accounts at two banks, a relatively small portfolio of stock investments, and one half interest in a joint venture investment in Colorado oil and gas leases. Depending upon the values assigned, the community property had a value of between $140,000 and $180,000.

Wallen and Mower then set up a joint conference with their respective clients for the purpose of working out an agreement first on the matters of temporary support and second upon a final property settlement. The former was settled with relative ease. John Jasper agreed to pay his wife $600 per month as alimony and temporary support for the children, to pay the regular charges on various family charge accounts, and in addition to bear all the expenses of maintaining the house. In addition, he agreed that he would remove himself from the house by 9:00 a.m. on Saturday, January 29. It was also agreed that Wallen would receive $500 as an initial payment on his fees, without admission that any additional fees would be proper.

Discussion of the property settlement agreement revealed that considerable difficulties would be encountered. Mower proposed, and Jasper frequently confirmed with vehemence, that an equal distribution of the community property was all that Thelma was entitled to, though he would consider making a proposal with respect to expenses of education and medical care for the children. Wallen responded that he could not even consider such a proposal until he knew more about the value of the Standard Meter and Gauge Co. as well as the other separate property of John Jasper, pointing out that the divorce laws of Washington empowered the court to dispose of a husband's separate property in making provision for his wife. Jasper refused to supply information concerning his business and other separate property, taking the position that it was a matter separate and distinct from that of determining how much Thelma would be entitled to upon termination of their marriage.

On February 25, 1966, Mower wrote to Wallen, and after making reference to their conference which they had attended with their clients, made the following offer for a property settlement. John Jasper would quit-claim the house, but not the furnishings, to Thelma Jasper at an agreed value of $95,000. He would continue to make his temporary alimony and support payments through September 1966, and he would then pay to Thelma any sum of money to which she might be entitled if her half of the community property exceeded $95,000 which was the value of the house. He added that he understood that Thelma would not want to keep the house, and that by selling it she could convert her share of the community property to cash or whatever form of property she desired.

Wallen telephoned Mower to inform him that the proposal was totally unacceptable, and suggested that Mower get in touch with him when he had been able to bring his client around to a more realistic view of matters. Nothing further transpired, however, except that the expected marriage of Eunice Jasper took place quietly. Wallen also agreed with Mower that February 23, 1967, be fixed for the trial date. On October 17, 1966, Wallen subpoenaed John Jasper to appear in Wallen's office on October 31, 1966, for the taking of his deposition, bringing with him the following:

1. Copies of all personal income tax returns filed by John Jasper and/or Thelma Jasper for the last 15 years;

2. Copies of all income tax returns filed by Standard Meter and Gauge Co. for the last 15 years;

3. All financial statements prepared for Standard Meter and Gauge Co. for the last 10 years;

4. All financial statements prepared for John Jasper and/or Thelma Jasper for the last 10 years;

5. The records of all salaries, bonuses, and dividends received by John Jasper and/or Thelma Jasper for the last 10 years;

6. Records of all business expenses for which John Jasper had received reimbursement from the Standard Meter and Gauge Co. during the last 10 years;

7. Records of all transactions with banks made by Standard Meter and Gauge Co. during the last 10 years;

9. Records of all transactions with banks made by John Jasper and/or Thelma Jasper during the last 10 years; and

10. All records of sales of personal and real property made by John Jasper and/or Thelma Jasper during the past 15 years, including all records of the investments made with respect to either their separate or community property.

On October 31, 1966, John Jasper and George Mower came to Wallen's office with the requested records. They agreed in the interest of saving time that Wallen could have copies made of the subpoenaed records. In addition, John Jasper testified that his gross income in 1965 had been $112,000, of which $32,000 was income received from his separate property, the balance being primarily salary and bonuses received from Standard Meter and Gauge Co. He further testified that he had received salaries and bonuses from the company in excess of $50,000 every year for the last 15 years, with the exception of 1962, when the company suffered a substantial loss because it became necessary to write off engineering and design expenses of a special metering device. The device had been developed for a business which failed to obtain what had seemed to be an almost certain government contract. At the present time the net worth of Standard Meter and Gauge Co. was $321,000 according to its books.

Wallen then inquired seeking more details concerning the condition of Standard Meter and Gauge Co. during its periods of difficulty in 1962. The company had never been insolvent in the sense of having its liabilities exceed its assets, but its liquid position had become very poor and at one point its current liabilities had equaled its current assets. This crisis was passed with the aid of an extension of credit of up to $100,000 by a Seattle bank. Actually, only $78,000 was actually borrowed from the bank. The documents which John Jasper signed in obtaining the line of credit obligated the company, himself separately, and the community of John and Thelma Jasper.

Wallen told Mower that he would be in touch with him after he had had an opportunity to review the financial records produced in response to the subpoena. On November 16, 1966, he telephoned Mower to say that, while he had not been able fully to digest the information contained in the records, it seemed quite apparent to him that John Jasper's separate property was worth close to two million dollars. For example, while the stock which he owned in Standard Meter and Gauge was carried in the account of his separate property at a value of $270,000, the company's own records indicated that it had a book value of $321,000. Moreover, the book values assigned to the assets of the company were quite unreal. The land upon which the plant and offices stood was by itself probably worth twice the amount at which it was carried on the books. In short, there was a tremendous amount of separate property, and the court in making a disposition of property should and would look to his separate estate. Moreover, during the 1962 financial crisis of the company, the credit of the community had been extended to save the company and the other separate property of John Jasper. If this was not sufficient to work a change of the property from separate to community property, it was in Wallen's opinion certainly enough to give the community a lien upon the separate assets and this was a factor which should be considered in determining how the admittedly community assets should be divided. He requested Mower to discuss the matter with John Jasper and come up with a realistic settlement offer.

Mower replied on December 5, 1966. He proposed that, giving consideration to the property which had already been given in trust to his son John, additional support in the amount of $65 per month would be appropriate. He would also agree to pay any medical bills incurred by John until he reached the age of 21. Moreover, he would pay all tuition, fees, room and board, and transportation costs incurred by John in attending any four-year college in the State of Washington until June of 1971. He would pay Thelma alimony of $500 per month for the next three years, unless she sooner remarried. If she became unable to work at any time during that period because of sickness or injury, as certified by their family physician, additional alimony of $6 per day would become payable. He further proposed that Thelma take the Vashon Island property and that he take the Cypress Island property as being of equal value, that the family house be sold, and that an equal distribution be made of the community property.

On January 6, 1967, Wallen replied by letter, saying he had discussed the offer with his client and they agreed that it was unacceptable. In particular, the provision made for the support of John, Jr. was insufficient; Jasper should be willing to provide medical care for his son beyond the age of 21; and provision should be made for education in addition to four years of college in the event that John, Jr. decided that he wanted to do graduate work or obtain a professional degree.. The alimony offered was entirely inadequate, both in amount and duration. Wallen's letter suggested that the discussion of the property settlement proceed on the basis that Thelma would receive all the community property and negotiations be restricted to fixing the additional amount she would receive. He again stated his view that the pledge of the community credit had created a lien on the separate property of John Jasper, if in fact it had not changed the nature of that property. In any event, John Jasper had been married to Thelma for more than twenty years, during which he had gotten her accustomed to a very high standard of living. The marriage now had to end because of John Jasper's refusal or inability to deal with his wife in a humane and sympathetic manner, but that termination should not and would not be accomplished by requiring Thelma to change all other aspects of her way of life. He asked again for what he called a realistic proposal, stating that otherwise they should expect a long trial.

On January 11, 1967, Mower telephoned Wallen to say that as a result of extended discussions with his client, he could now offer the following: Support for John, Jr. would be in the amount of $100 per month until John reached the age of 21; medical expenses incurred by John, Jr. until he reached the age of 24 would also be paid; in addition to the previously offered college educational expenses his client would pay for similar expenses incurred in pursuing a program of graduate education for a period of three years, provided that the course of education be completed by June 1974. As for alimony, the most he could do was to increase the amount to $600 per month for a period of three years.

Wallen said that the changes were desirable, but he was quite sure not enough to satisfy his client, particularly with respect to alimony. It was at this point that Mower said that Thelma might not be having problems with alimony for any period of time because, according to a private detective hired by John Jasper, a man, whom they had identified, had spent the night, or almost all the night with her at the family house several times during the Christmas season. Wallen said he would communicate the offer to his client and inform Mower in due course.

He did inform Thelma, and then queried her with respect to the allegations that a man had spent the night with her during the Christmas season. She denied that any man had stayed in her house for an entire night, but did admit that a friend had come and stayed very late and that they had had intercourse upon each occasion. She insisted that, while she had known the man for several years, there had been no such intimacy until a considerable time after the divorce proceedings had been instituted. The man involved was a widower.

Thelma wanted to know what this would do to the divorce proceedings. Wallen told her that it would make it a great deal more difficult to get as much as he had thought he would be able to produce for her in terms of a property settlement, but that he was sure he could get more than had been offered up to that time. He also advised discretion, or better yet, abstinence in her romantic affairs until the matter was closed.

Wallen waited until January 23, 1967, to arrange a meeting with Mower for the following day. He went to Mower's office and informed him that the latest offer had been, as he expected, unacceptable to Thelma. He stressed his certainty that he could and would be able to reach the separate property on the theories he previously mentioned. He suggested, however, that a single man in John Jasper's income tax bracket could make a much better arrangement by making substantial alimony payments which were deductible for income tax purposes and that, to the extent that Mower and Jasper would increase the amount of alimony, he would reduce his claim upon the separate property.

Mower suggested that Thelma's claim for either alimony or a share of the separate property was not particularly appealing in light of her boy-friends and that John Jasper might himself file suit for divorce on the ground of adultery. Wallen assured Mower that at most there had been but one boyfriend, and that even if Mower could prove at a trial that adultery had taken place, which he doubted, it was quite clear that there had been no impropriety until long after the divorce proceeding had been instituted. He thought the situation unchanged, and asked Mower to discuss the matter with his client, particularly in light of the income tax considerations they had discussed. Mower agreed to do so.

On January 27, 1967, Mower telephoned Wallen and informed him that he was authorized to increase the alimony offer to $1,000 a month. Wallen inquired if there was not also a concession with respect to the period of time during which alimony would be payable, and Mower said he was authorized to increase the time period to five years. Wallen asked whether there was any change in the offer beyond the former proposal that the community property be shared equally. Mower said that there was not. Wallen said in that case he would recommend that his client reject the offer, and that he would inform Mower in due course. He requested Mower to get some improvement in the offer in terms of the property settlement, suggesting that at least $100,000 of the separate prop-erty should be included in the package.

On February 2, 1967, Wallen telephoned Mower that the offer had been rejected and jokingly said that they'd better get ready for six or seven days of trial if something better were not forthcoming. Mower said he was authorized to offer alimony of $1,500 per month for the first year with $1,000 per month for the next four years. Wallen asked if there were nothing added to the property settlement. When told there was not, he suggested that Mower see if he could get in touch with his client, and that unless he heard otherwise he would plan to meet Mower in Mower's office that afternoon to see if they could not work out a settlement. He concluded the conversation by saying it was totally un-realistic of Mower and Jasper to think that with such a sizeable separate estate there should be no property transferred in addition to the division of the community property.

That afternoon Wallen went to Mower's office to discuss the matter. Mower said that because of tax considerations he was willing to increase the amount of the alimony for the first year to $1,700. Wallen expressed appreciation, but said that certainly no agreement could be made which did not involve a transfer of some property in excess of one half of the community. Mower then offered to pay the sum of $15,000 as a token payment in recognition of the claim on the separate property. Wallen said he would communicate the offer to his client, but that he could not recommend it because of the inadequacy of the property settlement.

Upon returning to his office he telephoned his client and informed her of the terms of the latest offer. She thought it satisfactory and authorized Wallen to accept it. He counseled her to reject it, saying that so much had come so fast in the last few days he was sure more would be forthcoming if they would only wait. Somewhat reluctantly Thelma agreed that he could reject the offer. He then called Mower and told him the offer had been rejected, and expressed regret that they had not been able to reach agreement.

The weekend passed without further developments, but on Monday, February 6, 1967, Mower telephoned Wallen and said that he had one last offer to make before going to trial. It was that instead of a token cash payment of $15,000, Jasper would give Thelma a promissory note in the amount of $50,000 payable within five years, and secured by a mortgage on the Cypress Island property. Wallen again expressed appreciation for the increase, and telephoned his client to report the increase. Thelma was, of course, willing to accept this offer and said so. Wallen did not, however, inform Mower of the acceptance until the following day.

Writing up the property settlement agreement involved the exchange of several drafts in which language was clarified and made more explicit. The only substantial matters not previously resolved were that agreement was reached that the interest in the Colorado oil leases would not be sold, but that instead John Jasper would convey an undivided one-half interest to Thelma Jasper, who would agree to be bound by John Jasper's business decision as to whether the lease should be sold or not and upon what terms. Since a purchaser for the house had not yet been found, it was agreed that the divorce decree should operate to transfer the house to Wallen as trustee, to hold the house until sold at a price no less than $95,000, with the expense of sale borne equally by John and Thelma. At Mower's insistence, the obligation to pay alimony of $1,700 per month for the first year and $1,000 per month for the next four years was to terminate if Thelma should die or remarry. The remainder of the divorce proceedings was accomplished in a perfunctory manner.

QUESTIONS

1. Wallen obtained for his client $68,000 in alimony, payable over five years, a $50,000 note payable in five years, approximately $90,000 as Thelma's share of the community property in addition to child support payments of about $3,600, plus medical and educational expenses. Would you have tried for still more? Remember that in 1966 the dollar had more than double its present purchasing power.

2. This property settlement was negotiated when the governing law required the party seeking a divorce to prove that the other spouse was at fault. Do you think "no-fault" divorce laws significantly affect the bargaining power of the parties in a case like this? In answering this question consider that, at least in some states, it was relatively easy for a party to prove that the other spouse had subjected the party to "cruel treatment, rendering life burdensome." See *Roebuck* v. *Roebuck*, 62 Wn. 2d 917, 385 P2d 50 (1963), applying a subjective rather than an objective test and looking to the effect of the conduct on the health and happiness of the complaining party. Will evidence of "fault" be admissible whenever there is a dispute over custody of children? Will evidence of "fault" be relevant to financial needs of the parties?

3. What effect do you believe the equal rights or women's liberation movement has had on cases such as this? Remember that most of the judges who exercise discretion with respect to property settlements in these cases are men past middle age.

4. Did John Jasper choose his attorney for this litigation wisely? Did Mower wisely decide to act as Jasper's attorney in this case?

5. What was John Jasper's attitude toward his wife? Would counseling on this subject have aided the negotiation process? Specifically, was the first offer unrealistically low? If so, do you think Mower and John Jasper erred in starting with this? How might it have been better for them if the original settlement figure had been higher? Was the temporary order so favorable that Thelma was under no pressure to settle?

6. How do you explain the frequency with which the settlement offered by Mower was increased? Was it wise to do so, or would fewer but more substantial improvements have been wise?

7. Why didn't Mower get Wallen to suggest a figure? How could he have done so?

8. Do you think it wise, from Mower's viewpoint, for the conference of January 1966 to have been conducted with the clients present, or would it have been better for Mower alone to be in contact with Wallen?

9. What do you think of Wallen's argument that the community had a lien on Jasper's separate property? Entirely apart from what you think of it, how much was it worth?

10. Should John Jasper have pretended that he wanted to save the marriage?

11. Do you think Mower made the best use possible of Thelma's indiscretion? Do you think it was worth more defensively than Mower obtained from it? Would it have been worth more if a countersuit for divorce had been filed? Would you have urged John Jasper to file such a suit if you had been his counsel?

12. Will John be obliged to pay alimony if Thelma takes on a new lifestyle and lives with but does not marry another man? See W. Wadlington, *Sexual Relations After Separation or Divorce: The New Morality and the Old and New Divorce Laws*, 63 Va. L. Rev. 249 (1977).

13. Why didn't the parties make all of the property settlement in the form of alimony to take advantage of the tax consequences?

14. Will John Jasper be entitled to deduct from his gross income the amounts which he agreed to pay to Thelma as alimony? See 26 U.S.C. 71, which provides in pertinent parts:

"(a) General rule.

"(1) Decree of divorce or separate maintenance. If a wife is divorced or legally separated from her husband under a decree of divorce or of separate maintenance, the wife's gross income includes periodic payments (whether or not made at regular intervals) received after such decree in discharge of (or attributable to property transferred, in trust or otherwise, in discharge of) a legal obligation which, because of the marital or family relationship, is imposed on or incurred by the husband under the decree or under a written instrument incident to such divorce or separation.

. . .

"(c) Principal sum paid in installments.

"(1) General rule. For purposes of subsection (a), installment payments discharging a part of an obligation the principal sum of which is, either in terms of money or property, specified in the decree, instrument, or agreement shall not be treated as periodic payments.

"(2) Where period for payment is more than 10 years. If, by the terms of the decree, instrument, or agreement, the principal sum referred to in paragraph (1) is to be paid or may be paid over a period ending more than 10 years from the date of such decree, instrument, or agreement, then (notwithstanding paragraph (1)) the installment payments shall be treated as periodic payments for purposes of subsection (a), but (in the case of any one taxable year of the wife) only to the extent of 10 per cent of the principal sum. For purposes of the preceding sentence, the part of any principal sum which is allocable to a period after the taxable year of the wife in which it is received shall be treated as an installment payment for the taxable year in which it is received."

15. Who will be entitled to the deduction for the support of John, Jr.? Was the greatest bargaining advantage obtained from this?

16. Consider how the bargaining process would have differed if Thelma had a large income even after divorce.

17. Why did neither lawyer make an attempt to effect a reconciliation of the Jaspers or to determine whether there was any possibility that such a reconciliation might be accomplished?

For practical suggestions concerning the defense of a husband in a divorce proceeding, see Griswold, *Representing the Husband in a Divorce,* 15 Prac. Law. (No. 7) 39 (1969). For a comparable article written primarily from the viewpoint of representing the wife, see Glieberman, *How to Negotiate a Divorce Case Settlement,* 10 Prac. Law. (No. 2) 63 (1964).

(4) *Plea Bargaining in Criminal Cases*

STEINBERG AND PAULSEN, A CONVERSATION WITH DEFENSE COUNSEL *

. . .

Question: Prosecutors frequently say, "We never bargain." What is the fact—do prosecutors ever bargain?

Answer: Well of course they do. They don't like to use the word "bargain" because they are afraid that the public will not understand the usefulness of a plea of guilty to something less than the facts might warrant if the case were pressed as hard as possible. Consider just a few facts. In New York County literally thousands of pleas of guilty, or compromises are effected each year on felony indictments. Less than 100 serious criminal cases go to actual verdict before the nine judges of the Court of General Sessions. Ninety to 95 per cent of the cases must thus be disposed of by a guilty plea or by some sort of compromise, or there would be a completely unmanageable backing-up of the caseload. The whole administration of criminal justice would grind to a halt if every one of the cases had to be tried to a jury. It would just not be physically possible. Unfortunately, the public generally doesn't fully understand the reality of this situation.

Question: What are some of the factors that enter into the acceptance of a plea to a lesser crime?

Answer: Well, the primary factor I suppose is the strength of the prosecution's case. If the prosecution's case has some weakness in it, the district attorney will be much more willing to agree to compromise than if he has all the elements of the crime fully documented. Furthermore, the prosecution is aware of the facts that I just mentioned. It is not possible to carry all the serious cases through a jury trial to verdict.

But another point must be made. These bargain pleas perform a useful function. We have to remember that our sentencing laws are for the most part savage, archaic, and make very little sense. The penalties that they set forth are frequently far too tough. In the state of New York we have an habitual-offender law, the so-called Baumes Law, which provides for life imprisonment in the case of a fourth-felony offender. The fourth felony may be far from serious, *i.e.,* snatching someone's purse, with a dollar in it. A purse snatcher who has been convicted of felony three times before, however, would be sent up for life. The prosecutors themselves realize the injustice of such punishment in such cases. Furthermore, as a practical matter, savage mandatory sentences are frequently seen as open invitations to juries to nullify the law by bringing in a ver-

* Copyright 1961 by The American Law Institute. Reprinted with the permission of *The Practical Lawyer.* Subscription rates $18 a year; $3.75 a single issue. "A Conversation With Defense Counsel," by Harris B. Steinberg and Monrad G. Paulsen, appeared in the May 1961 issue, Vol. 7, No. 5, of *The Practical Lawyer,* pp. 25-43.

dict of not guilty no matter what the evidence may be against the defendant, in order to avoid the unreal rigors of the required sentence.

The negotiated plea is a way by which prosecutors can make value judgments. They can take some of the inhumanity out of the law in certain situations. The law, for example, might in a given case require the death penalty—and yet the prosecutor may believe that the death penalty would be unfair, because of the defendant's age, lack of education, drunkenness, or other factors. Our sentencing laws are exceedingly severe and, if they were strictly applied, they would be great breeders of disrespect for the law.

. . .

NOTE

As indicated by the excerpt from Steinberg and Paulsen, in 1961 there were doubts about the propriety and respectability of plea bargaining in criminal cases. It was widely practiced, but not openly acknowledged. Indeed the *sub rosa* status of plea bargaining frequently led to concealment and even misrepresentation to a sentencing judge that no bargain had been made. See, e.g., *Blackledge* v. *Allison*, 431 U.S. 63 (1977). However, in *Santobello* v. *New York*, 404 U.S. 257 (1971), the U.S. Supreme Court placed its judicial seal of approval on plea bargaining. Speaking for the Court, Chief Justice Burger said, 404 U.S. at 260-261:

"The disposition of criminal charges by agreement between the prosecutor and the accused, sometimes loosely called 'plea bargaining,' is an essential component of the administration of justice. Properly administered it is to be encouraged. If every criminal charge were subjected to a full-scale trial, the States and the Federal Government would need to multiply by many times the number of judges and court facilities.

"Disposition of charges after plea discussions is not only an essential part of the process but a highly desirable part for many reasons. It leads to prompt and largely final disposition of most criminal cases; it avoids much of the corrosive impact of enforced idleness during pretrial confinement for those who are denied release pending trial; it protects the public from those accused persons who are prone to continue criminal conduct even while on pretrial release; and, by shortening the time between charge and disposition, it enhances whatever may be the rehabilitative prospects of the guilty when they are ultimately imprisoned."

A bargained plea cannot support a judgment of guilt unless it is voluntary in a constitutional sense, which requires that the defendant have an understanding of the elements of the offence to which he is pleading. *Henderson* v. *Morgan*, 426 U.S. 637 (1976). A prosecutor may not vindictively bargain for a guilty plea to a more serious charge because the defendant took advantage of a right under federal or state law. *Blackledge* v. *Perry*, 417 U.S. 21 (1974). However, the range for bargaining permits a prosecutor to give notice that he will seek an indictment for a properly chargeable, more serious offense if a defendant does not plead guilty to the lesser offense charged and carry through to conviction pursuant to that notice when the plea is withheld. *Bordenkircher* v. *Hayes*, 434 U.S. 357 (1978). On the other hand, it has been held that a state judge, who had earlier proposed a sentence for a plea of guilty, could not impose a more severe sentence upon a defendant after trial, absent reasons unknown to the judge when he proposed the earlier sentence. *Frank* v. *Blackburn*, 605 F.2d 910 (5th Cir. 1979). The defendant is entitled to withdraw a plea if the prosecutor does not perform in accordance with the agreement which produced a plea. *Santobello* v. *New York, supra; Blackledge* v. *Allison, supra*. Review by way of habeus corpus of 28 U.S.C. § 2255 is considerably narrowed after the entry of a guilty plea, and the defendant may not challenge antecedent constitutional defects, such as exclusion of blacks from the grand jury list or the deprivation of other rights prior to entry of the plea. *Tollett* v. *Henderson*, 411 U.S. 258 (1973).

An extensive study of plea bargaining in the United States was published in 1978 by the National Institute of Law Enforcement and Criminal Justice. H. Miller, W. McDonald, and J. Cramer, PLEA BARGAINING IN THE UNITED STATES. It reveals that the extent of plea bargaining varies from state to state, and differs within a given state between rural and urbanized areas, but that there is no fixed relationship between population and the guilty-plea rate. In some districts 100 percent of the convictions are the result of guilty pleas; in other jurisdictions as little as 50 percent of the convictions resulted from guilty pleas. A rate of conviction based on guilty pleas of in excess of 90 percent was not uncommon. Ibid., Chapter 1. Part II. The lack of correlation between population and the guilty plea rate casts substantial doubt that the extent of plea bargaining is regulated by case load.

A distinction may be drawn in the analysis of plea bargaining between bargaining over the charge to which a plea will be entered and bargaining over the recommendation for sentencing which the prosecutor will make to the sentencing judge. Attention must also be given to whether in a particular jurisdiction it is possible to predict or control the selection of the sentencing judge and whether the sentencing judge may participate in the plea bargaining process. Rule 11 (e)(1) of the Federal Rules of Criminal Procedure contemplates that bargaining will occur over both the charge and the sentence, but specifically provides that the court shall not participate in any such discussions. Rules governing discovery in criminal proceedings vary between jurisdictions, and obviously may affect the plea bargaining process.

A frequently expressed concern is that plea bargaining leads to the conviction of innocent persons. Analysis of this problem is assisted by drawing a distinction between legal guilt and factual guilt. See H. L. Packer, THE LIMITS OF THE CRIMINAL SANCTION 149-173 (1968). A factually guilty person is one who did the acts constituting the crime that is charged, whereas a legally guilty person is one whose guilt can be judicially established, overcoming the presumption of innocence with evidence that can be introduced in a procedurally regular fashion in a court of competent jurisdiction. There is an obvious tension between the traditional concept that it is better that ten guilty men go free than that one innocent man be found guilty and pursuit of a system which permits a prosecutor to obtain a plea on the basis that he might be able to obtain a conviction of an even more serious charge. No prosecutor should attempt to obtain a guilty plea in a case in which he believes the defendant is factually innocent. But to what extent does he properly serve the public interest by seeking to obtain a guilty plea in a case in which he believes the defendant may be legally innocent but factually guilty?

CHARLES HOAGUE'S CASE*

[The following is a Seattle attorney's narrative recollection of how he proceeded with the case of Charles Hoague, aged 18. The actual file of the case is relatively slim, consisting primarily of the formal papers and a few notes. As will be seen, most of what the attorney did for his client was accomplished in oral discussions, either in person or by phone.]

On Monday, July 19, 1965, after first telephoning me, Alex Hoague came to my offices to see me concerning his son Charles, who was then under arrest and held in the city jail upon a charge of suspected burglary. According to Alex, who is the manager of the local supermarket at which my wife and I trade, Charles and his friends Bill Marceau and Terry Amber were arrested Sunday afternoon upon charges of burglary growing out of some housebreaking which was apparently done in the course of a search for beer to supply a party they attended last Saturday night. I agreed to handle the case, but told Alex I could give him little advice until I had had a chance to talk with Charles and find out more about what had happened. Alex was very eager to post bail and get Charles out of the jail, but I told him that unless he thought the experience would be unbearably traumatic for Charles, it was probably better for him and certainly much better for his case if he spent a little jail time. I promised to give the matter my immediate attention, taking care to discuss with Alex the retainer and the possibility of additional expenses.

At the city jail I met Charles and told him his father had retained me to represent him. Terry Amber was not in the jail, but instead at the Youth Service Center because his case had to be handled as a juvenile court matter since he was not then 18 years of age. Charles then told me the following.

On Saturday night, July 17, 1965, he and his friends Bill Marceau and Terry Amber went to a party in the Rainier District of Seattle. When the beer began to run low, Marceau and Amber volunteered to get more, and, because they had come in Hoague's car, he drove them. A few attempts at purchasing beer failed when merchants refused to honor Marceau's false identification cards. Amber then suggested that he knew

* Reproduced by permission of the copyright holders, Robert L. Fletcher and Cornelius J. Peck.

several families who were away on vacation, and that they had most likely left beer supplies in their refrigerators. He led the group first to the home of Richard Roe, on Lake Washington Boulevard, where they forced entry by lifting the sliding door of the back patio off its runners. Inside they found only four cans of beer. According to Hoague, Amber then said, "Hell, if that's all they've got for us, we'll look for some real stuff." Ultimately he found the liquor closet and removed a nearly full bottle of Scotch and one full bottle and a nearly empty bottle of bourbon.

When they got outside, Hoague suggested that they go back to the party, saying that the housebreaking was too risky. But Amber and Marceau insisted upon "another try." The next house visited was that of Martin Kreist, also on Lake Washington Boulevard. Hoague did not enter the Kreist house, but stayed outside to serve as a lookout. Marceau and Amber apparently worked the same trick on another sliding door, and came out about 10 minutes later with a full six pack and four bottles of beer. They insisted upon one more try, and the party went to the house of David Codie. Here they had to break open the basement door, which they did with the force of their bodies. While searching the kitchen for beer and liquor supplies, they were surprised by Codie's mother, who apparently had not gone with the rest of the family on a camping trip. Amber seized a large carving knife from its rack in the kitchen and told Mrs. Codie to lie down on the floor and stay quiet for 10 minutes if she didn't want her throat slit open wide. Mrs. Codie did as directed, and the boys ran out. Amber dropped the knife on the back porch.

They returned to the party, and, after consuming some of the beer and liquor they had brought with them, began to boast of the evening's exploits and of how frightened and funny Mrs. Codie looked lying on the floor in her nightgown. Someone at the party apparently reported the events to his parents the next day, and the parents reported the matter to the police.

Charles admitted to the police that he had driven the car to the three houses, but denied any part in entering the houses, including that of Richard Roe. He did not know what Marceau or Amber had told the police, but the police must have thought they had enough because they informed me that they were transferring the file to the prosecutor's office that afternoon. I left the jail, after assuring Charles that I would do everything possible for him, but that we would just have to wait to see what could be done. When he inquired about the possibility of getting out on bail, I told him it was too soon to decide, but that he might have to spend some time in jail if we were to negotiate a reduction of the burglary charge. I suggested further that he discuss the case with no one else until he had heard from me.

Returning to my office, I called Irving Mark, the deputy who reviews the cases coming from the police to determine whether a defendant will be bound over for trial in the Superior Court on a felony charge or prosecuted in justice court on a misdemeanor charge. I asked him to delay making his decision as to which he would do until July 27. He agreed.

On Tuesday, July 20, Charles' case came before the justice of the peace who, of course, found probable cause for the burglary charge. As Mark and I had agreed, no decision was made then as to whether or not Charles would be bound over to Superior Court. I did not attempt to arrange for bail.

I then checked into Charles' school record. He graduated the June before from Franklin High, with a grade point average just a hair under 3.0. He had only minor disciplinary problems in high school, and apparently the same was true for his junior high school period. He worked since graduation in a Shell Oil gasoline station, at which he had been employed during previous years. His employer considered him a satisfactory employee, apparently with mechanical abilities, and appeared somewhat surprised by and interested in the difficulties into which he had gotten himself. He said he would be willing to reemploy him, and I urged him to do so when we got Charles out on bail, saying it would make a very favorable impression on the judge who heard Charles' case. Charles was a pretty good-looking boy, and I was comforted by knowing that he would "clean up" well in conservative clothing.

On Thursday, July 23, Alex Hoague and his wife came to see me. I inquired further about Charles' background and whether the Hoagues had ever experienced difficulties with him before. I was told that there had been none but the usual problems, including a fairly unpleasant period during which he had been denied the use of the car because he drove it alone one afternoon when he had only a learner's permit and not a driver's license. Alex and Mrs. Hoague were surprised somewhat that Charles and his friends had parties at which beer and even hard liquor were consumed, though they knew that Charles had smoked secretly since sometime before he was 15. Charles had a satisfactory relationship with his older brother and his younger sister. I also learned that a few years ago the Hoagues had considered the possibility of a divorce, but decided to remain together for the sake of the children.

I explained to them that technically Charles was guilty of burglary in the first degree, which carries a mandatory five-year term in the state penitentiary, reduced only by one third off for good behavior. I further explained that in light of Charles' lack of a police record we might be able to get the prosecutor to agree to reduce the charge to petit larceny if Charles would plead guilty, understanding that the prosecutor would recommend perhaps a six-month jail term, with five months suspended. This would have had the advantage that the case would remain in justice court and Charles would not have the record of having been convicted of a felony. Furthermore, it would involve at most a month in jail. On the other hand, we could have Charles bound over to Superior Court for trial on a burglary charge. In that event we would try to convince the prosecutor to charge burglary in the second degree, which does not have a minimum prison term. If the prosecutor would agree, we would then enter a plea of guilty, with the understanding that the prosecutor would recommend that the sentencing be deferred during good behavior for probably three years. If Charles made no more mistakes and had no further encounters with the law for that three-year period, the whole case would be washed out at the end and Charles would end up with no criminal record, even though he had pleaded guilty to the felony charge. Furthermore, he would not have to spend any more jail time.

The big question thus became whether we thought Charles could be depended upon to stay out of trouble for the next three years. His father thought he could, and urged that we take the route through Superior Court. Mrs. Hoague was not so certain, but left the matter up to her husband. I thought that there had been surer bets, but I was inclined to back Charles and bet on his ability to stay out of trouble for three years or so.

On the morning of Friday, July 24, I was distressed to see a newspaper story reporting that the Juvenile Court had waived jurisdiction of Terry Amber and referred his case to adult authorities for action. As Charles had indicated to me in the initial interview, Amber has had difficulties with the police on previous occasions. It also appeared that Mrs. Codie had recollections, perhaps not accurate, of close and menacing gestures having been made by Amber as he held the knife.

I called Irving Mark the same day to see if I could see him to talk about the Hoague case, but he suggested that I contact him Monday, after he had had more time to look into the case. When I did see him on Monday, July 26, he assured me that trial in the justice court on a gross misdemeanor charge was out. As he saw it, Charles was clearly guilty as a principal of three felonies, even if he had remained in the car all the time. And these included a burglary in which not only had one of the burglars armed himself with a deadly weapon, but he had also assaulted a human being in a way which could easily have led to bloodshed.

We then went into Charles' background and the prognosis with respect to future criminal conduct. Mark agreed that he looked like a pretty good bet, but in light of the way the burglary had taken place he had considerable reservations concerning reduction of the charge to second degree burglary with the recommendation that sentencing be deferred for three years during good behavior. Ultimately he agreed, and we took the case to Hailey (the county prosecutor) to wrap it up. After some consideration, Hailey gave his approval, saying that since Charles had not physically threatened anyone or been present when the threats were made, he was willing to give him the opportunity to clear himself and avoid the lifetime mark of a felony conviction.

On Wednesday, July 28, we completed the preliminary hearing and had Charles bound over to Superior Court on a charge of burglary in the second degree. I then arranged to have Charles released upon $2,000 bail, and he left in the custody of his parents. I told them that Charles should be sure to get back at work at the gas station as soon as possible.

I then went to Irving Mark's office to check on the plea calendar. He suggested that we set the date for the following Friday, July 30, but I didn't agree because the calendar indicated that Judge Denny would then be presiding over the plea calendar. On a few occasions in the past I've had difficulty with Judge Denny, and I'm inclined to think he sometimes believes in dealing out sterner medicine to erring youths than does the prosecutor. In any event, it wasn't worth the risk, so I suggested Monday, August 2. I must confess that I was partially influenced by thinking that Judge Richards would be presiding then and he almost always accepts the prosecutor's recommendation. He would most likely be impressed by the fact that Charles' employer had taken him back. It was also to our advantage that I could inform Judge Richards that Charles had spent almost two weeks in confinement, and therefore knew quite a bit about what prison life would be like should he encounter difficulties which would lead to earlier sentencing on the felony charge.

Judge Richards did accept the prosecutor's recommendation, and so far Charles has been in no difficulties. I believe that Pete Randolph was able to work out just about the same deal for Bill Marceau, but my recollection is that Terry Amber ended by spending some time at Monroe (a maximum security reformatory for youthful offenders).

QUESTIONS

1. Why did the attorney believe it would be "better for his case" not to get Charles out on bail immediately?

2. What was the significance of the newspaper story concerning Terry Amber? Would the negotiation possibility be less in a small town?

3. Suppose Charles had quit school in his senior year and had not yet found regular employment. Do you think the prosecutor would have agreed to either a deferred sentence or a reduction in the charge?

4. Suppose that in addition to quitting school and not having found regular employment, Charles had upon one occasion been taken into custody by the juvenile court authorities in connection with a beer drinking party. Do you think the prosecutor would have agreed to either a deferred sentence or a reduction in the charge?

5. Do you think the prosecutor would have agreed to a deferred sentence or a reduced charge if Charles had been the person who threatened Mrs. Codie with a knife?

6. For what additional and related reason did the attorney urge Charles' reemployment upon release on bail, i.e., besides the "favorable impression on the judge"?

7. In deciding that he was "inclined to back Charles and bet on his ability to stay out of trouble for three years or so," the attorney was not concerned solely with the welfare of Charles. Can you identify another factor in his judgment, one that would cause, perhaps, more caution than solely a concern for Charles' welfare? To what extent does a defendant's attorney's appraisal of his guilt and character determine what will happen to him?

8. What do you think would have happened if the attorney had advised Charles to plead not guilty? How would the prosecutor have proved his participation? Is bargaining on proof considerations less ethical than the bargaining in this case? Do prosecutors watch their "win" record?

9. Does consideration of the importance of negotiation in criminal cases give you additional insights as to the desirability of the rules announced in *Gideon* v. *Wainwright,* 372 U.S. 335 (1963), and *Miranda* v. *Arizona,* 384 U.S. 436 (1966)?

10. Chief Justice Burger has expressed serious concern about the number of incompetent lawyers who appear in trials. If he is right in his appraisal of the competence of attorneys in trials, what is the implication for those defendants who plead guilty on the advice of counsel that the agreement reached with the prosecutor is to be preferred to the risk of conviction or a longer sentence after trial? Will incompetent counsel more frequently seek to avoid trial by recommending that a client enter the bargained plea?

POLSTEIN, HOW TO "SETTLE" A CRIMINAL CASE*

. . .

FUNCTION OF COUNSEL FOR THE GUILTY DEFENDANT

There is, of course, one prerequisite before any criminal case can be disposed of by plea—the defendant must be guilty. In this context, the word "guilty" is meant in its strictest sense. If a client fully admits his culpability and freely acknowledges his willingness to plead guilty, then and *only* then, may counsel assume he is guilty.

Emotionally, it is easy to undertake the defense of one unjustly accused of crime. But it can be just as rewarding—and, unfortunately, even many lawyers do not appreciate this—to represent the guilty.

In the first place, far too many "beefed up" indictments are returned by grand juries—in much the same way that complaints in civil causes often contain exaggerated claims. The defendant charged with murder is far more willing to plead to manslaughter than he would be if the lesser crime were the only one charged. Further, although legal distinctions between accessories and principals are disappearing, there are often cogent reasons for treating co-defendants differently upon plea and sentence. The human element is always present, and intelligent administration of criminal justice dictates that the punishment should fit the criminal rather than the crime. Furthermore, there are always differing degrees of guilt, and even the guilty client usually cannot assess the degree of his own culpability. In short, when representing a guilty client

* Copyright 1962 by The American Law Institute. Reprinted with the permission of *The Practical Lawyer.* Subscription rates $18 a year; $3.75 a single issue. "How to 'Settle' a Criminal Case," by Robert Polstein, appeared in the January 1962 issue, Vol. 8, No. 1, of *The Practical Lawyer,* pp. 35-44.

who is willing to pay some penalty, it is defense counsel's responsibility to make sure that only the proper degree of guilt is acknowledged and only the fair penalty is paid.

FACTORS FACILITATING SETTLEMENT CLIMATE FOR PROSECUTION

Although the initial feelers concerning the possibility of a lesser plea normally come from defense counsel, it is the prosecuting attorney who will have the final say as to what plea is offered. In New York, as in some other jurisdictions, unless the prosecutor is willing to offer a lesser plea, defense counsel, the defendant himself, and the court are powerless to accept or enter one. Whether or not a particular prosecuting attorney will offer a lesser plea may depend upon a number of considerations— whether the plea that is acceptable to the defendant affords the court adequate scope of punishment, the strength or weakness of a particular case, whether the lesser plea offered can be justified to either his superiors or the public at large, and perhaps even the weight of his current case load.

The widely held opinion that prosecutors never bargain is a myth. As a practical matter they must in order to stay in business. No trial lawyer can afford to lose too many cases. The prosecutor, just as his colleagues in the civil courts, has to settle a weak case. Unlike England, where the barrister prosecuting a case on behalf of the Crown one week may be retained to defend a criminal case the next, prosecutors in this country are elected or appointed to represent the People only. The measure of a prosecutor's success is the amount of convictions he obtains. The public cares little whether nine out of 10 of such convictions result from pleas rather than trials. Statistically, at least, to a prosecutor a plea of petit larceny under a robbery indictment is as good for the batting average as a conviction of the top count upon trial. Thus, to protect his record, any prosecutor is usually willing to offer a lesser plea of guilt in a weak case.

TIMING AND TACTICS FOR EXPLORING SETTLEMENT POSSIBILITIES WITH PROSECUTION

The one thing that no defense lawyer should do is to wait until he is in court before exploring plea possibilities with his adversary. An appointment for a personal interview at the prosecutor's office should *always* be made. At that interview, defense counsel must be prepared to argue the merits of his case.

Whatever extenuating circumstances are present, whatever good can be said for one's client, whatever weaknesses there are in the prosecutor's case (short of educating one's adversary), should be brought to the attention of the prosecuting attorney at that time. One must be prepared to do a real piece of advocacy to convince the district attorney that the plea suggested is a fair one. This cannot be done in a few whispered words during the course of the calendar call. Too often, prosecutors have refused to recommend lesser pleas "off the papers" in court that would have been acceptable to them had they had the opportunity for some prior sober reflection in their offices.

The personal interview with the district attorney often serves another purpose. In discussing his case, the prosecutor may quite frankly disclose the reasons why he will not offer as low a plea as defense counsel thinks is warranted. If these reasons are valid, defense counsel then owes it to his client to discuss with him the altered circumstances and point out why the plea offered is reasonable. And *any* plea that shaves some time from a prison term is a fair one!

With sincere efforts on both sides, nearly every indictment can be disposed of by compromise. This is so because within the framework of most indictments there is included some lesser count that will be acceptable to both prosecutor and defense. For example, the usual armed robbery indictment in New York includes four counts—robbery in the first degree (10 to 30 years), assault in the first degree (up to 10 years), grand larceny in the first degree (up to 10 years), and an unlawful weapon count, as either a felony (up to seven years), or as a misdemeanor (maximum sentence of indeterminate term up to three years). This is the indictment filed whether the case involves a petty street robbery with a simulated weapon, or a professional payroll holdup. Under such an indictment, there are some 22 lesser pleas, with countless combinations, that could be entered—pleas that either tie the judge's hands by a statutory minimum sentence or give him the widest latitude. Often, the actual plea offered is a mere label. The scope of sentence, for instance, is the same (up to five years) whether the eventual plea is attempted robbery in the third degee, grand larceny in the second degree, or assault in the second degree. The ideal plea, as far as the prosecution is concerned, is one that effectively passes the buck to the bench. Then, if any criticism results, the prosecutor can always explain that the judge had adequate scope of punishment but chose not to exercise it.

There is one situation, however, where no one can fault the district attorney—where leniency is exchanged for needed co-operation against co-defendants. Whether such a bargain can be struck depends on a variety of factors; the weakness of the case against the co-defendants, the extent of the defendant's participation, the aid he can render, and who the prosecutor's real target is. The scared kid who waits behind the wheel of the getaway car while his prison-hardened confederate robs a bar and grill, and in the process guns down an innocent bystander, obviously deserves more consideration than his co-defendant. If his cooperation is necessary in order to convict the "real killer" (even though both are technically principals), no one will criticize the prosecutor for granting the lesser culprit some leniency. Thus, the possibility of co-operation in exchange for consideration is an avenue that should be explored in every serious case involving multiple defendants. Often, this is the only way out of an otherwise hopeless situation. It is not a very dramatic way to save a client from the execution chamber, but a practical one.

TIMING AND TACTICS IN PERSUADING JUDGE TO
ACCEPT COMPROMISE PLEA

Obtaining the offer of an acceptable plea from the prosecutor is merely the first hurdle. Defense counsel's next problem is to find a judge who will accept the plea. Normally, the judge before whom the plea is entered will later impose sentence. Personal predispositions and prejudices, therefore, become a major consideration in determining whether or not to plead guilty before a given jurist. Judges are human and are subject to human foibles and quirks. Some regard all crimes of violence as meriting stiff sentences. Others feel that only commercial frauds deserve a prison term. To some, any hint of publicity, with the resultant possibility of public criticism, dictates no leniency. In short, before entering a plea before a criminal court judge, defense counsel must learn all he can about that judge. This can be done easily enough by speaking with court personnel or lawyers familiar with that jurist's sentencing practices, or by actually sitting in one morning when the particular judge is disposing of his sentence calendar.

Despite individual differences, there is one generality that seems to apply to all criminal court jurists. For the most part, our sentencing statutes are cruelly medieval. Nearly all jurisdictions have barbaric, recidivist statutes that dictate minimum sentences for multiple offenders. In New York, for instance, a second or third conviction for robbery in the first degree carries a mandatory sentence of 15 to 30 years—despite any mitigating circumstances—and a fourth conviction for any felony means a life sentence. Judges do not, as a rule, like this encroachment upon their traditional prerogatives. They will usually communicate this distaste at the bench conference preceding the plea. In fact, the judge's general attitude toward both the specific crime and the particular defendant may be explored at that time. A judge occasionally feels so strongly that he will actually make a commitment to defense counsel that if the prosecutor's offer will not afford enough leeway on sentence, he will suspend sentence on the major counts of the indictment and impose sentence only on the lowest count. In other words, in the multiple count indictment situation, a plea to the entire indictment before a sympathetic judge is often more beneficial to the defendant than a plea to a single lesser count that precludes judicial discretion. In this respect it should be noted that the prosecutor is powerless to prevent the defendant from pleading guilty to the entire indictment.

RELEVANT FACTORS INFLUENCING SETTLEMENT POSSIBILITIES

The prime consideration in any negotiations between defense and prosecution is the particular crime charged. Obviously more consideration will be shown the youthful first offender who embezzles from his employer in order to buy medicine for his sick mother than will be shown or is deserved by the hardened graduate of two previous prison terms who commits a crime of violence. However, it must be remembered that publicity will often make even the most humane adversary or judge reticent to consent to a reduction of the charge. If the defalcations of the pathetic clerk have received any newspaper coverage, an irate employer may insist on a full prosecution. He doesn't want an easy plea or a lenient sentence to give other employees a green light for larceny. The prosecuting attorney and the sentencing judge, likewise, can't afford to be put in a position where they must excuse their conduct to an angry electorate. Accordingly, the best service defense counsel can perform when representing a guilty client is to stay out of the press! The less publicity, the better—as far as the client is concerned, at any rate.

It is a sad, but true, fact that *where* a crime is committed is often more determinative of the final outcome of the prosecution than *what* crime was committed. In large cities the casual theft of an automobile by a youngster bent only on a joy ride goes unnoticed by everyone but those immediately affected. In an outlying rural community, however, such a casual misadventure may assure the aspects of a major crime wave. Obviously, in terms of megalopolitan crime, the attorney representing the youth who "borrowed" a neighbor's car under somewhat suspicious circumstances is able to make a better deal for his client than the lawyer in the outlying community whose client stands in the glare of the spotlight. Accordingly, there appears to be an almost mathematical rule that "the more crowded the calendar, the lower the plea."

In those jurisdictions where an overcrowded prison has resulted in a backlog of trials, there is a real and immediate pressure on prosecutors and judges to dispose of cases by plea. The Constitution guarantees the right to a speedy trial, and undue delay may result in a dismissal of the indictment. If there is an inexcusable lag between indictment and trial, prosecutors react automatically by lowering pleas. Defense counsel can check calendar congestion easily enough by visiting the court clerk's office and looking up the dates of indictments currently being tried. By insisting on a trial when he knows the district attorney has a backlog of older cases, defense counsel can sometimes force a lesser plea. Obviously, this is somewhat risky. Prosecutors usually control the calendar and can insist upon the early trial of any given indictment. However, if the case is a minor one, defense counsel's pressure for an early trial is often worth this gamble.

The defendant, naturally enough, is really the key to the whole situation. As has already been indicated, his acknowledgement of guilt and desire to plead are prerequisites to any negotiations. But, in addition, the nature of the crime, the degree of participation, and the personality of the man himself are all major elements in obtaining a lesser plea. The first offender, whose sentence is not circumscribed by any recidivist statute, is usually more ready to plead guilty than the multiple offender whose sentence is statutory, whether he pleads or is convicted after trial. Even in jurisdictions where all participants are treated as principals, the degree of participation usually makes a difference in the plea that is offered.

Assuming that defense counsel has done his job well and convinced both prosecutor and judge that a favorable lesser plea is justified, the client still has to be sold the idea that he's getting a bargain. It is remarkable how many unsuccessful robbers think that petit larceny is the only fair plea. In this respect, however, it should be noted that, often, even the most obdurately "innocent" of felons will suddenly want to "cop out" when the first juror is impaneled.

Putting the prosecution to its proof, moreover, many times is a double-edged sword. The defendant who thinks the plea offered is too harsh usually has a change of heart when the parade of state's witnesses begins to march to the stand. Similarly, the prosecutor who has insisted on a harsh plea may come down to earth when defense counsel begins poking holes in the case. And, incidentally, defense counsel should not be taken in by the prosecutor's threat, "if we go to trial, all deals are off." If his case were weak enough for him to have offered a plea in the first place, he'll be no more anxious to try the case than is the defendant.

Too often, once the plea is entered and the sentencing date is set, defense counsel regards his task as done. There is nothing left but to diary the sentence date, appear in court, and say a few kind words on behalf of his client—more to assuage the feelings of the defendant's near and dear ones than to sway the judge, it might be added. The lawyer who adopts this attitude is not only doing a grave disservice to his client, but is also bypassing a golden opportunity to affect the ultimate sentence.

After trial, the presiding judge is fully familiar with all facts and circumstances of the crime and has also learned a great deal about the defendant. Even if the accused has not testified, the court has had an opportunity to observe his demeanor, hear eyewitnesses describe his acts, and listen to the prosecution's version of his postarrest admissions. If the jury returns a guilty verdict, the judge has a pretty good idea of how to treat the defendant on sentence. This is not so in cases that terminate in pleas. The defendant, except as a name on an indictment, is a complete stranger to the court. The indictment itself, other than setting forth the bare legal elements of the crime, is silent on details that will vitally affect the ultimate sentence. In such cases, the court's only basis upon which to decide the punishment will come from the presentencing report prepared by the probation department.

Today, as never before, the functions of probation departments are assuming ever increasing importance. Presentencing investigations are now the norm. The day is fast disappearing when a judge passes sentence immediately after conviction. Usually, a period of weeks will pass during which a probation officer, frequently a trained sociologist, will investigate and evaluate the background of the defendant for the purpose of assisting the court in determining what is a fair sentence. Such investigations range from a study in depth, supplemented by a battery of psychological tests and psychiatric interviews, to a cursory inquiry into only the most rudimentary facts of the crime and facets of the criminal's personality. Whatever the type of investigation, however, defense, counsel can usually make sure that all favorable factors are included in the presentence report.

In the first place, he should learn the identity of the probation officer assigned and make it his business to visit him. At that interview every favorable fact concerning the defendant and the crime, including names of prospective defense witnesses who would have testified at the trial, should be disclosed. Probation officers, these hectic days, at least, are overworked and will appreciate whatever assistance counsel can give. This assistance may take a variety of forms.

Initially, counsel should emphasize to his client the purpose of the investigation and that this is the defendant's last chance to help himself. The fact that complete, truthful, and frank answers are necessary must be stressed! Too often do the terms "subject seemed evasive— refused to co-operate" in a probation report convince an otherwise uncertain jurist that prison is the only answer. Counsel should ask the probation officer whom he wants to interview and make sure that these people keep their appointments. Copies of hospital records, doctors' reports, military records, and any other similar documents casting light on the defendant's physical or mental condition should be obtained by counsel and made available to the probation officer. An attempt should be made to solicit favorable character references from the defendant's employer, schools, clergyman, and neighbors, and such material should be placed at the disposal of the investigating officer.

In assault cases, defense counsel should try to obtain the court's permission for the defendant to pay the complainant's medical and hospital expenses. Similarly, in larceny or commercial fraud situations, a schedule of restitution should be worked out with the probation officer, including either the establishment of an escrow account or arrangements for regular payments into court. Such procedures serve a dual purpose. In the first place, the victim's vindictiveness will be softened, and this fact will be included in the presentence report. Secondly, it may insure a suspended sentence. Restitution cannot be made by a prisoner earning a dime a day making license plates, and, no matter how incensed a judge may be at the defendant, he's not likely to penalize the victim further by preventing him from recouping his losses.

CONCLUSION

Now, the above suggestions are not intended as a blueprint by which the guilty defendant may evade the consequences of his anti-social act.

They are offered, however, as an aid in unstacking the deck with which the accused are forced to play in criminal courts. Even though the cards are not arranged by the prosecutor or judge, the fact remains that any criminal prosecution is inherently unfair to the defendant, semantic presumptions of innocence notwithstanding. The defendant is not being sued for some real or imagined civil debt. He is being accused of a crime against the community, an assault upon the *status quo*. The plaintiff is the People. The complaint doesn't contain vague allegations drawn by some lawyer trying to earn a fee, but is an indictment returned by a grand jury. Plaintiff's counsel is no unknown attorney, but the public prosecutor. "Accused," "crime," "grand jury," "indictment," "district attorney," "People,"—these are words that evoke an emotional response. All of the majesty of the law, all of the dignity of the prosecutor's office, all of the outrage of the community, is working to the prejudice of the defendant. And, if he is guilty, so much the worse for him.

This, then, is the responsibility of defense counsel. He must insure that guilty defendants get a fair deal. He must strive for an equitable settlement on behalf of the client who is willing to pay a fair penalty, but should not be forced to pay the full amount demanded in the complaint. As officers of the court, as law-abiding members of the community and as guardians of the liberties of all citizens, not just the innocent, defense counsel must fight, within the framework of the judicial processes, to protect the rights of the guilty client.

An angry faith in the justness of one's cause is one of the advocate's most powerful weapons. However, this is a luxury that criminal lawyers can seldom afford in run-of-the-mill cases. Nevertheless, defense counsel has the obligation to provide the best possible representation to his guilty client. This he can most effectively achieve, consistent with his divided responsibilities to the client, the court, and the community, by vigorously negotiating for the fairest possible disposition of each individual case. More than this, no defendant is entitled to. But less than this, no enlightened legal system can force him to accept.

. . .

ADDITIONAL READINGS

Alschuler, *The Prosecutor's Role in Plea Bargaining*, 36 U. Chi. L. Rev. 50 (1968).

Alschuler, *The Defense Attorney's Role in Plea Bargaining*, 86 Yale L.J. 1179 (1975).

Berger, *The Case Against Plea Bargaining*, 63 ABA J. 621 (1976).

Lagoy, *An Empirical Study on Informational Usage for Prosecutorial Decision Making in Plea Negotiations*, 13 Am. Crim. L. Rev. 435 (1978).

Newman, CONVICTION: THE DETERMINATION OF GUILT OR INNOCENCE WITHOUT TRIAL (1966).

Owens, *Plea Bargaining . . . Agreeing . . . Recommending,* 26 Legal Aid Briefcase 55 (1967).

Note, *Guilty Plea Bargaining: Compromises by Prosecutors to Secure Guilty Pleas,* 112 U. Pa. L. Rev. 865 (1964).

HARRIET WINTERS' CASE*

March 7, 1963: Rex Mitchell phoned to ask if I would be willing to take over the defense of the case of Harriet Winters, who shot and killed her husband yesterday. Rex handled a divorce action against Mr. Winters which Harriet started and then dropped about four years ago. He doesn't want to handle the homicide charge. I agreed to look into the case. Charles Winters, eldest son of the deceased, and Mrs. Thelma Warner, sister of Harriet, then came to my office to tell me about it.

Harriet is 46 years old. Charles is 22 and now lives in Portland. There are two other boys, Michael, aged 16, and William, aged 12, who have been living at home. George Winters was 48 years old and employed as a welder at Pacific Car and Foundry at the time of his death. Yesterday, at about 7:00 a.m. and after breakfast, Harriet shot him once in the back as he was opening the front hall closet. He stumbled back to the kitchen and told Michael, "I'm shot!" Michael called an ambulance and the police. George was dead on arrival at Harborview.

Harriet sat in the living room until the police came. There had been no quarrel or argument during breakfast. She told the police she had had to kill her husband because he was going to kill her and the younger two boys. Apparently she is in some kind of psychotic state at present. In any event she is now in the security ward of the King County Hospital rather than in the county jail. No charge has yet been filed. Mrs. Warner believes something mental has been wrong with her sister for several years, and that it has been getting worse, as indicated by the weird stories and interpretations of events which Harriet related to Mrs. Warner over the last few months. Two years ago Harriet spent about three weeks in Western State Hospital for the Mentally Ill. Just last Monday, March 4th—two days before the killing—Harriet had gone again to Western State Hospital for outpatient treatment, and had been cleared by the three doctors who examined her.

The gun with which she shot George was a 38-calibre pistol which George had kept loaded in his bedroom dresser at all times.

Mrs. Warner has taken the younger two boys in with her temporarily. How long this can last depends in part upon how well they get along with the Warners' four children and how well the Warners can get along with the additional people in the house.

I discussed my fee arrangements with Charles and Mrs. Warner, and agreed upon the schedule of payments. There will be sufficient assets in the estate to pay the fee if Harriet is not disqualified. Mrs. Warner and

* Reproduced by permission of the copyright holders, Robert L. Fletcher and Cornelius J. Peck.

her parents will make initial retainer payment. Also will set up a trust account for expenses. Gave them the usual explanation of criminal procedure and the alternatives which may lie before us.

March 7, 1963: Visited Mrs. Winters at King County Hospital to obtain her approval of the selection made by Mrs. Warner and Charles. She approved, but seemed confused and uninformative. Insisted her husband was going to kill her and the two younger boys, probably by poisoning. Husband's alleged motives not clear, except that he wanted to be rid of them all. She also inconsistently suggested that he might injure William, leave him with her, and skip town taking Michael with him.

March 8, 1963: Talked to Joel Langen, deputy prosecutor. Medical report obtained by prosecutor's office (Dr. Ritchie) indicates that Harriet Winters is now in a state of paranoid schizophrenia, a danger to society and not to be at large, and that she cannot now intelligently assist in the preparation of her own defense. Joel has not yet decided whether he will charge murder in the first degree, but will go along with a stay of the proceedings until such time as Mrs. Winters can assist in the preparation of her defense. Joel indicated that he may be willing to reduce charge to murder in the second degree to avoid a jury trial.

I requested Dr. Cooper to examine Harriet and give me a report.

March 12, 1963: Arraignment on a charge of murder in the first degree. Pleaded not guilty and not guility by virtue of insanity. Trial set for April 10, 1963.

March 14, 1963: Received Dr. Cooper's first written report. He concludes that Harriet is now suffering from paranoid schizophrenia, that she is not capable of intelligently assisting in the preparation of her own defense at the present time, and that she now poses a danger to society and is not safe to be at large. He wants more time for determining whether at the time of the shooting she knew right from wrong or the nature and quality of the act which she performed, but he is inclined to think not. Apparently her late husband frequently called her crazy, threatened to have her confined at Western State, and upon occasion beat her rather severely.

Called Joel Langen. He is awaiting further reports from Dr. Ritchie, but indicated that the charge could almost certainly be reduced to second degree. Will agree to putting off trial, but wants to obtain the additional medicals.

April 2, 1963: Order, approved by Joel Langen, was entered by Judge Sacks, staying further proceedings until such time as Harriet will be capable of assisting at her own defense. Order further provides for transfer of Harriet from King County Hospital to Western State Hospital for the Mentally Ill.

April 15, 1963: Mrs. Warner decides to become guardian for Michael and William. I am appointed guardian ad litem for Harriet Winters, to serve as such in the proceedings involving the guardianship of the children and the settlement of the estate of George Winters. Charles will be administrator of his father's estate, and Rex Mitchell will serve as his attorney in settling the estate.

June 19, 1963: Dr. White of Western State staff reports Harriet is making some progress, but not yet ready to assist in her own defense. She still believes that she had to kill her husband to protect the children and herself, and seems not to understand the seriousness of what she did. Responding well in group therapy, as well as individual treatment. He will testify that she did not know right from wrong at the time of the shooting.

November 12, 1963: Dr. White of Western State staff believes that Harriet is as well as she will ever become in a hospital and that she is ready for trial. So informed Joel Langen.

November 19, 1963: Dr. Ritchie believes that Harriet should stay in the hospital for a few more months, without tranquilizers.

April 21, 1964: Dr. Ritchie believes that Harriet is as well as she will ever be. He believes that she should be kept in a nursing home or some other controlled environment until it is possible to say with greater certainty that she does not pose a threat to society. He also believes she can now assist in the defense of her trial.

April 24, 1964: Harriet was transferred to the county jail. When I visited her she seemed greatly improved. She is somewhat anxious to get the trial over. I again explained that the charge might be reduced to second degree, but that she may have to spend additional time, possibly in a nursing home, receiving treatment.

April 29, 1964: Agreed with Joel Langen on the trial date of June 1, 1964. Went to Bailey's office (the prosecuting attorney) to discuss the case. Langen and Bailey agree that (1) the charge will be reduced to second degree; (2) the case will be tried without a jury, with me attempting to get a finding of not guilty by virtue of insanity; (3) Harriet will be kept in a private place, or possibly with her family, but under court order to report for further treatment by psychiatrists.

May 1, 1964: Mrs. Warner phoned to inquire about the forthcoming trial. I explained arrangements made, and told her that, while one can never be certain, in my opinion there is better than a 90 percent chance that Harriet will be found not guilty, but required to submit to treatment until she has made a complete recovery.

June 2, 1964: Trial completed today. All three doctors (Cooper, Ritchie, and White) testified that at the time of the shooting Harriet did not know right from wrong or the nature and quality of the act which she committed. Doctors Cooper and White were of the opinion that she had now recovered sufficiently so that she does not constitute a threat to society, but Dr. Ritchie believed that treatment should be continued before she is given full freedom.

Judge Reagh entered findings and conclusions suggested by Langen and me. Specifically he found that Harriet did shoot her husband with the intent to kill him; that she was insane at the time and did not know right from wrong or the nature and quality of the act; that she was presently sane and capable of assisting intelligently at her trial; but that he would not make a determination that she was safe to be at large until she had undergone a period of psychiatric treatment. She will continue as an outpatient at Western State, reporting monthly until January 1965. At that time a further hearing on her sanity will be held and appropriate disposition made of her case.

January 18, 1965: Hearing before Judge Jones on Harriet's sanity. Doctor James testified that she is now safe to be at large and poses no threat to society. Judge Jones entered an order so finding and concluding the criminal proceeding.

February 16, 1965: Order entered terminating my guardianship of Harriet.

February 22, 1965: Orders entered terminating guardianship proceedings of Michael and William, who have been living with their mother since last September.

QUESTIONS

1. What were the negotiated aspects of this case?

2. Why didn't the attorney press for trial as soon as he obtained the medical opinions indicating that Harriet Winters was legally insane at the time of the homicide?

3. What was the importance of Harriet's visit as an out-patient at Western State two days before the shooting took place?

4. Why did Mrs. Winters' attorney consider it important to have a trial without a jury? Why would the prosecutor's deputy state (p. 61) that "to avoid a jury trial" was a reason for him to agree on a reduction of the charge?

5. Why did the prosecutor agree to reduce the charge to second degree?

6. Suppose that the fact pattern differed from that stated above in that Mr. Winters had upon occasion had extramarital relations and that Mrs. Winters' delusion was that he was going to kill her and the children so that he might be free of them. Do you think the prosecutor would have agreed to reduce the charge even if the medical testimony were just as positive and firm to the effect that Harriet was insane at the time of the killing?

7. Suppose that the fact pattern differed from that stated only in that Harriet Winters believed it was a neighbor who was going to harm or kill the children. Do you believe the prosecutor would have agreed to reduce the charge?

(5) *Settling a Case With the NLRB*

The National Labor Relations Board is an agency with a heavy case load in the critical and sensitive area of relations between employers, employees, and unions. According to its chairman, its intake of cases, now at about 60,000 per year, is expected to grow to 80,000 per year by 1982. 1978 DLR 127: A-1. In its 1977 fiscal year, 68.7 percent of the unfair labor practice cases were dismissed or withdrawn before the issuance of a complaint, 24.8 percent of the cases were disposed of by settlements and adjustments, and only 3.8 percent of the cases resulted in an order in a contested case. Of those unfair labor practice cases deemed "meritorious" by the general counsel, 78.9 percent were disposed of by formal or informal settlements made in the regional offices of the NLRB whereas only 12 percent produced a decision by the Board in a contested case. 42 NLRB ANN. REP. 5 (1977).

The NLRB's Statements of Procedure, Series 8, 29 C.F.R. 101.7 and 101.9 describe the procedure followed in making informal and formal settlements. Informal settlements are those made prior to the issuance of a complaint and require the approval of the regional director. Formal settlements are made after the issuance of a complaint and require the approval of both the regional director and the Board. A formal agreement provides that the Board may issue an order requiring the respondent to take action appropriate to the terms of the agreement, and ordinarily also provides that the Board may apply to the appropriate court of appeals for a decree enforcing that Board's order. An attempt is made to have all parties join in the agreement, but it sometimes occurs that the general counsel's representative and a respondent will find satisfactory an agreement which the charging party believes to be inadequate. In such cases the charging party may take an appeal to the general counsel from the decision of the regional director to approve the settlement. If the settlement occurs after the opening of a hearing it must obtain the approval of the administrative law judge. If any party will not join in the settlement, the administrative law judge will give that party an opportunity to state on the record its reasons for opposing the settlement.

Early versions of 29 C.F.R. 101.9 did not make provision for review by the Board of settlement agreements made over the objections of a charging party, although the standard informal agreement itself did provide for review by the general counsel. See 29 C.F.R. 101.7, 101.9 (1955). The addition of such a provision was apparently made in response to decisions such as *Retail Clerks Union 1059* v. *NLRB,* 348 F.2d 369, 59 LRRM 2618 (D.C. Cir. 1965), holding that a labor organization named as a "sweetheart union" in charges filed with the NLRB was entitled to be heard on its objections to a settlement agreement made between the regional director and the employer charged. See also *Leeds & Northrup Co.* v. *NLRB,* 357 F.2d 527, 61 LRRM 2283 (3rd Cir. 1966). The view that the NLRB may settle a case over the objection of the charging party is predicated on the proposition that the NLRB acts to vindicate the public interest rather than to protect private interests. See *Amalgamated Utility Workers* v. *Consolidated Edison Co.,* 309 U.S. 261, 6 LRRM 669 (1940). The Court of Appeals for the Second Circuit has concluded that the policy of the Act "requires that the Board be recognized as empowered to determine when the possibly slight merit of a charge is outweighed by the sure and speedy concessions, the industrial harmony restored and the saving of Board resources which a settlement can achieve." *Local 282, IBT* v. *NLRB,* 339 F.2d 795, at 799, 58 LRRM 2065, at 2067 (2nd Cir. 1964).

Accord: *Oshkosh Truck Corp.* v. *NLRB*, 530 F.2d 744, 91 LRRM 2561 (7th Cir. 1976).

The following case involves a settlement which was neither formal nor informal within the meaning of the NLRB's Statements of Procedure but had instead been arrived at by the union and the employer charged and approved by the administrative law judge over the objections of the general counsel's representative.

COMMUNITY MEDICAL SERVICES

236 NLRB No. 102, 98 LRRM 1314,
reconsideration denied, 239 NLRB No. 179,
100 LRRM 1100 (1979)

The relevant facts of this case may be succinctly stated. In accordance with the allegations of the consolidated complaint the General Counsel offered to prove by a preponderance of the evidence that the Respondent violated Section 8(a)(1) and (5) of the Act by unilaterally terminating, without notice or bargaining, the existing employee health plan and submitting therefore a health plan that provided diminished benefits, by insisting to impasse on changes in the scope of the recognized bargaining unit, and by failing and refusing to furnish the collective-bargaining agent with relevant information which the bargaining agent requested during negotiations. The General Counsel is also prepared to prove that Respondent violated Section 8(a)(1) and (3) by its failure and refusal to reinstate a large number of employees to their former or substantially equivalent positions of employment after the employees made an unconditional offer to return to work (the employees had been engaged in a strike against Respondent which the complaint alleges was caused and prolonged by Respondent's unlawful conduct). Finally, the complaint alleges that this Respondent engaged in independent violations of Section 8(a)(1) of the Act by threatening employees with job loss, closure, and other retaliation if they persisted in their protected activity, by warning employees there would be no union unless the Union came to terms, and by interrogating employees about their protected activity.

The non-Board settlement approved by the Administrative Law Judge provided for the execution of a collective-bargaining agreement between Respondent and the Charging Party, the reinstatement by August 15, 1977, of 14 strikers who had not yet been reinstated at the time of the hearing, and the full reinstatement of three strikers who had been returned to work but not to their former or substantially equivalent positions. Finally, the settlement agreement provided no backpay for the many employees who may have been discriminatorily denied reinstatement upon their unconditional offer to return to work.

The legal principles which the Board will apply in determining whether or not to approve a settlement agreement and withdrawal of unfair labor practice charges are well settled. In *Jack C. Robinson, doing business as*

Robinson Freight Lines, 117 NLRB 1483, 40 LRRM 1035 (1957), the Board pointed out at 1485.

". . . the Board's power to prevent unfair labor practices is exclusive, and, . . . its function is to be performed in the public interest and not in vindication of private rights. Thus, the Board alone is vested with lawful discretion to determine whether a proceeding, when once instituted, may be abandoned. Such discretion to dismiss charges will be exercised only when the unfair labor practices are substantially remedied and when, in the Board's considered judgment, such dismissal would effectuate the policies of the Act."

The Board has also long recognized that the willingness of a charging party to withdraw charges is not necessarily a ground for dismissal of a complaint "for once a charge is filed, the General Counsel proceeds, not in vindication of private rights, but as the representative of an agency entrusted with the power and the duty of enforcing the Act in which the public has an interest." *The Ingalls Steel Construction Company,* 126 NLRB 584 at fn. 1, 45 LRRM 1353 (1960). And the Board has observed that "when a matter has ripened to the point of being before the NLRB for decision, we must, of course, give paramount weight to the public interest affected by withdrawal of the underlying charges." *Retail Clerks International Association, Local Union No. 1288, AFL—CIO (Nickle's Pay-Less Stores of Tulore County, Inc.),* 163 NLRB 817 at fn. 1, 64 LRRM 1433 (1967).

Turning to the facts of the case before us, we note at the outset that there is nothing minimal about the unfair labor practices of which this Respondent stands charged. Rather, the allegations of the consolidated complaint, once established, would show a respondent who willfully and persistently flouted not only its basic collective-bargaining obligation under the Act but also its obligation to respect the exercise by employees of their protected rights. Thus, as the General Counsel points out in his request for special permission to appeal, this Board and the courts have long recognized that insistence to impasse on a nonmandatory subject of bargaining, here the composition of the established bargaining unit, constitutes an unlawful evasion of the basic duty to bargain in good faith which the statute mandates and this Board is required to enforce. The General Counsel also contends that Respondent's insistence on altering the scope of the recognized unit, coupled with its adamant refusal to furnish the Union with relevant information and its numerous and flagrant acts of interference with employees' statutory rights, triggered a long and apparently bitter unfair labor practice strike during which Respondent never receded from its unlawful position. And, finally, the General Counsel submits that Respondent demonstrated its contempt for its employees' protected rights by discriminatorily failing and refusing to reinstate 71 unfair labor practice strikers on their unconditional offers to return to work, and by delaying the reinstatement of 51 unfair labor practice strikers who had made unconditional offers to return. It is axiomatic that such conduct, if proved, is discriminatory conduct that "goes to the very heart of the Act." *NLRB* v. *Entwistle Mfg. Co.*, 120 F.2d 532, 8 LRRM 645 (C.A. 4, 1941).

. . .

In our judgment this settlement agreement must be rejected as a wholly inadequate vehicle for effectuating the purposes and policies of the Act. First of all, we note the absence of any effective notice to employees concerning the rights of unfair labor practice strikers, including, *inter alia,* their right to full reinstatement even if their employer has hired replacements and must discharge those replacements. Moreover, inasmuch as the proposed settlement agreement also totally ignores the Respondent's alleged violations of Section 8(a)(1) of the Act, there is no notice language communicating to employees their right as employees to engage in or to refrain from engaging in protected concerted activity or their employer's undertaking to avoid conduct which would interfere with, restrain, or coerce them in the exercise of such rights. Nor is the absence of such a notice, particularly given the circumstances of this case, a trifling omission. For, as we have pointed out, this Respondent has been charged with conduct that amounts to a rejection of the fundamental purposes of the Act, the resolution of industrial strife by peaceful means, and the protection of employees' right to engage in concerted activity for their mutual benefit.

Of equal moment in reaching our conclusion that the proposed settlement is inadequate is the abrogation therein of this Respondent's liability for backpay. In this connection General Counsel contends that the amount of backpay to which the discriminatorily treated employees are entitled will likely exceed $60,000. We find it inconceivable that the public interest in the vindication of statutory rights will be advanced or the underlying purposes and policies of the Act effectuated by acceptance of a settlement agreement that trades off employees' rights to be made whole for a wrongdoer's agreement to execute a contract.

Finally, we would be remiss if we failed to challenge our dissenting colleagues' analysis of this case. They claim we should approve this settlement because it "fully protected the interests" of employees and a majority of employees voted to ratify it. They also predict that our disapproval of the proposed settlement will prove destructive of the parties' bargaining relationship and will frustrate the goal of industry harmony. And last, they suggest that the Board's time and money could be better spent on matters other than litigating this case.

In the first place, as we have indicated previously, we are at a loss to understand how a settlement agreement that surrenders employees' entitlement to backpay can be said to protect their interests. Nor do the dissenters offer any illumination on this point for, in addition to glossing over the fact that this Respondent is charged with numerous and serious violations of Section 8(a)(1) and (3), as well as violations of Section 8(a)(5), they also gloss over the absence of any provision for backpay with the cryptic observation that the wage rates contained in the new contract "were negotiated with the backpay expectations of the employees in mind."

The dissenters also make much of the 60-to-14 employees vote in favor of the settlement. We find it not at all surprising that most employees, after having been embroiled in a long and unsuccessful strike allegedly caused by their employer's unlawful conduct, might feel themselves constrained to forgo the opportunity for the full vindication of their statutory rights in exchange for a "bargain basement" settlement. And, in any event, statutory rights are not, and cannot be, a matter for referendum vote. For, as we have taken pains to point out herein, there is an overriding public interest in the effectuation of statutory rights which cannot be cut off or circumvented at the whim of individual discriminatees.

Nor do we find merit in the dissenters' suggestion that by approving settlements of the sort proposed here we would encourage the friendly resolution of labor relations disputes and husband the Board's limited resources for other, and presumably worthier, matters. If we read our colleagues' opinion rightly, and we think we do, in effect they endorse the notion that employees should be asked to "foot the bill" for an employer who has long avoided its obligation to bargain in good faith (and, in the process of so doing, has trampled on employees' statutory rights), all in exchange for that employer's undertaking to "play fair" to the extent of negotiating a new collective-bargaining agreement.

The essential unfairness of such a proposition aside, we wonder how our approval of settlements of this nature could be thought to serve as a deterrent to the commission of unlawful conduct or as a spur to the speedy and peaceful resolution of labor disputes by collective bargaining. To the contrary, we think it is clear that we would encourage wrongdoers to subvert the collective-bargaining process by flouting their obligation to bargain in good faith if we approved settlements whereby they could wipe the slate clean by offering to execute a contract on condition that employees be denied full remedial relief. Such settlements are neither fair nor effective as to past misconduct and would encourage further unlawful misconduct in the future to the detriment of the stability of bargaining for which our colleagues hope. In this connection we agree with the General Counsel's contention that the Board's strong policy in favor of securing settlements must be balanced against the need for an effective remedy. We also agree that, if respondents can expect to win approval of settlements of the sort proposed here from Administrative Law Judges at the time of hearing, the whole settlement process at the prehearing stages will be undermined and, ultimately, the litigation burden of the Board increased.

Finally, the weakness of the dissenters' case is made clear by their response to our reasons why this settlement must be rejected. Sidestepping the real issues, they attack a variety of strawmen, with an argument perhaps more adjectival than logical.

First, it is simply illogical of the dissenters to chide us for our supposed failure to distinguish properly between the allegation of a complaint and the actual finding of a violation. We would not have thought it necessary to point out that, for the limited purpose of passing on the acceptability of a proposed settlement, of necessity we begin with the assumption that the case is meritorious and the General Counsel is prepared to carry his burden of proof. Indeed it is, or should be, evident that taking the allegations of unfair labor practices as proved is, in cases of this nature, an essential part of the settlement procedure. Hence, any unqualified reference to "wrongdoers" or the like in this Decision is solely a consequence of this fundamental and necessary assumption and of our obligation to explain why, more generally, settlements of the sort proposed here are unacceptable. The use of such terms obviously does not, in such circumstances, indicate any inclination on our part to decide the case on its merits before a hearing and in derogation of this Respondent's unquestioned right to a full and fair trial.

For the rest of it, the dissenters' response to our views requires but little comment. Thus the dissenters' assertion that the absence of an effective notice should be charged to the General Counsel's refusal to agree to the settlement is plainly unfounded. As we have taken pains to point out herein, the proposed settlement is deficient for myriad reasons and the General Counsel's refusal to join in it is plainly warranted. Hence, in seeking to shift to the General Counsel the blame for the absence of an effective notice, the dissenters are looking at the hole instead of the doughnut.

The dissenters are correct, however, in suggesting that the issue of backpay deserves careful consideration. One wonders, nonetheless, what point they wish to make by stating that it is within the Board's discretion under Section 10(c) of the Act whether to grant backpay even if the allegations of the complaint are proved in their entirety. In its 43-year history the cases in which the Board has ordered reinstatement without backpay as a remedy can be counted on the fingers of one hand. And the Board has taken such action only in the most extraordinary, indeed singular, circumstances. More germane to the backpay issue is our colleagues' apparently unhesitating acceptance of Respondent's computation of its potential backpay obligation in the vicinity of $30,000, as contrasted with the General Counsel's claim that Respondent's liability will exceed $60,000. The dissenters' unconcern for the amount of backpay liability is perhaps not surprising; they are, after all, satisfied with a settlement that denies backpay entirely.

. . .

IT IS FURTHER ORDERED that the above-entitled proceeding be, and it hereby is, remanded to the Regional Director for Region 6 for further appropriate action.

. . .

PENELLO AND MURPHY, Members, dissenting:

Although this case does not involve any major principle of substantive labor law, we think it is one of the most important in which we have participated since becoming Members of the Board. We say that because the decision of the majority exhibits an attitude toward administration of the Act which we find to be repugnant to its basic purposes and policies. At issue is whether our job is to force unwilling employers and unions to continue lengthy and expensive unfair labor practice litigation detrimental to both sides and to the employees concerned, or whether it is to promote the settlement of union-management differences at the bargaining table on terms which are just and acceptable to employer, union, and employees alike. That may appear to be a rhetorical question, but the facts will testify that it is neither an exaggerated nor unfair description of the issue resolved by the Board today.

. . .

The only sensible yardstick against which to measure the settlement is the remedy to which the Union would be entitled if it won the entire case on the merits. To remedy the 8(a)(5) violations, the Board would order the Employer to rescind the change in the employees' health plan, to bargain with the Union in good faith, and to provide the Union with the relevant and necessary financial information for bargaining. The intent of such an order, of course, would be to facilitate the execution of a collective-bargaining contract by the Union and the Employer. However, under the settlement agreement, the Union and the employees have achieved the desired end—the benefits and protection of a labor contract—without need of such an order. In addition, if the Union should prevail on all counts in the litigation, the Board would order that all the strikers be returned to their former or substantially equivalent positions, and that they receive backpay for the period between 5 days after their unconditional offer to return to work and the time when they were actually reinstated. The settlement agreement provided for the reinstatement of the strikers, and according to the union attorney, the wage rates contained in the labor agreement were negotiated with the backpay expectations of the employees in mind. In sum, the Union gained more for the employees with the settlement agreement than it would through litigation.

. . .

These comments [of counsel for the union concerning the meeting at which employees ratified the agreement] graphically show that the agreement was entered into by the parties for legitimate reasons, that the agreement fully protected the interests of the employees, and that, with full knowledge of their rights, the employees endorsed the agreement.

Equally important with the advantages of settling the case on this basis for all involved, it is important to consider the destructive impact of upsetting the agreement on the parties' collective-bargaining relationship and upon the lives of the individual employees. The contract contains a clause stating that, if the settlement agreement is set aside by the

Board, the collective-bargaining agreement becomes void *ab initio*. This means that the majority decision will cause the employees to lose immediately the higher wage rates and all the benefits of the contract. It means that the Union will be required to give up the contract reached with the Employer on the *hope* that it can eventually get something *less*—a bargaining order. Bargaining may not even begin until after a court of appeals decision in the far future. In any event, by pitting the Employer against the Union in unwanted, protracted litigation, the Board is likely to make process of ultimately reaching a contract that much more difficult.

Although the General Counsel has objected to the settlement, we believe the agreement serves the public interest as well as that of the private parties. Approval of the settlement would have obviated the necessity of considerable expenditures in time and money by the Board in trying and deciding the case. This Agency, with limited staff and resources, is currently staggering under a load approaching 60,000 cases annually. For the Board to deal speedily and effectively with those cases that must be litigated, we have to accept settlements which attain the ends we desire without the need for going to trial. Today's decision, however, amounts to a public announcement that the Board wants litigation for litigation's sake and that even settlement of an 8(a)(5) case by the execution of a collective-bargaining agreement is an inadequate substitute for litigation.

Although we find the emotionally charged language used throughout the majority opinion highly entertaining, our colleagues cannot make up in rhetoric what they lack in logic. We feel constrained to point out first that the majority has taken but little care to preserve the distinction between a complaint alleging that a respondent violated the Act and an actual finding to the same effect. In fact, we regret to say that our colleagues' intemperate remarks leave the reader with the impression that they have already decided the case on the merits. Thus, the members of the majority refer to what the allegations of the complaint "once established," not if established, would show regarding Respondent's conduct. They refer twice without qualification to Respondent as a "wrong-doer," and to the "commission of unlawful conduct" and to "past misconduct" by Respondent. They term Respondent an employer "who has long avoided its obligation to bargain in good faith (and, in the process of so doing, has trampled on employees' statutory rights) . . ." And they refer to the employees' so-called entitlement to "backpay" and the settlement's alleged "abrogation of this Respondent's liability for backpay," although the employees have neither a right to backpay nor Respondent a backpay liability at this point.

. . .

One last matter remains to be addressed. The majority says that Respondent "has been charged with conduct that amounts to a rejection of the fundamental purposes of the Act, the resolution of industrial strife by peaceful means, and the protection of employees' rights to engage in concerted activity for their mutual benefit." But Respondent, which was entitled to litigate whether it had committed any unlawful acts at all, instead voluntarily executed a collective-bargaining contract with the Union that was accepted by the overwhelming number of the represented employees, and further agreed to reinstate all strikers to their former or substantially equivalent positions. Respondent has therefore shown its good faith in attempting to meet its obligations under the Act without compulsion from the Board. We hardly perceive this, though our colleagues apparently do, as the action of a "willful and persistent" flouter of the labor laws.

In voiding the settlement reached in this manner by the Union and the Employer, the Board has turned a blind eye to the overarching purpose for which it was established 42 years ago—the alleviation of industrial strife through the furtherance of collective bargaining. In so doing, it has set a short-sighted, pettifogging course, which insists upon litigating every alleged violation of law regardless of its negative consequences for the parties and the presence of a just and efficient alternative.

We emphatically dissent.

NOTES AND QUESTIONS

1. The wisdom of the Board's decision in *Community Medical Services* is the subject of a debate between two members of the ABA Committee on Development of Law Under the National Labor Relations Act, 1976-1978. A. Bioff, *"Capitulate or Litigate"—The Labor Board's Settlement Policy and the Objectives of the National Labor Relations Act,* 47 UMKC L. Rev. 289 (1979); C. D. Whipple, *"Capitulate or Litigate"— The Labor Board's Settlement Policy and the Objectives of the National Labor Relations Act—A Reply,* 47 UMKC L. Rev. 309 (1979). Mr. Bioff points out that the *Robinson Freight Lines* case upon which the majority relies involved a settlement agreement made after a trial which had resulted in findings and conclusions that unfair labor practices had been committed, which he believes justified the Board's refusal to compromise. Mr. Whipple responds that in *Retail Clerks Int'l Ass'n Local 1288,* 163 NLRB 817, 64 LRRM 1433 (1967), the Board had applied the same standards in rejecting a settlement agreement after a trial examiner [administrative law judge] had decided the respondent had not committed unfair labor practices. Do you believe the three types of cases should be treated by the Board in the same manner?

The major criticism made by Mr. Bioff is that the Board has mistakenly concluded that the purpose of the NLRA is preventing unfair labor practices instead of encouraging the process of collective bargaining. Does this rephrasing of the purposes of the NLRA affect the determination of whether a settlement agreement should be approved by the Board? Is it significant that the Board has no power to initiate unfair labor practice proceedings, and can issue a complaint only when a charge has been filed by an aggrieved party?

2. Soon after the decision in *Community Medical Services*, the general counsel of the NLRB issued the following memorandum:

GENERAL COUNSEL MEMORANDUM 78-41

July 6, 1978

TO: All Regional Directors, Officers-in-Charge, and Resident Officers
FROM: John S. Irving, General Counsel
SUBJECT: Settlement Status Report

The continuing ability of this Agency to achieve a high rate of settlement has been of paramount importance in the Agency's efforts to effectuate the purposes of the Act. This ability can be attributed in part to the continuing emphasis upon the successful achievement of settlement in each Regional Office.

Thus far in this fiscal year, the Agency was presented with a number of unusual factors which significantly affected settlement potential in many Regional Offices. For example, a shortage of Administrative Law Judges, the curtailment of travel in October and November pending final approval of the Agency's Fiscal Year 1978 budget, and reduced scheduling of unfair labor practice hearings during May and June by the Division of Judges substantially increased the period between complaint issuance and formal hearing in many cases and diminished the prospect for early settlement of disputes scheduled for hearing. Similarly, the 1977 decision of the Fifth Circuit in *Robbins Tire Company*, 563 F.2d 724 (96 LRRM 3128), which required the prehearing disclosure of the statements of witnesses in pending unfair labor practice proceedings, resulted in the postponement of a large number of cases scheduled for hearing and substantially reduced, or at least delayed, settlement possibilities in these situations pending the Supreme Court's decision. These factors severely tested the Agency's ability to achieve settlements. Although the Agency has experienced some recent slippage in its national rate of settlement to a present rate of 80 percent, the fact that the settlement rate has not more substantially decreased during this period demonstrates the extent to which each Region has committed itself to achievement of settlement, and the success of the Regional efforts in this regard.

Many of the factors which made settlement particularly difficult during the past several months no longer exist or are abating. Thus, the Division of Judges has resumed the regular scheduling of unfair labor practice hearings and are in the process of hiring additional judges, and the Supreme Court overturned the decision of the Fifth Circuit in *Robbins Tire* (98 LRRM 2617). Further, the Board has reiterated its intent to carefully examine the remedy provided by settlement agreements accepted at hearing over the General Counsel's objection, balancing the Board's strong policy in favor of securing settlements against the need for an effective remedy. *Community Medical Services of Clearfield, Inc., d/b/a Clear Haven Nursing Home*, 236 NLRB No. 102(98 LRRM 1314). This restatement may affect the efforts of some respondents to delay settlement until the hearing in an attempt to obtain a more favorable adjustment.

The Regions have already demonstrated their ability to maintain a high rate of settlement, even when confronted with unusual settlement problems, and I am confident that as the Regions renew their settlement efforts in the coming months, the Agency will again achieve the high rate of settlement which is necessary for the timely remedying and adjustment of meritorious unfair labor practice cases.

Do you agree with the general counsel's suggestion that the decision in *Community Medical Services* will discourage respondents from delaying settlements until the hearing? Will the general counsel have to use criteria different from those of the Board in determining the acceptability of informal settlements if delay until hearing is to be discouraged? An indication that he will do so is found in a more recent address before the American Newspaper Publishers Association by NLRB General Counsel John Irving. He stressed the importance of settlements to disposition of the Board's case load, urging that a "settlement mentality" was necessary on the part of both the general counsel's representatives and the named respondents. "Do We Need A Labor Board?" 101 LRR 15, 16 (May 7, 1979).

3. The NLRB earlier called upon its administrative law judges to exert their best efforts, consistent with their role as impartial triers of cases, to present to the parties full opportunity for settlement. Fanning, "The Role of the Hearing Examiner in the Settlement of Formal Complaints by the National Labor Relations Board," reprinted in LABOR RELATIONS YEARBOOK—1966 at 324 (1967).

(6) *The Equal Employment Opportunity Commission's Experience With Conciliation and Negotiation*

The Equal Employment Opportunity Commission (EEOC) was created by Title VII of the 1964 Civil Rights Act. Originally EEOC had no enforcement powers and was limited to attempting to achieve compliance with the Act through conciliation. In 1972 EEOC was authorized to file suits in federal district courts to enforce the Act's prohibitions against employment discrimination, but it made no attempt to integrate its newly created litigation function with its former conciliation function. The conciliation stance both before and after 1972 was to treat each charge filed as the basis for a class action and to ensure that a charging party settled for no less than the full measure of his or her statutory rights. The consequence was that charged parties had little incentive to settle. Conciliation efforts were largely unsuccessful because of EEOC's lack of realism about the negotiation process. Peck, *The Equal Employment Opportunity Commission: Developments in the Administrative Process 1965-1975*, 51 Wash. L. Rev. 831, 852-853, 861-864 (1976).

In 1977 EEOC amended its procedural regulations by adopting a provision relating to negotiated settlements which authorizes district directors to approve any settlement agreement which is agreeable to both parties. 29 C.F.R. 1601.20, 42 F.R.55,388 (1977). More recently, EEOC announced the transfer of its enforcement attorneys from regional litigation centers to its 22 district offices. In those offices the attorneys work in a "team approach" with compliance personnel. An attorney will be assigned to every case identified as "a potential litigation vehicle" and will work with the investigator in every phase of development of the case through to litigation if necessary. *House Oversight Hearings on EEOC*, 1978 DLR 229: A-5, E-1-E-8. These changes suggest that EEOC has adopted a standard for determining what is a proper settlement which uses comparison with what is likely to be achieved through litigation.

At an earlier date, and before it had obtained power to sue to enforce Title VII, EEOC negotiated effectively by associating its activities with those of other government agencies, in effect borrowing power from those agencies. The Newport News Agreement—the first important agreement concerning the elimination of discrimination in employment—became possible because, after EEOC opened negotiations, the Secretary of Labor suspended further contracting by any government agency with the Newport News Shipyard. The Justice Department was persuaded to accept the agreement negotiated by EEOC instead of filing suit. The agreement was found by the company to be an acceptable substitute for the expectable results of litigation. Later, EEOC established the basis for negotiating a settlement agreement with AT&T by opposing a rate increase proposed by the company. The Federal Communications Commission set the petitions of EEOC and certain civil rights organizations for hearing to investigate the relationship between the alleged discriminatory employment practices of AT&T and the determination of just and reasonable rates. In addition to the threat of economic consequences the hearing posed for AT&T the danger of public disclosure and discussion of employment practices which might have been inconsistent with the image the company wished to project to the public. Once again the terms of the proposed settlement appeared to be preferable to the anticipated results of the hearing, even though the cost to the company was over $50 million. Peck, 51 Wash. L. Rev., *supra*, 854-957.

(7) *A Dispute Over a Government Contract*

CRAIG CONSTRUCTION COMPANY
AND THE
LIQUID FUEL STORAGE CONTAINERS *

On January 20, 1961, the United States Navy awarded to Craig Construction Co. of Pugwash, Lowerstate, a contract for the construction of three containers at the Pugwash Naval Base for the storage of liquid fuel used in certain missiles with which Navy vessels are armed. The total contract price was $1,475,350. It was a government standard-form construction contract, which contained the following provisions pertinent to subsequent developments:

(b) *General Provisions—Standard Form 23A:*
"3. CHANGES.

"The Contracting Officer may at any time, by a written order, and without notice to the sureties, make changes in the drawings and/or specifications of this contract and within the general scope thereof. If such changes cause an increase or decrease in the amount due under this contract, or in the time required for its performance, an equitable adjustment shall be made and the contract shall be modified in writing accordingly. Any claim of the Contractor for adjustment under this clause must be asserted in writing within 30 days from the date of receipt by the Contractor of the notification of change: Provided, however, that the Contracting Officer, if he determines that the facts justify such action, may receive and consider, and adjust any such claim asserted at any time prior to the date of final settlement of the contract. If the parties fail to agree upon the adjustment to be made, the dispute shall be determined as provided in Clause 6 hereof. But nothing provided in this clause shall excuse the Contractor from proceeding with the prosecution of the work as changed. Except as otherwise herein provided, no charge for any extra work or material will be allowed."

"9. INSPECTION.

"(a) Except as otherwise provided in paragraph (d) hereof, all material and workmanship, if not otherwise designated by the specifications, shall be subject to inspection, examination, and test by the Contracting Officer at any and all times during manufacture and/or construction and at any and all places where such manufacture and/or construction are carried on. The Government shall have the right to reject defective material and workmanship or require its correction. Rejected workmanship shall be satisfactorily corrected and rejected material shall be satisfactorily replaced with proper material without charge therefor, and the Contractor shall promptly segregate and remove the rejected

---

* Reproduced by permission of the copyright holders, Robert L. Fletcher and Cornelius J. Peck.

material from the premises. If the Contractor fails to proceed at once with the replacement of rejected material and/or the correction of defective workmanship, the Government may, by contract or otherwise, replace such material and/or correct such workmanship and charge the cost thereof to the Contractor, or may terminate the right of the Contractor to proceed as provided in Clause 5 of this contract, the Contractor and surety being liable for any damage to the same extent as provided in said Clause 5 for terminations thereunder.
. . .

"(d) Inspection of material and finished articles to be incorporated in the work at the site of production shall be made at the place of production, manufacture, or shipment, whenever the quantity justifies it, unless otherwise stated in the specifications; and such inspection and written or other formal acceptance, unless otherwise stated in the specifications, shall be final, except as regards latent defects, departures from specific requirements of the contract, damage or loss in transit, fraud, or such gross mistakes as amount to fraud. Subject to the requirements contained in the preceding sentence, the inspection of material and workmanship for final acceptance as a whole or in part shall be made at the site. Nothing contained in the paragraph (d) shall in any way restrict the Government's rights under any warranty or guarantee."

(c) *Supplement A to General Provisions—Standard Form 23A:*

"A. 1. DEFINITIONS. Clause 1 in Standard Form 23A is deleted and the following clause substituted in lieu thereof:
"As used in this contract:
"(a) The term 'Contracting Officer' means the person executing this contract on behalf of the Government and includes his successors or his duly authorized representative.
"(b) The term 'Navy' means the United States Navy or any duly authorized representative, including the Contracting Officer except for the purpose of deciding an appeal under the clause entitled 'Disputes'."
"6. DISPUTES.
"(e) Except as otherwise provided in this contract, any dispute concerning a question of fact arising under this contract which is not disposed of by agreement shall be decided by the Contracting Officer, who shall reduce his decision to writing and mail or otherwise furnish a copy thereof to the Contractor. Within 30 days from the date of receipt of such copy, the Contractor may appeal by mailing or otherwise furnishing to the Contracting Officer a written appeal addressed to the Commission, and the decision of the Commission shall, unless determined by a court of competent jurisdiction to have been fraudulent, arbitrary, capricious, or so grossly erroneous as necessarily to imply bad faith, or is not supported by substantial evidence, be final and conclusive: Provided, that if no such appeal to the Commission is taken, the decision of the Contracting Officer shall be final and conclusive. In connection with any appeal pro-

ceeding under this clause, the Contractor shall be afforded an opportunity to be heard and to offer evidence in support of its appeal. Pending final decision of a dispute hereunder, the Contractor shall proceed diligently with the performance of the contract and in accordance with the Contracting Officer's decision.

"(b) The provision of paragraph (a) of this clause shall not apply to disputes arising between the Contractor and his subcontractors."

STATEMENT OF WORK

"(A) *Work to be done.* The work consists of furnishing all labor, equipment and materials, and performing all work in strict accordance with these specifications and schedules and drawing forming parts thereof for construction of three liquid fuel storage containers at the Pugwash Naval Base."

PRINCIPAL FEATURES

"Construction of the three liquid fuel storage containers is to provide facilities for the storage of liquid fuel for missiles used by the United States Naval Forces, and includes the following:

"1. Each container shall consist of a steel containment shell of ellipsoid shape, the major axis of which shall be forty five feet in length and the minor axis of which shall be thirty two and one-half feet, to be constructed in accordance with ASME [American Society of Mechanical Engineers] Boiler and Pressure Vessel Code. Each such container shall be placed underground in a steel reinforced concrete vault. The bottom half of each container shall rest upon a concrete foundation, except as indicated openings are to be provided for access."

The specifications for the work to be performed, which were incorporated as a part of the contract, contained the following pertinent statements:

"15. *Container Design and Fabrication.* Each container shall be designed and fabricated in strict conformance with the 1956 Edition of ASME Boiler and Pressure Vessel Code, as supplemented by addenda of 1956, 1957, and 1960."

"h. Container shall be of all-welded construction."

"k. Welders and welding procedures shall be qualified and all welding shall be done in strict conformance with the ASME [American Society of Mechanical Engineers] Code."

"17. *Vessel Erection.* Each vessel shall be erected in two stages to allow placement of interior concrete baffles, temperature sensitizers, and temperature control devices. The first stage erection of the container shell shall stop at the horizontal midsection. All welds made in the first stage of erection shall then be radiographed and tested for leak tightness before those welds are made inaccessible. The completion of the container shall constitute the second stage of erection."

"21. The concrete foundations for each container shall be free from voids and shall provide full and continuous bearing for the container, except for indicated access openings."

On April 24, 1961, Craig Construction Co. entered into a contract with H H & C Iron and Metal Co. of Elgin, Upperstate, for the fabrication of the steel containers, the price at a total contract price of $417,000.

"On April 28, 1961, the United States Navy appointed Universal Dynamics, the manufacturer of the missiles which would use the liquid fuel, to serve as its agent for inspection and acceptance of work done on the storage container facilities. Universal Dynamics accepted the appointment under an agreement indemnifying it against any and all liabilities it might otherwise incur as inspecting agent.

On January 25, 1961, the government contracting officer gave Craig Construction Co. notice to proceed, thereby starting the running of time within which the various phases of the construction were to be completed. The contract established four general construction phases, for each of which a required completion date was stated in terms of the number of days following notice to proceed. Those phases were (1) excavation of the underground sites in which the containers were to be placed, (2) construction of all of the reinforced concrete vault in which the containers were to be placed, except the covering head, but including the foundations for the containers, (3) erection of the steel shells of the storage containers, (4) all other work, including the connecting of all fuel transfer lines and pumps as well as the construction of the covering head of the vault. Liquidated damages of $1,500 per day were provided for failure to complete any phase of the construction within the period established by the contract.

Excavation of the underground sites and construction of the reinforced storage vault proceeded expeditiously, and with only minor difficulties through most of the second phase of construction. On May 19, 1961, which was 119 days after notice to proceed had been given, Craig Construction Co. requested H H & C to furnish its template of the bottom of a container shell for use in molding the concrete foundations upon which the container shells were to rest. H H & C then informed Craig that it had formed the container shells using only sectional templates, and that it did not have a complete template for the bottom half of the containers. Moreover, the subcontract between Craig and H H & C did not specify the manner in which H H & C would undertake to shape the steel shells nor did it require H H & C to furnish such a template. Craig then instructed H H & C to manufacture such a template, which H H & C did, giving notice that it considered this to constitute work not covered by its contract, for which it expected reimbursement of costs, plus 20 percent for overhead and 10 percent for profit. The template did not arrive until June 2, 1961, which delayed the pouring of the foundations by four days. To make up some of the time thus lost, Craig ordered work done by its ironworkers and cement masons over the weekend of June 3 and 4, although this obligated it to pay time and one half for the work done on Saturday and double time for the work done on Sunday.

On June 20, 1961, H H & C began to weld the partially assembled sections of the bottom half of the first container together in place on their foundations. On June 29, 1961, the inspector designated by Universal Dynamics informed Craig's project manager that this method of construction did not conform to contract requirements, pointing out that the specifications required that the foundations provide full and continuous bearing for each container and that the method of assembly used by H H & C gave no assurance that in fact each shell would be so supported. Craig's project manager consulted with the H H & C representative. The following day he discussed the matter with the Universal Dynamics inspector, contending that while it was theoretically possible to shape the container so that the foundations gave full and continuous support, in fact, no way existed to achieve complete continuous support and that this would have been the case even if H H & C had utilized a complete template of the bottom half in fabricating the shells. The Universal Dynamics inspector replied that it was his obligation to get what the contract required, and that he would be satisfied with nothing less.

Irving Craig, president of Craig Construction Co., was informed of these developments. On July 5, he proposed by letter the following to ensure the full and continuous support of the foundations: Eight grouting channels would be cut in each of the foundations under the steel shells. After the shell bottoms had been fabricated, grout would be forced into the grouting channels under pressure, beginning with a moist and penetrating mixture and ending with a firm and standard grout. On July 11, 1961, the Universal Dynamics inspector replied by letter, giving his approval to the proposed method for dealing with the problem. By this time, however, H H & C was nearing completion of the bottom of the first storage container shell and had begun work on the second.

In order to cut in the grouting channels it was necessary to require H H & C to do no work on the second container from July 11 through July 17, which obligated H H & C to pay travel expense for its metal workers from Pugwash, Lowerstate, to Elgin, Upperstate, and return. It then became necessary for Craig Construction to rent a crane capable of lifting the bottom of the first shell and holding it off its foundation while the grouting channels were cut. This was made possible by having H H & C employees attach and later remove temporary pad eyes from the shell.

On July 20, Irving Craig wrote to the U.S. Navy's contracting officer, informing him that in the opinion of Craig Construction Co. the Universal Dynamics inspector had ordered the performance of additional work not required by the contract and that when additional cost data had been accumulated it would submit that data to him for his approval. He also requested that Craig Construction be granted an eight-day extension of time for completion of the contract because of this additional work. On the same date he wrote to H H & C requesting that it prepare a statement showing the extra costs to which it had been subjected by virtue of the delay associated with the grouting operation.

On August 24, 1961, Universal Dynamics' inspector delivered to Craig Construction Co. and H H & C his report on the welds made on the bottom half of the first container vessel. This report was based upon both

X-ray films make of the welded seams and visual inspection of the seams. It required that at 59 places the existing welds be cut out and replaced. H H & C then undertook to replace the welds as directed. Before the replacement work on the first container had been completed, the inspector issued his report on the second container. It required that at 43 places the existing welds be cut out and replaced. The report on the third container required that at 56 places the existing welds be cut out and replaced.

This replacement work was completed on November 19, 1961. H H & C then wrote to Craig Construction Co. stating that it had cost H H & C $24,790 to replace the welds as required by the Universal Dynamics inspector; that the welds replaced had been in conformance with the ASME code as required by its subcontract; and that accordingly it expected payment from Craig of the costs incurred, plus 20 percent overhead and 10 percent profit.

Craig Construction Co. replied, asking for substantiation that the welds replaced had conformed with the ASME code. Its letter of reply further stated that it had been delayed 35 days in its work under the contract by H H & C's failure to perform the welding to the satisfaction of the Inspector, and that when the costs attributable to this delay, including any liquidated damages assessed for failure to complete work as scheduled, were determined, it would furnish a statement of those costs to H H & C for use in connection with the final settlement under their contract.

On November 22, 1961, H H & C replied to the letter of Craig Construction Co., denying any responsibility for delays caused by the rewelding work. As proof that it had been required to perform work over and beyond that required under its contract, H H & C enclosed a copy of a letter from J. R. Shulman, a member of the American Society of Mechanical Engineers, stating that he had examined the X-rays taken of the welds which were required to be replaced, and that in his opinion only four of them did not conform to ASME standards.

About this time the Chief of the Construction Branch of the U.S. Navy at the Pugwash Naval Base wrote to Craig Construction Co., pointing out that work on phase 3 of the contract (erection of the steel shells of the storage containers) appeared to be 40 days behind schedule, and that if the work on that phase were not completed by December 20, 1961, it would be necessary to assess liquidated damages of $1,500 per day. Craig replied to this letter, enclosing a copy of Shulman's letter to H H & C, and stating that at least 35 days of the existing delay was due to the unreasonably high standards established by the inspector for welds and that another eight days of the delay had occurred because Craig had been required to perform additional work in connection with grouting between the shells and the concrete foundations. He accordingly requested that Craig Construction Co. be granted an extension of 43 days for the completion of phase 3 of the contract. Nevertheless, Craig Construction then hired and established a second shift of its own employees, and directed H H & C to do the same with respect to the welding crew. H H & C complied with these directions, informing Craig that it considered them a direction to perform new and additional work for which additional compensation would be required. Despite these measures, phase 3 of the construction was not completed until December 29, which resulted in the Navy contract administrator sending notice that liquidated damages for nine days delay would be assessed.

Work on phase 4 of the contract proceeded with relatively few problems, other than scheduling difficulties produced by the delay in completion of phase 3. Craig Construction Co. continued to utilize a second crew in the attempt to make up time lost on phase 3, and in fact succeeded in doing so. Work on the contract was completed on February 27, 1962. At this point Craig Construction Co. was able to assess its total situation with respect to the contract. It had spent or incurred obligations amounting to a total of $1,773,950. Among other things it still owed H H & C Iron and Metal Co. a total of $83,500 on the subcontract, and had in addition been presented with claims for $97,000 for work required in addition to the contract.

Pursuant to the notice previously given to the Navy contract administrator, the sum of $13,500 had been withheld as liquidated damages for delay in completion of phase 3 of the contract. At this point Irving Craig decided that he should get in touch with Gene Stason at the firm of Cosway, Katz, Stason, and Cooper.

Stason immediately wrote to the Chief of the Construction Branch of the United States Naval Base, informing him that the law firm had been retained to present claims on behalf of Craig Construction Co. in connection with the work which it had performed on the contract, and requesting time within which to familiarize himself with the complicated facts of the case. He received a reply stating that the Chief of the Construction Branch would wait until March 21 before submitting the claims previously made by Craig Construction to the contracting office for disposition. At the same time Stason wrote to George Berter in Elgin, Upperstate, who he had learned was counsel for H H & C, informing him of the plan to submit a claim to the Navy and requesting his cooperation.

He received a phone call in reply from Mr. Berter, in which Berter stated that the only conditions upon which H H & C would be willing to cooperate with Craig Construction in presentation of claims to the Navy were that (1) Craig immediately pay H H & C the $83,500 remaining due on the subcontract, (2) Craig and H H & C execute mutual releases of all other claims against one another, and (3) any award received from the Navy be shared on a basis of one share for H H & C and three shares for Craig—this being the approximate ratio of their expenses in addition to the contract prices. Stason stated that in his view this was an unrealistic proposal, since it gave no consideration to the potential and very sizable claims which Craig might have against H H & C. Stason, nevertheless, discussed the proposal with Irving Craig, who decided to reject it and Berter was informed by letter accordingly. Berter phoned again to state that H H & C was unwilling to cooperate with Craig Construction on any basis other than that previously stated, and that if those conditions were not accepted, H H & C would commence action to recover the balance due on the contract as well as the amount of its claim for additional work. Stason expressed his regret that they were not able to cooperate with one another in settling their problem and in the presentation of their claims to the Navy.

On March 21, 1962, Stason forwarded to the Chief of the Construction Branch a claim for additional compensation. The claim consisted primarily of an explanation of the difficulties encountered, as summarized above, and the assertion that all the demands made were demands above and beyond that required of Craig Construction under the terms of the contract. In dollar amounts there was a claim for $124,785 for additional expenses and damages caused by delay associated with the demand that each container have 100 percent continuous support on the concrete foundations and a claim for $173,815 as damages caused by the delay attributable to the excessive demands made with respect to the quality of the welding done by H H & C. More specifically, the additional expenses claimed consisted primarily of increased labor costs resulting from the hiring of additional crews to make up the time lost, although there were items claimed for additional materials and equipment rentals, as well as allowances of 20 percent for overhead and 10 for profit. Stason received in reply a letter from Dennis Newman, attorney for the contracting officer, informing him that some time would be required for study of the claim.

Approximately one month later, Newman, the attorney for the contracting officer, wrote to Stason requesting that arrangements be made to permit inspection by Navy representatives of the X-ray films made of the various welds rejected by the Universal Dynamics inspector. The films were in the possession of H H & C. Stason arranged through Berter to make the films available to representatives of the Navy at the offices of H H & C in Elgin, Upperstate.

Two weeks later the attorney for the contracting officer wrote to Stason, stating that in preparation of data for submission to the contracting officer he wished to know the following:

1. Under which article of the contract was it claimed that the Navy could award additional compensation?

2. Why was the claim not time-barred for failure to submit it within 30 days after the changes allegedly were ordered, in light of the contract provision relating to changes? [See p. 76, *supra*.]

3. The reasons for the statement that in fact no way existed to achieve complete and continuous support of the storage containers even if a complete template of the bottom halves of the containers had been used in fabricating the shells.

Newman further stated that claims for breach of contract by the Government are matters to be settled by the Comptroller General or the Courts, and do not come within the disputes clause of government contracts, under which the claims were being submitted to the contracting officer.

On May 14, 1962, Irving Craig received a telephone call from the president of H H & C, making what was called a final demand for payment before the filing of suit for both the $83,500 due on the original contract and $97,000 to cover the work required in addition to that provided for in the contract. In the course of the conversation the president of H H & C made reference to a letter which he had received from Craig's project manager, stating that Craig had been damaged only to the extent of $23,500 by the delays in welding, and that its presentation to the Navy would destroy the pending claim of Craig Construction. Craig responded that H H & C could submit the letter to the Navy if they thought it the proper thing to do, but that he was sure that it would be a mistake from their viewpoint because it would only prejudice H H & C. If Craig did not get compensation from the Navy it was going to pursue H H & C, who it believed was primarily responsible for the welding delays as well as the expenses and delays associated with providing continuous support for the containers.

On May 22, 1962, suit was filed by H H & C Iron and Metal Co. against Craig Construction Co. in the United States District Court for the Western District of Lowerstate. The jurisdiction of the court was invoked under the Miller Act, 40 U.S.C. § 270a et seq., and the bonding company which had issued the payment bond on Craig's prime contract was joined as a party defendant. The bonding company promptly tendered defense of the suit to Craig Construction Co., which accepted the tender. H H & C was represented in this action by Merrill Bobbs, a member of the bar of Lowerstate with whom Berter had associated for litigation of the claim.

Stason sought and obtained Bobbs' agreement to extend the time within which pleadings were to be filed until July 15, 1962, and the appropriate stipulation was prepared. Prior to July 15, 1962, Stason prepared and served on Bobbs a motion to stay the entire proceeding until a determination had been made by the contracting officer on the claims which had been submitted to him. Because of mutual difficulties in their schedules of court appearances and other commitments, Stason and Bobbs agreed to put over argument on the motion to stay until September 17, 1962. In the meantime, Stason filed a third party complaint and brought in Universal Dynamics as a third party defendant, alleging that Universal Dynamics had prepared the plans for construction of the storage containers and acted as the inspection agent for the U.S. Navy. The third party complaint alleged negligence on the part of Universal Dynamics in drafting plans requiring full and continuous support for the containers when in fact this could not be achieved and wrongful inspection practices with regard to welding, causing damages to Craig Construction Co. of a total of $298,600. In addition, the third party complaint sought recovery from Universal Dynamics of any additional sums of money for which Craig might be held liable to H H & C. Subsequently, by letter, Stason tendered defense of the action against Craig, to Universal Dynamics, whose attorney rejected it.

In addition, Stason telephoned Bobbs and informed him that Craig was considering filing a countersuit against H H & C. He suggested that if the motion to stay was denied, a cross complaint against H H & C would be filed, and suggested that Bobbs look into the possibility of H H & C being held liable to Craig. (Actually, Stason had very considerable doubts that the court in a Miller Act proceeding would have jurisdicition of his cross complaint.)

Scheduling problems complicated by the involvement of Universal Dynamics and its attorneys required that the case be put over until November 15, 1962. At that time the court heard arguments on Craig's motion to stay the proceeding pending determination of the claims before the contracting officer, as well as the arguments of Universal Dynamics' motion to dismiss the third party complaint. At the conclusion of the arguments, the count denied both motions. Stason then prepared and on November 22, 1962, filed a motion to certify the order denying the stay for appeal pursuant to 28 U.S.C. § 1292(b). Argument was heard on that motion on November 30, 1962, and the motion was denied.

On November 30, 1962, after the motion to certify had been denied, Stason and Bobbs had a short conversation which Stason initiated by asking if Bobbs had found time to give consideration to the possible liability of H H & C to Craig Construction. Bobbs said that he had, and indicated that he was willing to listen to any proposal Stason had to make. They parted with an agreement to meet at Bobbs's office on December 4, 1962.

Bobbs indicated that H H & C could see no reason why they should not be paid immediately, and that they were quite confirmed in this view because Berter had repeatedly told them that he could see no reason why Craig Construction would not pay what they so clearly owed H H & C. Stason agreed that, except as a matter of set-off or recoupment, there was no valid reason for refusing to pay the $83,500 that remained due to H H & C on the original subcontract price. However, the losses that Craig had suffered on the contract left it somewhat short of working capital. If Craig were to receive compensation on its claims before the contracting officer, it would be in a better position to make payment to H H & C. Moreover, if it were successful on its claims against the Navy, it would not have to pursue its possible claims against H H & C. He further suggested, and Bobbs gave some indications of agreement, that the basic cause of difficulty was the strictness of Universal Dynamics' inspection and construction of the contract—a strictness that had brought about loss to both Craig and H H & C.

Bobbs then suggested that they might be able to come to an agreement if Craig Construction agreed to pay H H & C the balance due on the original subcontract price, that it amend its claim before the contracting officer to include the claims of H H & C for additional work, that H H & C would assign to Craig all its claims for extra compensation and that any award received from the Navy be shared by them on the basis of one share for H H & C and three shares for Craig. Stason responded that this was little better than Berter's proposal. He suggested instead that Craig pay only one half of the balance due on the original subcontract price, that the pending Miller Act suit be dismissed, and that the claim before the Navy contracting officer be amended to include H H & C's claim. H H & C would agree to cooperate with Craig in the presentation of all claims, but it would be understood that Craig would have control of that presentation and any subsequent litigation, and that H H & C's claim for extra compensation would be assigned to Craig.

Discussion of the problems that might arise if a settlement offer were received from the Navy led to the following proposals. If the Navy made an offer that was unacceptable to Craig, H H & C could inform Craig that it elected to take the amount offered, or $41,750 (the remaining half due on the subcontract), whichever was less. In the event of such an election, H H & C would waive all additional claims against Craig and all interest in the claim pending before the contracting officer. If Craig decided to. accept any settlement for less than $41,750, it would pay $41,750 to H H & C, and that in turn would satisfy all claims which H H & C might have against Craig. If Craig elected to settle the claim for any amount in excess of $41,750, the amount received in excess of that amount would be divided into four equal shares, one of which would be allocated to H H & C and three to Craig, provided that in no event was H H & C to receive more than the $97,000 it had claimed was due and owing to it for extra work. Stason and Bobbs agreed to submit Stason's proposed settlement to their respective clients for approval.

On January 7, 1963, Bobbs telephoned Stason to tell him that he had a belated Christmas present for him: H H & C would accept his proposal. Stason thanked him, and replied that interestingly enough he had a similar present for Bobbs: Craig Construction Co. would also accept the proposal. Stason undertook the preparation of the first draft of the settlement agreement. Three exchanges of drafts followed, including one which incorporated suggestions made by Mr. Berter substituting covenants not to sue for releases of claims.

On January 22, 1963, Stason filed an amended claim with the Navy contracting officer, requesting an additional $97,000 as the sum due to its subcontractor for changes made in the original contract and performed by H H & C on its subcontract. Subsequently, Irving Craig discussed the pending claims with the Chief of the Construction Branch, U.S. Navy, suggesting that the root of the difficulties for both Craig and H H & C lay in the inspection work done by Universal Dynamics. The Chief of the Construction Branch indicated that this might be the case, but when Craig raised the matter of reaching an informal settlement, the best he could obtain was a statement that the matter probably could be settled if Craig would accept payment of $50,000.

On February 27, 1963, the Navy contracting officer issued his decision, in which he allowed Craig only $35,000 for additional work in designing and developing the grouting techniques which gave near to full and continuous support to the storage containers. The claim for damages arising out of rejection of welding was denied upon the basis that no formal change order had been issued, and that, as known by Craig Construction Co., Universal Dynamics was authorized to act only as an inspecting agent and was not empowered to issue change orders. An additional reason for denying all relief on these claims was the failure of Craig to request an equitable adjustment within 30 days after the change had been ordered, as required by the change article of the contract. [See p. 76, *supra*.]

Stason filed notice of appeal from the decision of the Navy contracting officer with the Armed Services Board of Contract Appeals on March 11, 1963. He then prepared a draft of the complaint to be filed on the appeal, and sent copies to Bobbs and Berter for their comments. On March 29, 1963, he filed the complaint. Upon motion of the attorney for the contracting officer, time for answering the complaint was extended to May 15, 1963. In essence, that answer, when filed, reaffirmed the position taken by the contracting officer in his decision. A request for admission of facts filed by the attorney for the contracting officer made it necessary for Stason to call upon Bobbs and Berter and H H & C for considerable detail relating to welding procedures and welding tests, and this too required an extension of time. In the meantime, the chairman of the Armed Services Board of Contract Appeals notified the parties that he had designated Mr. Albert Black to serve as the hearing examiner of the board on the appeal of Craig Construction Co. Soon thereafter, the parties received from Mr. Black a telegram suggesting that a prehearing conference of all the parties be held at Pugwash, Lowerstate, on June 24, 1963.

Stason suggested to Bobbs and Berter that it would be wise to obtain still another expert's opinion of the weld X-rays for use at the conference, and they agreed. In essence, the second expert opinion then obtained conformed to the earlier one, although it listed two additional welds as not conforming to ASME standards and raised some questions as to whether the X-rays were satisfactory because surface markings had not been removed prior to the taking of the X-rays. The material developed by H H & C for response to the request for admission made it quite clear that after November 1961 it had encountered much less difficulty in obtaining approval of the welding work done, and that in fact there was no serious contest as to the welding corrections ordered on the upper halves of the storage containers.

Upon filing his response to the request for admissions of facts, Stason also filed a motion with the hearing examiner to require the Navy to produce its copies of documents relating to this case to discover any evidence or records of discussions and letters which may have been kept by the Navy but which were not included in or had been lost from the files of Craig Construction Co. In addition, he specifically requested that he be permitted to discover any instructions given by the Navy to Universal Dynamics as to the manner in which it was to inspect the quality of welding performance.

Various conflicts and scheduling problems of the parties involved resulted in a postponement of the prehearing conference the hearing examiner had fixed for June 24, 1963. On July 8, 1963, Dennis Newman, the attorney for the contracting officer, requested permission to have the X-ray films made available for examination by experts selected by the Navy. This permission was granted, and the suggestion made that the contracting officer and Craig Construction Co. agree to exchange the reports they had received from experts concerning the quality of the welding work.

Upon receipt of a letter from the hearing officer inquiring as to the parties' views concerning a prehearing conference on September 16, 1963, the parties agreed. At the hearing Stason argued that the hearing examiner should take evidence and rule upon the amount of damages to which Craig was entitled, whereas the attorney for the contracting officer argued that the examiner should rule only on the issue of liability, and if he found liability, remand the case for determination of the damage issue by the contracting officer. The attorney for the contracting officer also formally moved to dismiss the complaint upon the ground that the claims for extra work had not been submitted within 30 days after the alleged change orders were issued. There was considerable discussion of the presentation of the testimony of expert witnesses, and it was agreed that the testimony of the experts relating to welding would be reduced to writing. It was also agreed that the parties should reserve the week of January 20, 1964, for the hearing of the case.

On November 11, 1963, the hearing examiner issued his decision on the motion to dismiss made at the prehearing conference. He denied the motion upon the ground that a claim need be filed within 30 days only in those cases in which a written change order had been issued, and that in this case the changes allegedly ordered were not made in writing. He also issued an order defining the issues to be litigated, making it clear that one of them was the right of Craig Construction Co. to equitable adjustments if changes had been in fact ordered.

As the time for hearing approached, there was an exchange of information relating to the expert testimony concerning the quality of the welds rejected. Stason furnished the contracting officer's attorney the letter statements of the two experts who had been retained by H H & C during the period of the contract and controversy. He did not receive the written reports of the X-ray experts retained by the Navy, but he learned that they did not differ substantially from those of the H H & C experts. Newman, the contracting officer's attorney, suggested that it seemed quite likely that the case should be settled, if the proper basis for arriving at a figure might be established. In particular he asked for substantiating details concerning certain cost figures. Further discussion led to the suggestion that a conference looking forward to a settlement be held at Pugwash, Lowerstate, on December 9, 1963.

The conference was attended by Attorneys Stason, Bobbs, Berter, and Newman, by Irving Craig for Craig Construction, by the project engineer of H H & C (the president was away in connection with a project which H H & C had undertaken in Latin America), by the contracting officer, and by the Chief of the Construction Division of the Navy. Conspicuously absent were representatives of Universal Dynamics, though, so far as Stason knew, there was no reason why they were not qualified to attend and represent the Navy.

The discussion of the merits of the claims began somewhat slowly. The attorney for the contracting officer pointed out that Craig's claims totalled $298,600, which, added to the $97,000 claimed on behalf of H H & C, made a total of $395,600 claimed as extra compensation on a contract that was supposed to have been performed for only $1,475,350. He suggested that this proportion was too great and must be reduced. Stason replied that he recognized the relatively large size of the claims, but suggested instead that attention be directed to the merits. The attorney for the contracting officer suggested that the 10 percent profit and the 20 percent overhead claimed could be eliminated, which would substantially reduce the claims. Stason responded that overhead costs were in fact real, and could not and should not be overlooked by some accounting technique that would attribute those costs to other projects. As for the profit allowance, he suggested that this was a regular factor in any contract price, and he saw no reason for excluding it if Craig were to receive what was truly an equitable adjustment for increased work. Berter added that certainly profit was a legitimate factor insofar as H H & C was concerned in its position as a subcontractor. After further discussion, the parties left the room for caucuses.

Upon returning, Stason held to the claim for overhead and profit, as agreed upon in the caucus, and the attorney for the contracting officer indicated a rather firm conviction that these items should be eliminated. Bobbs then suggested that perhaps progress might be made if attention were directed to the separate elements of the claims—the claims associated with the support changes and the claims associated with the welding changes. He suggested that discussion be directed first to the support changes, as had been agreed in the caucus. [The theory was that the welding claims were stronger—and ones upon which the Navy would have to and would give most—and that Craig would be in a weaker position to hold out for more than the $35,000 given by the contracting officer on the support claim if the Navy had appeared to be generous on the welding claim.] The attorney for the contracting officer agreed to this procedure, but noted that any agreement reached as to one branch of the claims would of necessity be tentative because the Navy had to view the claim as a whole, and what could be agreed upon with respect to one aspect of the claim affected what could be agreed upon with respect to other aspects.

At this point the discussion turned to the details of the support construction work and the grouting operation, involving Irving Craig, the project engineer of H H & C, and the Chief of Construction of the Navy. The contracting officer's attorney pointed out that a portion of that claim was for the extra labor costs resulting from hiring additional crews to work on extra shifts, and that the premium pay received by the crews exceeded the $1,500 per day liquidated damages which would have been assessed for delay in completion. After prolonged discussion and several caucuses, the Navy representatives agreed that perhaps as much as $50,000 of the costs claimed could be recognized as valid, without allowance for profit or overhead. Stason demurred as to $50,000 being adequate compensation on this aspect of the claim, but suggested they turn attention to the welding claim. At this point it was suggested that the parties recess for lunch, the time being 1:15.

Returning from lunch, which had been a continuing caucus for both sides, the parties took up the welding claims. The contracting officer's attorney agreed that Universal Dynamics' inspectors had been too strict. He emphasized, however, that neither Craig nor H H & C had called this to the attention of the Navy until the end of November 1961, by which time work on the project had fallen at least 15 days behind schedule. He further noted that the fact that there had been many fewer rejections of welds for the top halves of the containers showed not only that the earlier inspection had been unduly rigid but that discussions between the Chief of Construction and Universal Dynamics representatives could have produced a change in attitude much earlier if the strictness of inspections had been called to the Navy's attention. He further noted that the increased labor costs accumulated by both Craig and H H & C exceeded the amount of the liquidated damages which would have been assessed for the delay. Giving consideration to these factors, he suggested that the allowance of a percentage of the costs for either overhead or profit was not proper, which, even by the figures submitted by Craig and H H & C, would reduce their total claims to slightly less than $190,000. Even these, he suggested, were excessive, and an upward adjustment of $125,000 was the most that would be required as an equitable adjustment.

Comments on and criticism of the arguments of the attorney for the contracting officer continued for some time, and the parties caucused again. Upon returning Stason suggested that a settlement could be worked out on the basis of an allowance of $60,000 for the support construction work claim and $150,000 on the welding claim. The Navy representatives caucused, and retired with an offer of a flat $200,000 in settlement of both claims. Agreement was then reached at this figure.

The contracting officer's attorney then suggested that the settlement be worked out in the form of an agreement to be filed as of record in the pending appeal of Craig Construction Co. This required the exchange of drafts between Stason and Newman, the contracting officer's attorney. As finally worked out, the stipulation called for the issuance of change orders by the contracting officer with respect to both construction of the support foundations and with respect to expediting work by hiring extra shifts, with the total equitable adjustment of $200,000. This agreement in the form of a stipulation was filed with the hearing examiner on December 17, 1963.

By return airmail Stason and Newman received a letter from the hearing examiner stating that he considered the matter to be of such importance that a hearing should be held before him during which a record could be compiled to set forth the basis upon which the agreement was reached. He expressed the view that a one-day hearing would suffice, and suggested that it be held at Pugwash, Lowerstate, on January 20, 1964. Stason and Newman agreed, and Stason informed Bobbs and Berter that the case unfortunately would not be closed out that year.

The hearing held on January 20, 1964, was largely a pro-forma affair, with Stason and Newman supporting one another in the presentation of the factual data supporting the compromise at which they had arrived. On a few occasions the hearing officer's questioning attitude carried the suggestion that he might not approve the stipulation. He did so, however, at the close of the hearing.

Payment of the claim was made by the Navy on February 21, 1964, and with the intervening weekend it was not until February 24, 1964, that Stason was able to send Bobbs a check for $81,312. In his letter of transmittal he expressed regret that the Christmas present he had almost been able to deliver was two months late, but offered the consolation that by virtue of the delay Bobbs would not have to pay all the tax on his fee until a year later.

QUESTIONS

1. What would you consider the most significant development in the course of these negotiations?

2. What significance would you attribute to the appearance of Merrill Bobbs in the negotiations? Why did he continue to take part once the agreement was reached to dismiss the Miller Act proceeding?

3. What significance do you attribute to the fact that Craig Construction Co. could not obtain a stay of the Miller Act proceeding?

4. How do you account for the change of attitude on the part of representatives of the Navy after the appeal had been taken from the decision of the contracting officer?

5. Do you believe the Navy representatives acted in these negotiations as would the representatives of privately owned companies? If not, how would you describe the differences?

6. Why were the Navy representatives interested in getting the basis of settlement into the record of the appeal?

7. Did Craig Construction Co. wait too long before consulting its attorneys? At what point would you have been able to give them assistance, minimizing the difficulties they accomplished?

8. Can you point to certain costs to Craig incident to preparation for trial that are somewhat unusual, likely to be extraordinarily high, and not so likely to be incurred by the Navy?

9. Do you believe you could have improved upon the services Stason rendered? If so, how?

ADDITIONAL READINGS

California Continuing Education of the Bar, GOVERNMENT CONTRACTS PRACTICE (1964).

B. SINGLE PHASE COMMERCIAL TRANSACTIONS—EXCHANGE MODELS

NIERENBERG, SALE OF THE REMAINING LEASEHOLD IN A BUILDING TO BE DEMOLISHED*

. . .

Once I was retained by a client who was the last tenant in an office building scheduled to be demolished. The new owner planned a sky-scraper in place of this four-story building. All the other tenants had moved out. My function, in addition to protecting my client's rights, was to work out a solution acceptable to both parties.

The landlord recognized that, to get my client out of the building, he would have to pay money. His question was, "How little?" The landlord first approached me personally. (In my opinion, this was a mistake. Later we will take up the value, in certain situations, of bargaining through an agent who has only limited authority.)

"How much do you want?" the landlord asked. "I'm sorry," I replied, "You are the one who is buying. I am not selling." This placed the burden of opening the negotiations upon him. So far so good. We both recognized that my client was in a very strong position. He had two years to go on his lease, and the landlord needed to get started immediately.

The opening offer indicated the landlord's willingness to pay moving expenses and the differential in rent. I declined to get into anything other than the cash figure he was offering—"How much?" After some byplay he offered $25,000. I refused even to consider it. He left the office.

The landlord's next tactic was delay. But this worked against him, because my client was perfectly willing to stay put. When delay did not work, the next approach came through the landlord's attorney. I told the attorney that when he came up with a figure that was in the "ball park," we would negotiate. "Fifty thousand," he said. "Not in the ball park," I replied.

Approaches continued, with the offer getting higher. I never named a figure until the final stages. But I did do some homework, figuring out what the landlord had paid for the building, what it would cost him to keep the building vacant, what it would cost him to hold the mortgage commitments until the end of my client's lease.

I came up with a figure of a quarter of a million dollars. Knowing that this was speculation, and not wanting to squeeze the last dollar, I cut this

---

* From Nierenberg, THE ART OF NEGOTIATING 27-28 (1968). Reproduced by permission of the copyright holder, Gerard I. Nierenberg.

in half. The landlord's lawyer was forced to bid against his own figure and finally settle for $125,000. It seemed to me that this was a solution that satisfied everyone.

However, I was in for a surprise. When the landlord's lawyers delivered the check, a young attorney said to me, "Five dollars more and you might have had a crane hit the building." The crane was on the property, and it just might have struck the old building—"accidentally"—so that it would be declared a hazard that had to be torn down. In that case my client might have gotten nothing.

Now a few things may be noted about this. It was not the most intelligent thing in the world for the opposing lawyer to say. However, I realized that he meant what he said. (When a negotiation is over and the opponent is upset, his tendency is sometimes in the other direction—to make you feel bad by indicating that there was a lot more to be had if you had just held out for it.)

My client was vulnerable. If I had realized how close I was to the top figure, I would have settled at a lower price. The danger of going too far is not worth the risk.

. . .

NOTE

Nierenberg, FUNDAMENTALS OF NEGOTIATING (1975), combines THE ART OF NEGOTIATING with Nierenberg's later book, CREATIVE BUSINESS NEGOTIATIONS (1971), in a single readable volume, which also contains an elaborate analytical treatment of the negotiation process.

HENDERSON, BRINKMANSHIP IN BUSINESS *

This article could be entitled, "How to Succeed in Business by Being Unreasonable." Most businessmen are very skillful in this respect, athough their behavior is popularly called negotiation, gamesmanship, or, perhaps most apt of all, brinkmanship. The art of being unreasonable is not, of course, restricted to smoke-filled rooms at corporate headquarters. The principles are regularly applied by labor union negotiators, diplomats, and extortionists as well as by businessmen.

ANATOMY OF VICTORY

The real dynamics of competition in the U.S. economy are frequently obscured by rationalization. A businessman often convinces himself that he is completely logical in his behavior when in fact the critical factor is his emotional bias compared to the emotional bias of his opposition.

Writers and teachers, too, are likely to describe the decision-making process in purely rational terms, with perhaps a decision tree or simulation exercise suggested as a device for making it even more rational.

Several elements seem basic to success in the cold wars of business. The executive must know the character, perspective, motivation, and values of his competitors. Using such knowledge, he may be able to achieve competitive success with a minimum of actual conflict by convincing the competition that it can gain more by accepting a compromise of its objectives than by having a test of strength. There is plenty of evidence, it seems to me, that such persuasion takes place often. It accounts for the fact that most business competitors achieve stability in their relationships with one another. Indeed, as we shall see presently, cooperation with one's competitors appears to be an unofficial goal of competition.

The personal element is crucial in all this. Unfortunately, some businessmen and students take the attitude that competition is some kind of impersonal, objective, colorless affair, with a company competing against the field as a golfer does in medal play. A better case can be made that business competition is a battle royal in which there are many contenders, each of whom must be dealt with *individually*. Victory, if achieved, is more often won in the mind of a competitor than in the economic arena. Consider situations like the following:

¶ The labor union calls a strike. The wages lost during the strike can easily exceed the added benefits which the union hopes to gain. On the other hand, if there is a strike, the employer accepts losses far greater than the cost of meeting the union demands without a strike. Thus, both parties lose by the strike. Both gain if they can agree without the strike. But who gains the most in the settlement?

If either party assumes that the other is unreasonable and sufficiently stubborn, then the logical thing to do is settle in advance without incurring the additional costs of the strike. The obvious deterrent to such surrender is the fear that the next time such an event happens, the other party will make exorbitant demands. Either way it is not logic, but the assessment of the opponent's attitude, which counts.

¶ A metal manufacturer can supply molten metal to a nearby foundry and save it a substantial sum in transportation and remelting costs. The molten metal can be sold to no one else, and the foundry can buy molten metal from no one else. How should the profit be shared?

Here the situation is clearly a standoff. Both parties lose unless they can agree. Any division of the profit is arbitrary. The only leverage either party possesses is the threat to break off negotiations, and that would clearly be an irrational, emotional decision.

¶ A steel manufacturer and an electrical manufacturer enter into a joint research agreement. They develop a very superior electric steel. With this steel, transformers cost far less and perform better. The steel can be sold only to the research partner. What should the price be? That is, how should the profit be shared?

No escape from agreement is possible here. Although there are many arguments that have some validity and bear on the price, the only possible agreement depends on a compromise which is primarily based on the attitude of the two partners.

. . .

NEGOTIATION TECHNIQUES

The negotiator's skill lies in being as arbitrary as necessary to obtain the best possible compromise without actually destroying the basis for voluntary mutual cooperation or self-restraint. There are some common-sense rules for success in such an endeavor:

1. Be sure that your rival is fully aware of what he can gain if he cooperates and what it will cost him if he does not.

2. Avoid any action which will arouse his emotions, since it is essential that he behave in a logical, reasonable fashion.

3. Convince your opponent that you are emotionally dedicated to your position and are completely convinced that it is reasonable.

It is worth emphasizing that your competitor is under the maximum handicap if he acts in a completely rational, objective, and logical fashion. For then he will cooperate as long as he thinks he benefits at all. In fact, if he is completely logical, he will not forgo the profit of cooperation as long as there is *any* net benefit. If he acts in this manner, and you have followed the preceding rules, you can give him a token reward and keep the rest for yourself.

If this statement seems theoretical or contrived, consider everyday experience in business. Here are some typical examples I know of:

¶ A muffler manufacturer sells only in the automobile "after-market." Another supplier who has previously been active only in the original equipment market wants to obtain distribution in the after-market. To gain entry, he cuts prices on his equipment. The first muffler manufacturer retaliates by going to original equipment manufacturers and offering to sell to them at drastically reduced prices (even though he has no contracts). The second muffler manufacturer must meet the price cuts or lose a major amount of his former business. Instead he stops his efforts to cut prices in the after-market—and, coincidentally, the first manufacturer withdraws his cut-price offer to the original equipment manufacturer on the plea of insufficient capacity.

These two manufacturers are having a border incident which verges on a hot war. They pull back when they realize the risk of mutual damage. This is a case of tacit cooperation between competitors. The tacit agreement is completely dependent on the mutual evaluation of attitudes.

¶ A major steel company makes it widely known that it will meet any competitive price shading by quoting an equivalent price publicly to all of its customers. While this is an illogical policy (it will cost the steel company more than anyone else), it effectively removes any potential benefits of price competition and stabilizes prices at a satisfyingly high level. The threat is effective as long as competitors believe that a price concession to a single customer will indeed precipitate an across-the-board price cut to all of the steel company's customers.

This episode represents a pure form of psychological warfare and tacit cooperation between competitors. The entire relationship is dependent on mutual self-restraint, which in turn is based on an assessment of the probable behavior of competitors.

¶ A paper company builds a large new mill. It is very expensive but has a low operating cost. The company then starts cutting prices to get added business in the new mill. Many competitors refuse to meet the prices, reasoning that the new mill has to get its share and obviously must cut prices until it does. They feel it is better to let the new mill get its share than to start a price war to keep it out. They assume that the new mill's low out-of-pocket cost should enable it to sell effectively below their own out-of-pocket cost.

In short, the conviction that conflict will not win produces a willingness to exercise self-restraint without forcing a test of strength. The case suggests that actual conflict is often waged solely for the purpose of producing a *conviction* about the consequences of economic war in the mind of a competitor.

. . .

We can now outline the behavior rules which are the most effective in cooperation-conflict confrontations. They apply in labor negotiations, politics, and international diplomacy as well as in business competition:

Rule #1: Be as cooperative and friendly as possible. (Minimize emotional responses and arbitrary behavior as much as possible.)

Rule #2: Be uncompromisingly stubborn in the attitudes you take. (Convince the opponent that you are indeed dedicated and immovable in your convictions.)

Rule #3: Be as friendly and warmly responsive as possible. (Leave the possibility of compromise open if necessary. Discourage a hostile emotional posture by your opponent; if he should start to take such a posture and see he is inducing an equally hostile response in you, the danger of his tactics will be more obvious to him.)

THE NAME OF THE GAME

In view of the foregoing, one might conclude that the art of negotiation has certain inherent characteristics. In the first place, real success requires an accurate and objective assessment of exactly what each party has to gain or lose. This assessment determines the absolute limits of a mutually profitable settlement. It also determines how much is at stake when emotional behavior or brinkmanship is involved.

Secondly, it is important to demonstrate to the opponent that you know exactly what he has to gain or lose. This reduces his ability to act irrationally or arbitrarily outside this range and to be convincing. Conversely, the less an opponent knows about your own situation, the greater his handicap. If he thinks you do not understand your own limits, he is under an even greater handicap.

Finally, a full understanding of the opponent's characteristic behavior is essential. It is particularly important to know how intelligent he is, how logical, and how emotional. And it is a great advantage to know his typical biases. The name of the game is this: Be as sweetly unreasonable as possible in a convincingly logical fashion without permitting your opponent to decide that it is impossible to deal with you!

STRATEGY & ATTITUDE

It is obvious that strategy must be concerned with inducing cooperation from competitors. This explains some of the examples cited earlier in this article:

¶ The labor negotiator agreed to a contract because he was *convinced* that he would lose on balance if he did not agree. The same thing was true of both sides of the bargaining table.

¶ The metal supplier and the foundry agreed on price because they were *convinced* they could negotiate terms no more favorable. The same was true of the steel company and the electric manufacturer.

¶ The two muffler manufacturers quit cutting prices because they were more *afraid* of a price war than they were *anxious* to get more volume.

¶ The steel company could enforce price stability because it *seemed* willing to accept a loss. Its competitors refrained from price cutting because they were more *afraid* of potential punishment than they were *anxious* to obtain added volume.

¶ The paper company's competitors were *convinced* that it would cut prices further if they did not voluntarily refrain from matching the price cuts.

In all of these examples, the action words—*convinced, seemed, afraid, anxious*—are subjective evaluations. Victory must be won first in the competitor's mind. Then it can be obtained in the factory and market.

Many strategic losses are the converse of the foregoing situations. If you believe your advantage is so great that you are invulnerable, you are likely to assume that your competitor sees it the same way. If he does not, however, he may well catch you without your defenses prepared. A classic example of this was Control Data Corporation's entry into the computer business. When it started marketing the world's largest and most sophisticated design to the most sophisticated users, it was a very small, unknown newcomer. It had already succeeded before IBM and other major competitors recognized it even as a threat.

The purest kind of strategic victory occurs when your competitive advantage is minimal or nil, but your competition can be induced to believe that your behavior will be so irrational that both of you will be involved in unacceptable costs or risks. If you can convince your competitor that you are reckless enough or irrational, you can win without actually playing Russian roulette. The classic example is the bank robber who threatens to blow up everyone, himself included, unless his demands are met.

. . .

DIFFICULTY ALONG THE DUWAMISH *

Charles Evans became the attorney for the estate of Dr. Arthur Celli in December 1964, having been retained by Anne Celli, the executrix of the estate. Anne was Evans' cousin, and had been a family friend since childhood. Dr. Celli died at the early age of 31 from leukemia, leaving his wife, Anne, aged 29, and two children aged 4 and 2. Dr. Celli had completed his residency in 1962, and had just begun to develop a successful practice when symptoms of the disease had appeared. At that time he still had not made a will, but in preparation for what seemed inevitable he consulted his friend Leslie Taylor who drafted the will.

Through conversations with Anne and with Taylor, Evans learned that Dr. Celli had accumulated very little property during his short period of practice. He did, however, own an undivided one-fifth interest in about 50 acres of farm land in the Duwamish River Valley, south of Seattle, which had been left him by his father. Taylor informed Evans that at the time the will had been drafted the estate of the father, Carlos, had been in probate for more than twenty years, with Dr. Celli's oldest sister, Allegra, serving as executrix. Indeed, Taylor discovered that the will had also contained a specific bequest of $15,000 to Arthur, of which he had received only $5,900 during the years he spent in obtaining his college and medical school education. (Arthur thought the $5,900 had been given him by Allegra as her personal gifts to assist him, and, upon learning of the bequest he and Anne speculated about the number of economic hardships they might have avoided during the time when they lived largely on her earnings, since his income as a medical student, intern, and resident had been negligible.)

Allegra urged Dr. Celli to make his will so as to put his property in trust for his wife and children, with Allegra and Anne serving as co-trustees. Dr. Celli's older brother, Carl, supported Allegra in this suggestion, pointing out that Anne had been converted to Catholicism prior to marrying Arthur and that she might leave the Church after his death. He thought that some control should be established to ensure that Anne would raise the children in the Catholic faith. Leslie Taylor, who drafted the will, advised Arthur not to put property he left to Anne in trust because of the difficulty of anticipating needs which might require the use of the principal. He also suggested that co-trusteeships between in-laws might be the source of much family bickering. When Dr. Celli's will was

* Reproduced by permission of the copyright holders, Robert L. Fletcher and Cornelius J. Peck.

executed, it provided that all of his property, both his half of the community property and his separate property, be divided into two shares, one of which went to his wife, Anne, directly and the other of which went to her as co-trustee with Puget Sound Bank for herself for life, with the remainder to be divided equally among his children.

In fact, the estate of Carlo Celli had not been closed at the time of Dr. Celli's death, nor had the balance of the bequest been paid. Because of the immediate need for cash to support Anne and the children, Evans asked Allegra to make immediate payment of the $9,100 remaining due. Allegra's response to Evans was that she would first consult the family attorney, Howard Pleas of Auburn, Washington, and let Evans know. When more than a week had passed, Evans again telephoned Allegra. Her response was that at the time the cash accumulated from rentals of various parcels of family property would hardly suffice to make the payment, but that it appeared possible. She thought, however, since the matter had arisen, it was time to get an understanding on how the property owned by the family should be handled. She thought it would be desirable to continue what had been the practice before her brother's death: whenever she thought a matter merited consideration by the family, it would be discussed in a family meeting, with decisions to be governed by the majority vote of family members.

Evans avoided an immediate confrontation on the voting issue, saying he would have to discuss it with Anne. However, he said it seemed to him that the payment of the balance of the bequest was not a matter for family decision but simply an obligation of the estate to the estate of Dr. Celli, and one which should be paid promptly in light of the financial needs of the widow and children. He urged prompt payment, and, indeed, further suggested that the probate of the estate of Carlo Celli be concluded as soon as possible.

When he reported on this conversation to Anne, he inquired about her relationship with her Celli in-laws. Her husband, Dr. Celli, was the youngest of the five Celli children, which made the others somewhat older than Anne. Allegra, the eldest, was about 50, married to an accountant, but without children. She lived in Auburn, where her husband maintained his office and practice. Allegra, who was executrix of her father's estate, served as manager of the Celli properties, collecting rent on the three or four houses the estate owned, as well as the land rented to Carl, the second child, who used it in his farming operations. Carl, who was probably in his late 40s, maintained a dairy herd on land rented from the estate and adjoining property. In addition, under contracts with the nearby Longacres Race Track and a number of riding stables, he regularly collected horse manure which he delivered to a large commercial mushroom producer. Carl had not married, and lived in a small house near his farm. The other two Celli children, Laura and Antoinette, were both in their 40s. They had both married and had children, but since they both lived in eastern Washington—one in Walla Walla and other in Yakima— Anne had not seen much of them and did not know many details of their lives. Antoinette, according to a recent report, however, had not been feeling well recently and had made a number of trips to the University of Washington Medical School for consultation and examination.

Of the five children, only Allegra and Arthur had gone to college. Allegra had taught grade school for several years before her marriage, and Arthur, of course, had become a doctor of medicine. As Evans knew, Anne was the daughter of Professor Charles Bender, who was recognized as a leading scholar in oceanography. Her mother, who played an active part in civic activities in Seattle, was well known for her position of leadership in the League of Women Voters. As it appeared to Anne, the brute fact was that neither she nor her deceased husband had much in common with his brother and sisters and their social exchanges had become limited to ritualized family occasions.

Obviously, this relationship made agreement to the proposal of majority rule unacceptable, even if there had been a basis for advancing it. Moreover, as Evans then said to Anne, it seemed likely that there would be difficulty in getting the Celli children to agree to breaking up the Celli estate so that Anne could realize anything on the share of the estate which had been left to her and her children. It might become necessary, he thought, to become an irritant, or a "burr under the saddle," in order to bring about a separation of interests.

Sensing that something of an adversary position might be developing, Evans allowed another week to pass, and then phoned Howard Pleas, who was the Celli family attorney. He requested Pleas to take action to close out the estate of Carlo Celli, stating that the death of his son and the necessity of settling the estate of Dr. Celli made imperative what otherwise might have not been considered of prime importance. Pleas agreed to see to it that the probate proceedings for the estate of Carlo Celli be concluded promptly, and, upon Evan's reminder, agreed that this would necessitate the payment of the $9,100 remaining due on the specific bequest. Early in January 1965, Evans and Anne Celli went to Pleas' office in response to his request for a meeting at which they could discuss the $9,100 remaining due on the specific bequest to Arthur. When they arrived, Allegra was present, but she let Pleas do most of the talking. Pleas stated that in his opinion the bequest to Arthur had been a specific bequest for the purpose of advancing his education, and that no longer being possible the balance was not due. Evans pointed out that there were no specific words of limitation in the bequest, and claimed the amount was due to Arthur's estate. Pleas then suggested that the disagreement could be disposed of and payment of the balance made if Anne would agree to the principle of majority rule with regard to the property held in undivided shares. Evans refused, asserting that Anne had a veto power which she intended to keep and most certainly would not give up for payment of a sum of money clearly owed Arthur's estate. Voices became angry on both sides, and Evans left, taking Anne with him and warning that if payment were not made promptly legal action would be taken to compel payment. In late January 1965, the balance due was paid to Anne, as executrix of the estate of her husband, but the estate of Carlo Celli was not settled until May 1965, during the negotiations hereafter described.

In February 1965, Evans was informed by Pleas that Allegra had been negotiating about a possible sale of a portion of the Celli estate lands to J. L. Oelwein, the president and principal shareholder of TR & RP, Inc. (Truckers' Rest and Recreation Parks, Inc.), which operated what are called truck stops in Spokane, Washington, and Boise, Idaho. Truck stops are installations which include low price motel and restaurant accommodations as well as complete service and repair facilities for long distance truckers.) TR & RP considered the Celli farm land well-suited for such an operation because of its location near Seattle and less than a mile and one-half from a proposed interchange on the principal freeway under construction between Seattle and Portland. The Duwamish Valley portion of the freeway was scheduled to be opened in nine months. The Celli farm did suffer a disadvantage in that the only access right was by way of a private easement over land owned by others, its entire western boundary being the unutilized but still existent rail right-of-way of Seattle Power & Light Company.

TR & RP was interested in acquiring only a portion of the 50 acres, probably the southerly 10 acres, and for that reason Oelwein acknowledged that a premium price would have to be paid for the land. Both Pleas and Evans retained the services of realtors and professional engineers, who rendered the opinion that sale of 10 or 11 acres of the land would not work to the disadvantage of the development of the remainder of the land if the matter were properly handled. Proper handling, as the consultants saw it, required a number of protective covenants. Among them were that the sellers retain their rights of ingress and egress for all types of traffic over the private easement from the south of the property, as well as an extension of that easement over the property to be conveyed. Maintenance of proper surface drainage, installation of a 12-inch water main leading to seller's property, proper setbacks of buildings and fences from public streets, easements, and property lines, as well as high construction standards for any buildings erected, prohibition of billboards and advertising signs, and safety standards for fuel storage were considered essential to proper development.

Negotiations between Oelwein and other representatives of TR & RP extended over several months, and concluded in September 1965 with an agreement that Oelwein would purchase on behalf of TR & RP a parcel of 11 acres on the south portion of the Celli farm at what all the sellers considered the phenomenal price of $275,000. [This is parcel No. 1 on the attached map.] The contract provided for payment over a period of five years, with interest at 6 percent on the remaining balance. The contract also included the protective covenants recommended by the development engineers, and in addition the following "boiler-plate" provision:

"8. No noxious or offensive trade or activity shall be carried on, nor shall anything be done thereon which may be or become an annoyance or

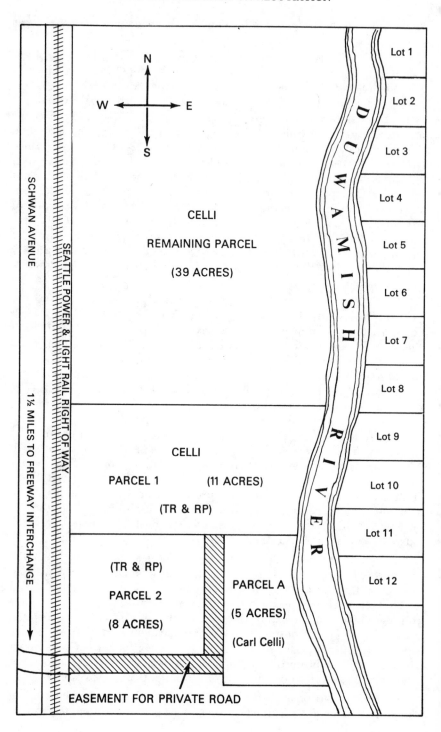

nuisance to the sellers' remaining property by reason of unsightliness or the excessive emission of odors, dust, fumes, smoke or noise."

The contract of sale was executed and the first two installment payments made and distributed without further incident. The estate of Dr. Arthur Celli was settled, and the financial needs of Anne Celli and her children satisfied with their share of the proceeds from the sale of the 11 acres to TR & RP. Her personal situation became even more secure in September 1966, when she married Byse Fletcher. Byse Fletcher had become president of Fletcher Chair Co. upon the retirement of his father a few years before. Fletcher Chair Co., which has plants in Seattle, Los Angeles, and Houston, is engaged in the manufacture of folding chairs. It is a substantial business, and Byse Fletcher had through his work in the company gained considerable experience with investments and business practice. This made it possible for Evans to leave to Fletcher some of the advising function for which Anne had previously relied upon Evans. However, nothing further of significance occurred until December 1966.

Early in December 1966, Mr. Jay Collins of Cooper & Bok, realtors, got in touch with Mr. Evans to learn whether the joint owners of the remaining Celli land would be interested in selling either all or one half of the remaining land to North-South Truck Lines. This resulted in a number of meetings with members of the Celli family, except Antoinette, whose health did not permit her to attend. Allegra expressed opposition to the sale of the land, stating that the land had already appreciated so much in value that it had made them wealthy, and that they should hold onto the land in order to realize on further appreciation. Evans, backed with the business judgment of Fletcher, urged upon them the view that the land had either reached its peak value or, even if some additional appreciation were possible, it would not be sufficient to justify retention of such an asset in a nonincome producing status. If the land were sold, each of the common owners would be able to place his share of the proceeds in income producing investments, which was economically the more sound way to deal with the valuable piece of property. Or, if one desired to continue land investments, other land, with a greater potential for increase in value, could be purchased at much lower prices. From time to time Laura, the youngest of the surviving Celli children, indicated agreement with Evans, but Allegra held out against the idea of sale. Carl Celli was somewhat noncommital, stating a willingness to sell if the price were good enough, but that there should be no need to dispose of the land in haste. Finally Evans obtained a group decision to at least consider proposals for purchase of the entire remaining land, and on this basis he authorized the realtors to obtain offers from North-South Truck Lines. He cautioned, however, that nothing could be finalized until after December 31, 1966.

The initial discussions with Richard Kyert, North-South's president, took place on December 16, 1966. It did not get off well. Kyert insisted that as sellers it was the obligation of the Celli interests to name a price, but Evans and Fletcher explained that because of the attitude of some of the persons involved, it was necessary instead for North-South to make a proposal which could be taken to the group. Somewhat reluctantly, Kyert indicated that North-South would pay $0.60 per square foot (or $26,136 per acre) for the entire remaining tract, or $0.75 per square foot (or $32,670 per acre) for a tract of 25 acres.

The prices suggested by North-South constituted a substantial increase over the $25,000 per-acre price which had been established just a year and a half earlier for the sale of only 11 acres to TR & RP. The effect was to strengthen the resistance of both Allegra and Carl to a sale of the land, confirming their view that it was better to hold on to it and realize an even greater appreciation. Evans was not able to get a counter proposal from them, but immediate difficulties with North-South were avoided when illness prevented Mr. Kyert from continuing negotiations. Fletcher wrote to Allegra, explaining that he had participated in the conference with the North-South people because the trust people at the Puget Sound Bank desired him to do so. He further reported his belief that an improved offer might be obtained from North-South if they were able to take a substantial parcel near the river, leaving the more valuable property near the Seattle Power & Light right-of-way for future disposition.

Nothing further developed in the negotiations with North-South, but Fletcher, whose business connections served well in this respect, did receive an inquiry from another real estate broker who wanted to discuss the possibility of a cash deal in acquisition of the property. What seemed to be an unrelated matter took place on March 6, 1967.

On that date Howard Pleas wrote to Evans enclosing two copies of a proposed supplement to the real estate contract for the sale of the 11 acres to TR & RP. It added to the "boiler plate" provision against noxious uses, quoted above, the following language:

"Provided, however, that the use of the premises for the construction and operation of a truck terminal and related activities shall be permissible."

In the accompanying letter, Pleas explained the proposed change by saying:

"Oelwein's position is that the sellers at the time of consummation of the sale were aware of his proposed use of the property for operation of a truck terminal and related activities so that the proposed additional language will clarify that point, and assist him in his quest for financing in connection with the construction of improvements on the property."

Evans forwarded a copy of the letter to Anne (Celli) Fletcher, along with a copy of the proposed amendment. Noting that Oelwein had apparently run into some financial difficulties in financing which was related to the restrictive covenant, he said:

"The difficulty with the requested language is that it provides carte blanche for construction and operation of a truck terminal and related activities. We have no idea what these 'related activities' would involve, and the reason we originally included such stringent restrictive covenants was to insure that the truck terminal proposed by Mr. Oelwein would not cause unreasonable interference with the remaining property.

"In my opinion, paragraph 8 of the contract, which is quoted in Howard Pleas' letter, is unobjectionable, and I do not recommend that you authorize any amendment to its language. I see nothing inconsistent with operation of a truck terminal within the framework of the restrictions of paragraph 8. While you certainly did consent in essence to the operation of a truck terminal on the property, there is no reason why such operation should cause the objectionable items referred to in paragraph 8. If we adopt the supplement requested by Mr. Oelwein, we are in essence changing the contract to mean that paragraph 8 applies only to the extent that the noxious or offensive activity or emission of odors, dust, fumes, smoke or noise is not a normal incident of a reasonably operated truck terminal. I don't think we should go that far."

He sent a copy of the letter to the Puget Sound Bank, which was co-trustee with Anne of the trust established under the will of Dr. Celli for Anne and her children.

After discussing the matter with her husband, Anne (Celli) Fletcher agreed with Evans' analysis and rejected the proposal. Evans telephoned Pleas and informed him of her decision, which seemed to disappoint Pleas, who said he did not understand why Anne should be so concerned about preserving the standard form clause without regard for what everyone knew Oelwein intended to do. Evans suggested that they should attempt to expedite the negotiations with North-South, or explore other means of effectuating a sale of the land. Pleas agreed, but nothing specific was agreed upon.

On March 14, 1967, Evans received a telephone call from John Stewart of Webster, Hoffman, Nickerson, and Adams. Evans was somewhat surprised to hear that the firm represented North-South Truck Lines and that he was interested in discussing the reasons for Anne Fletcher's refusal to release the restrictive covenant in the contract of sale to TR & RP. Stewart explained that North-South wanted to buy the land to use it as a truck terminal, but that it would not do so if the covenant remained in the contract of sale to TR & RP. When Evans expressed surprise that the tract of land was large enough for North-South's terminal needs, Stewart informed him that TR & RP also owned a parcel of about 8 acres to the south [parcel 2 on the attached map] and that it had acquired options on other land in the immediate area, so that taken together the various parcels would be sufficient. Evans repeated the analysis he had given Anne in his letter, indicating that he did not believe that a release or modification of the covenant could be obtained on the basis suggested. A telephone conversation with Jay Collins of Cooper & Bok, Realtors, confirmed North-South's interest in acquiring the TR & RP land. It also produced pretty reliable indications that the price which North-South would pay for the land was $1.05 per square foot, or $55,758 per acre.

On April 24, 1967, Evans met in his office with Allegra, Laura, Anne and Byse Fletcher, and a representative from the Puget Sound trust department. Allegra's opposition to sale of the land continued, but at the urging of Fletcher and Evans she finally agreed to go along with the sale if a substantial portion of the proceeds were reinvested in Duwamish Valley land farther south where values had not appreciated as much as in the area of the Celli holdings. The plan was to acquire approximately the same area of land, paying $15,000 per acre, or perhaps as much as $0.50 or $0.70 per square foot [$21,780 or $32,492 per acre]. Twenty-five acres of land would be offered to North-South at $1.05 per square foot, with the possibility of dropping the price of $0.98 per square foot. North-South would be expected to preserve access easements to the remaining property, and would also be requested to pay the broker's fee on the sale. These terms were given to Jay Collins of Cooper & Bok for transmittal to North-South. It was further agreed between Allegra, Laura, and Anne that they would not release the covenant against noxious uses except for a substantial payment, using it for leverage to compel North-South to purchase their land.

The next day Evans received a phone call from Lester Jayson, who had been a very good friend of his in high school. Jayson, who now lived in San Mateo, Calif., told Evans he was visiting relatives in Seattle, and wondered if they could meet for lunch sometime that week at the Washington Athletic Club. Evans agreed, and on Friday, April 28, they met. Jayson's father had come with him, and joined them at their table. Despite some urging, Evans did not join the Jaysons in cocktails, but enjoyed hearing about his friend's activities during the years of their separation. As the waiter took the order for a second round of cocktails, Evans was reminded that the senior Jayson was a vice president of North-South Truck Lines, and the conversation was quickly directed to the subject of that company's desire to purchase the TR & RP land. A number of letters from businesses located near other North-South terminals were offered to Evans, most of which were to the effect that North-South was a very desirable neighbor whose presence tended to increase the value of the industrial property. The senior Jayson questioned Evans as to why his client should refuse to permit modification of the restrictive covenant, stating that North-South recognized the superior qualities of the TR & RP location, but that it could not wait through the summer for a decision. Evans again repeated his analysis of why the modification should not be permitted on the terms suggested, and refused to agree to urge any change of position upon his client. He emphasized that his client's interest was in selling the land and not in granting a release from the covenant. After a rather long but unproductive lunch, he and Lester Jayson parted, agreeing that it had been good to see one another again.

North-South made no immediate response to the Celli group offer to sell 25 acres at $1.05 per square foot, and Evans, with Fletcher's help, worked up another proposal for possible solution of the disagreement between Anne and the Celli sisters and brother as to whether the remaining land should be sold in the near future. It was that seven acres of land in a rectangular shape and adjacent to the TR & RP property be set aside and quitclaimed to Anne, individually and as trustee, if she should find a purchaser for the land. She in turn would quitclaim all interest in the remaining portion of the land and in addition would execute a modification of the restrictive covenant on the contract to TR & RP.

On May 3, 1967, Evans received a telephone call from Howard Pleas, who, after some preliminary comments, said that the Celli group desired to grant the modification of the restrictive covenant, and asked that Anne join with them. In justification, he explained that a number of years ago Carl Celli had purchased about five acres of land along the river, and adjacent to the TR & RP property. Less than two weeks ago, according to Pleas, Carl had entered into an agreement to purchase all the TR & RP land at $1.05 per square foot. North-South was now interested in acquiring that land, plus the five acres owned by Carl, provided the covenant was modified. Evans inquired as to what benefit would come to the rest of the group from the modification which would result in a very profitable sale of Carl's land. Apparently none were anticipated. He requested time to discuss the matter with his client and her husband.

After a lengthy discussion and consideration of various courses of action with Byse Fletcher, on May 4, 1967, Evans wrote a three-page letter to Pleas. After informing Pleas that Anne and her husband were upset to learn that the group had abandoned its common front for the purpose of dealing with North-South, he said:

"Carl Celli has seen fit to strike his own bargain, at the expense of the entire group. Anne and Byse had understood that as a last resort the noxious activity clause would be released only if North-South paid an appropriate fee. By getting North-South to instead agree to purchase Carl Celli's land as part of the overall package, it is obvious that the leverage the group once held by virtue of the clause has already been used to harvest a profit. Unfortunately the profit accrues solely to Carl rather than to the group.

"Anne and Byse are also distressed because their most recent understanding had been that the group was considering buying them out entirely or at least allowing them to sell one-fifth of the property to North-South. This opportunity has also been thrown by the wayside as a result of the direct contact with North-South in the last few days."

In light of these events, the letter continued, Anne would not sign the modification of the restrictive covenant except on either of two conditions:

1. Simultaneously with execution of the modification, Carl Celli or other members of the family would buy out the entire one-fifth interest of Anne and the children for the sum of $394,000, or

2. Simultaneously with execution of the modification, Carl would pay to Anne the sum of $25,000 and in addition the Celli interests would

agree to allow Anne to sell one-fifth of the land to any willing purchaser, without limitation on use.

He concluded the letter by urging that the first solution be adopted.

The following Monday, May 8, Evans received a reply from Pleas, informing him that the Celli family members had rejected both proposals. In addition, the letter requested that if any matters arose concerning the Celli properties Evans consult Pleas, who was acting as counsel for the Celli family. Evans telephoned Pleas to assure him that Anne would not agree to modification of the covenant, and in the course of the conversation informed Pleas that Anne was no longer willing to allow Allegra to handle the accounts of the Celli interests but that Anne wished to be a co-signer of every check drawn on the checking account in which rental funds were deposited. He also suggested that certain utility bills and a telephone bill were not properly chargeable to the joint account.

One week later, on May 15th, Evans received a telephone call from Pleas, who said that the Cellis were still not interested in either of the propositions which Evans had suggested, but they did think they might negotiate with North-South for a consideration for agreeing to modification of the restrictive covenant. They suggested that they might ask for $15,000. Evans telephoned Anne, who said she was not interested in releasing the covenant, even for $15,000. As she saw it, if Carl got $200,000 for the sale of his five acres he would have no interest in selling any of the main parcel of land held in common. Accordingly, she would agree to modification of the covenant only if the group either permitted her to sell her share of the land to North-South or else agreed to purchase her interest. Evans immediately conveyed this information to Pleas.

Three days later Pleas sent to Evans a counter-offer he had received from Oelwein, in which Oelwein offered to pay $40,000 to the Celli estate beneficiaries if they would agree to the proposed modification of the restrictive covenant. Evans telephoned this information to Anne, but it produced no change in her views. She still wanted either to sell her share of the land to North-South, or to have the group buy out her interest. Evans then telephoned John Lowman, the attorney for Oelwein, whose name he got from Pleas, and informed him of Anne's views. Comments made in response by Lowman led Evans to believe that Carl had gotten himself into what he considered a difficult position by suggesting to North-South that the covenant might be released if North-South agreed to purchase Carl's land. The conversation produced an agreement for representatives of all the Cellis, Oelwein, and Anne to meet the following day for further discussion. In preparation for the conference, Evans met with Byse Fletcher and they agreed that they lacked precise information concerning the acreage remaining in the large parcel. This led them to reformulate their proposal to be that Anne would take either $1.05 per square foot for her share of the land after a survey, or $340,000 as an appropriate amount without a survey.

The meeting took place the following day, Friday, May 19, with Allegra, Carl, and Laura present and represented by Pleas, Oelwein represented by Lowman, and Evans and Fletcher representing Anne, who did not attend. In the preliminary small talk, Evans inquired as to whether Antoinette would be present. Allegra and Laura both looked somewhat disturbed and said that things had taken a very bad turn for Antoinette. It appeared that cancer had now spread through her body so that neither an operation nor radiation would be of help to her. The discussion then turned to the various proposals before the group but produced no change of position, even though Evans pointed out that Carl was about to make a profit probably in excess of $200,000 while offering Anne only her one-fifth share of $40,000 for permitting the transaction to go through. Evans and Fletcher then urged the Cellis to buy out Anne's interest or to sell the property. Evans added to their usual arguments the observation that the disturbing news about Antoinette made it clear that the property would have to be sold sometime in the near future to provide enough cash to meet the estate tax which would have to be paid after Antoinette's death. The Cellis would not agree, however, and the parties separated.

As they drove back to Evans' office, Evans and Fletcher discussed the matter and decided in light of the unreasoning attitude of the Cellis, the best thing for Anne to do was to agree to the modification of the covenant and get her share of the $40,000 offered for its release. As they saw it, the Cellis would not agree to sale of the land, and the covenant, which otherwise had little value, would lose the premium value it currently had if North-South abandoned its interest in the site. It was agreed that Byse would so advise Anne.

Anne, however, declined to accept the advice. She repeated her view that Carl would become so comfortable with the profit from the sale of his five-acre tract that he would have no interest in selling the remaining land. He would reinforce Allegra in her opposition to making a sale; Laura would never oppose either of them; and they both had such a fixation on keeping the land that they would very probably work out some way for payment of the estate taxes after Antoinette's death. The price offered was not sufficient in her opinion to keep her interest locked up so unproductively. After all, she pointed out, even at a 5 percent return, $300,000 would return an income of $15,000 a year, and she didn't want to lose that for several years just for the $8,000 she would receive as her share of the price paid for release of the covenant.

The next week, on May 24, Evans received a phone call from Lowman, who represented Oelwein, in the course of which Lowman expressed the extreme necessity of reaching some conclusion to the negotiations. It seemed that North-South had begun in earnest negotiations for purchase of another site and that the possibilities for Oelwein, Carl Celli, and the Celli interests generally were about to evaporate. The discussion turned to the inequality of profit that would be realized if the transaction were completed as proposed, and Lowman ventured the opinion that Carl had planned to pay $5,000 or $6,000 to each of his sisters as conscience money. He suggested that Carl might be induced to make such a payment to Anne in addition to her share of the $40,000 which Oelwein was prepared to pay for release of the covenant. Evans then suggested that in light of the fact that Oelwein was about to make in excess of $200,000 if the sale were to go through, he might increase his payment for release of the covenant to $100,000. Lowman brushed this aside, saying that it obviously would be better for Oelwein to hold the property for sale to some other purchaser and realize the gain for himself, rather than share it with the Celli interests. The conversation ended on this inconclusive basis.

The next day, May 25, Evans received from Pleas a letter stating that Carl Celli was willing to buy the one-fifth interest held by Anne in her own name and as trustee for the price of $340,000, without a survey being made to determine the exact area of the land. The initial down payment would be in the amount of 29 percent of the purchase price, the balance to bear 6 percent per annum, with Carl having the right to make payment of the entire balance within one year of the closing without penalty. Anne and the Cellis were to execute the requested modification of the restrictive covenant. Moreover, the entire transaction was to be contingent upon sale by Carl of his land to North-South. The offer was stated to be good for five days.

Evans quickly arranged a conference with Byse Fletcher and a representative of the Puget Sound trust department to discuss the offer. He also obtained appraisals of the value of the lots and houses on the other side of the river owned by the Celli interests, and from these calculated that a one-fifth interest had a value of approximately $35,000. Allowing the weekend for reflection, Evans called Pleas on Monday, May 29, to outline a counteroffer. The terms of the counteroffer, which Evans confirmed by letter mailed that day, were as follows:

"1. The total price shall be $373,461 OR a price computed on the basis of $1.05 per square foot, on a surveyed basis, for the square footage attributable to the one-fifth undivided interest in the large piece of property of approximately 35 to 39 acres, plus $35,000 for the remaining miscellaneous pieces of Celli property. The price of $373,461 is based on an assumed acreage of 7.4 acres for a one-fifth interest, priced at $1.05 per square foot.

"2. The parties will execute an earnest money agreement, providing, *inter alia,* for the following terms:

"(a) An earnest money deposit of $5,000.

" (b) A down payment at closing in the sum of 29 percent of the purchase price, less the earnest money already deposited, and the balance payable at the rate of 25 percent after December 31, 1967, and before January 10, 1968, 25 percent or more payable after December 31, 1968, and before January 10, 1969, and the balance remaining on or before January 10, 1970, with 7 percent interest per annum on declining balances. This will permit Carl to prepay the balance of the contract at any time after January 1, 1969, but he will have until January 10, 1970, to satisfy the balance if he chooses to wait that long.

"(c) Upon execution of the real estate contract the sellers will execute amendments to the Oelwein real estate contract to include the proposed modification of the restrictive covenant.

"(d) The proposed purchase will be contingent upon the sale of acreage owned by Carl Celli individually to Oelwein and/or North-South freight lines, and his earnest money will be refunded if either of those parties refuse to exercise the existing option with Carl Celli.

"(e) Execution of the real estate contract will be contingent upon obtaining court approval for the sale of trust interest in the Celli property."

Evans stated that his clients placed no firm deadline upon acceptance of the offer but suggested that it probably would not be held open for longer than seven days. He also added a cautionary reminder that the transaction did not include a sale of Anne's one-fifth interest in the real estate contract covering the earlier sale of land to Oelwein.

Telephone conversations with Pleas ensued, during which discussion centered about the interest rate applicable to the remaining balance and the schedule for payment. Finally, on June 16, 1967, Evans received from Pleas the original and two copies of a proposed earnest money agreement, together with a certified check in the amount of $5,000. The total purchase price agreed upon was $371,461 for all of Anne's interest in the Celli properties except her interest in the real estate contract covering the earlier sale to Oelwein and TR & RP. The schedule of payments provided for $109,303.69 to be paid as a down payment; $93,365.25 to be paid after December 31, 1967, and before January 10, 1968; and the remainder, except the last, in annual installments of $56,019.15. Interest on the declining balance was fixed at 7 percent per annum. Anne agreed to execute the modification of the restrictive covenant, and the whole transaction was stated to be contingent upon the sale by Carl Celli and by Oelwein (TR & RP) to North-South of lands appropriately described. Copies were soon signed by Carl Celli and Anne Fletcher.

The establishment of the escrow arrangements to handle the now complicated transaction required painstaking attention to detail, but posed no major problems for negotiation, and the same was true for the drafting of the real estate contract. The technical complications delayed closing of the transaction until October 10, 1967, by which time Antoinette was represented by her husband, who had been appointed guardian of her estate because of her serious and final illness.

QUESTIONS

1. Do you believe that the various positions taken by the parties in the negotiations were entirely based upon economic considerations? If not, identify other considerations affecting the conduct of the parties.

2. Do you believe the restrictive covenant had the significance which the parties attributed to it? If not, why did it assume such major significance in the negotiations? Were there any ways in which Carl Celli,

Oelwein, or North-South could have eliminated the covenant as a significant consideration? What kind of relief could have been obtained for violation of the covenant?

3. What would have happened if Anne had agreed to majority rule by family members with regard to decisions affecting the Celli property?

4. Do you think Pleas was frank and made full disclosure when he first knew about Carl's plans to sell his five-acre plot to North-South?

5. Was it an error on the part of the attorney for North-South to telephone Evans to request the release of the covenant? If you think it was, what should or could he have done to avoid committing such a mistake?

6. Notice how much the value of the land changed in a short time. Do you think Anne was well-advised to sell her interest at the time she did, or do you think she has lost the opportunity to realize an additional appreciation of land values? Is there any way one can develop reliable information on price trends?

7. What do you think about the episode with Jayson, Evans' high school friend? Do you think they should have expected to succeed in obtaining a modification or release of the covenant? Did they in fact reveal more about how much North-South desired the tract than they should have?

8. What was accomplished by the request that Anne become a co-signer of all checks drawn on the account maintained for the Celli properties?

9. Would you have suggested to the other Celli family members that Antoinette's death would require sale of the property in the near future? Why or why not?

10. Were Evans and Fletcher wrong in advising Anne to accept a share of the $40,000 for modification or release of the restrictive covenant? In what sense was her decision to the contrary a business or economic decision?

11. What do you think will happen if Carl Celli is unable to meet his scheduled payments on the real estate contract?

C. COLLECTIVE BARGAINING RELATIONSHIPS

NLRB v. REED & PRINCE MFG. CO.

205 F.2d 131, 32 LRRM 2225 (1st Cir. 1953), cert. denied,
346 U.S. 887, 33 LRRM 2133 (1953)

MAGRUDER, Chief Judge.

In the petition now before us, the National Labor Relations Board asks us to enforce a Board order entered October 16, 1951, directing Reed & Prince Manufacturing Co., upon request, to bargain collectively with United Steelworkers of America, CIO, as the exclusive representative of all the production and maintenance employees of respondent at its

plant at Worcester, Massachusetts. An earlier phase of this case is reported in *N. L. R. B.* v. *Reed & Prince Mfg. Co.*, 1 Cir., 1952, 196 F.2d 755.
. . .

Coming then to the merits, this is not a simple case where the employer has made a clear refusal to recognize or bargain with the certified representative of its employees. Rather, it is one where the employer engaged in a lengthy series of bargaining conferences, which got nowhere. In such a case the question is whether it is to be inferred from the totality of the employer's conduct that he went through the motions of negotiation as an elaborate pretense with no sincere desire to reach an agreement if possible, or that it bargained in good faith but was unable to arrive at an acceptable agreement with the union. Particularly in this area of mixed fact and law, a court will not lightly disregard the over-all appraisal of the situation by the Labor Board "as one of those agencies presumably equipped or informed by experience to deal with a specialized field of knowledge, whose findings within that field carry the authority of an expertness which courts do not possess and therefore must respect." *Universal Camera Corp.* v. *N. L. R. B.*, 1951, 340 U.S. 474, 488, 71 S.Ct. 456, 465, 95 L.Ed. 456.

Section 8(a)(5) of the Act, 61 Stat. 141, makes it an unfair labor practice for an employer "to refuse to bargain collectively with the representatives of his employees." Correspondingly, § 8(b) (3) makes it an unfair labor practice for a labor organization "to refuse to bargain collectively with an employer, provided it is the representative of his employees." More or less declaratory of the law as it had been expounded in judicial decisions under the original Act, § 8(d) of the Act, as amended, provides that for the purposes of this section "to bargain collectively is the performance of the mutual obligation of the employer and the representative of the employees to meet at reasonable times and confer in good faith with respect to wages, hours, and other terms and conditions of employment, or the negotiation of an agreement, or any question arising thereunder, and the execution of a written contract incorporating any agreement reached if requested by either party, but such obligation does not compel either party to agree to a proposal or require the making of a concession."

It is true, as stated in *N. L. R. B.* v. *American National Ins. Co.*, 1952, 343 U.S. 395, 404, 72 S.Ct. 824, 829, 96 L.Ed. 1027, that the Board may not "sit in judgment upon the substantive terms of collective bargaining agreements." But at the same time it seems clear that if the Board is not to be blinded by empty talk and by the mere surface motions of collective bargaining, it must take some cognizance of the reasonableness of the positions taken by an employer in the course of bargaining negotiations. See *Wilson & Co., Inc.,* v. *N. L. R. B.*, 8 Cir., 1940, 115 F.2d 759, 763. See also Smith, *The Evolution of the "Duty to Bargain" Concept in American Law*, 39 Mich. L. Rev. 1065, 1108 (1941). Thus if an employer can find nothing whatever to agree to in an ordinary current-day contract submitted to him, or in some of the union's related minor requests, and if the employer makes not a single serious proposal meeting the union at least part way, then certainly the Board must be able to conclude that this is at least some evidence of bad faith, that is, of a desire not to reach an agreement with the union. In other words, while the Board cannot force an employer to make a "concession" on any specific issue or to adopt any particular position, the employer is obliged to make *some* reasonable effort in *some* direction to compose his differences with the union, if § 8(a)(5) is to be read as imposing any substantial obligation at all.

After an attentive examination of the entire record of the bargaining negotiations herein, we are definitely of the opinion that this is a case in which, under the standard laid down in *Universal Camera Corp.* v. *N. L. R. B.*, supra, we should accept the ultimate finding of the Board that respondent did not participate in the bargaining negotiations with the good faith required of it by law.

As the outcome of a representation proceeding and a subsequent election held on July 12, 1950, the Board on July 20, 1950, certified United Steelworkers of America, CIO, as the exclusive bargaining representative of certain of respondent's employees. There was no dispute at that time, nor is there now, as to the appropriateness of the designated bargaining unit. On or about August 1 following, the chief negotiator for the Union called upon respondent's president with the request for a bargaining conference as soon as convenient. He was informed by the president that because of other commitments no definite date could be set at that time. On or about August 9 the Company sent word to the Union that it would be impossible to arrange a meeting before Labor Day in view of the fact that various members of the Company's negotiating committee were on vacation until that time. After Labor Day it was finally agreed that the initial bargaining session would be held on September 15. In its decision the Board questioned "whether the Respondent would have delayed, for such a relatively long period of time, negotiations for a business contract or a bank loan it was desirous of concluding." The Board went on to say that although "the Respondent's conduct in this respect, standing alone, might be deemed equivocal, appraising it in the context of the Respondent's whole course of conduct we conclude that it was another aspect of the Respondent's calculated effort to avoid reaching an agreement with the Union while preserving the appearance of bargaining."

Meanwhile, on or about August 9, the Union by telephone requested permission to post certain non-controversial notices on the Company bulletin boards. It was told that this request could not be granted at that time but that the matter should be brought up at the first meeting. By letter of August 9 the Union requested respondent to furnish it with wage rates and classifications and the age and length of service of all employees in the bargaining unit, "In order to enable the United Steelworkers of America to bargain intelligently" with the Company. Although the Union made several further requests for this data, the Company did not supply it in full until some time in October. Commenting upon this, the Board observed that "the Respondent's delay in supplying the requested data may be viewed legitimately as a significant part of its entire course of conduct in determining whether or not the Respondent has exercised good faith in its bargaining negotiations with the Union."

On September 15 the first meeting took place as scheduled. Apparently the Union wanted to begin the discussions on a broad base, exploring potential areas of agreement and disagreement. The Company, however, insisted that the Union submit a written list of its contract proposals, which the Union immediately did.

Subsequently there were twelve further meetings between the parties running from the beginning of October through early in February, 1951. The first five of these conferences were devoted to a discussion of the suggested contract submitted by the Union. The principal Union proposals were (1) a substantial wage increase; (2) some form of union security, either a union shop or a maintenance of membership clause as an alternative; (3) a check-off provision; (4) grievance procedure with arbitration as the ultimate resort; (5) six paid holidays annually; (6) a seniority provision, and (7) some form of insurance and pensions.

With respect to the matter of wages, the Company offered a general wage increase of ten cents per hour, with the express condition that if the offer were accepted there would be no further negotiations on this subject. The Union, having originally requested fifteen cents, or maybe more, was unwilling to accept the offer on these terms; however, it repeatedly stated that it would regard all the various economic benefits as a single "package," and hence might be able to agree to the ten-cent increase, once the Company's position was made known on certain other demands, *e.g.*, pensions, insurance, and paid holidays.

The Company announced its general opposition on principle to any form of union security and to arbitration.

On the check-off proposal, the Company registered its opposition, mainly on the ground that this was not a proper subject of collective bargaining. In this the Company was mistaken. The Company added that in any event it could not accept a check-off provision because its administration would be too much of a bookkeeping burden. As the Board observed, an employer who takes the erroneous position that a particular subject matter is not bargainable "can hardly approach the discussion of this subject with an open mind and a willingness to reach an agreement."

As to the proposed grievance procedure, the Company took exception to the first step, providing that an employee complaining to his foreman be accompanied by the steward, and to the ultimate provision for arbitration. The Union manifested some willingness to yield on these matters, provided the other terms of the contract could be worked out. But when in response to the Company's request the Union submitted a more detailed proposal with reference to grievance procedure, the Company objected that this was too "complex". Apparently it did not point out any particulars in which the proposal might be simplified, though the Union claimed that it had submitted a typical grievance clause which worked effectively at other plants.

The Company also rejected the Union's demand for six paid holidays, referring to its current practice of giving year-end bonuses. When the Union urged the Company as an alternative to commit itself in the contract to a continuance of this practice, the Company declined.

The seniority proposal submitted by the Union was found by the Company to be unacceptable in various items, for instance, in the provision allowing seniority to accumulate during absences not exceeding two years on account of lay-offs or disability. Subsequently the Company submitted its own seniority proposal, which was culled from the 1941 contract negotiated between respondent and the labor organization then representing its employees.

Finally, as to pensions and insurance, the Company listened to an exposition by a union expert, but expressed the view that these areas were sufficiently covered by Social Security and Blue Cross, to both of which the Company contributed. It added, however, that it would consider the Union proposals and would offer some of its own, which so far as we can discover the Company never did. The Union submitted certain fairly detailed written proposals on the subject of pensions and insurance; but respondent's vice president, testifying before the trial examiner, conceded on cross-examination that the Company's final position on insurance and pensions was never communicated to the Union.

In addition to the foregoing major issues, there were several lesser items brought into the discussion:

(1) At the first meeting the Union again raised the question of bulletin board space. The Company replied that while it could not comply with this request, it might be able to arrange for posting of Union notices on plant gates. Despite repeated requests by the Union, the Company never took definite action in this matter. The Board observed that the granting of such posting permission is a common industrial practice, and expressed the opinion "thus the Respondent's handling of the bulletin board matter, taken in the context of this case, indicates the Respondent's basic unwillingness to accept the principle of collective bargaining and further strengthens our conclusion that the Respondent has not bargained in good faith."

(2) At the end of the recognition clause proposed by the Union, the Company wanted to insert the first proviso of § 9(a) of the statute, recognizing the right of individual employees to present grievances directly to the employer. The Union agreed to this on the condition that there also be inserted in the recognition clause the second proviso in § 9(a), "That the bargaining representative has been given opportunity to be present at such adjustment." The Company took this countersuggestion under advisement, but presumably ultimately rejected it, since the recognition clause in the proposed contract which the Company submitted to the Union on November 22 contained only the first proviso of § 9(a). On

this matter the Board stated: "We cannot conceive of a good faith basis for a refusal to incorporate a statutory obligation into a contract in the very words of the statute. This type of quibbling conduct is consistent only with the conclusion that there was bad, not good, faith bargaining."

(3) The Union suggested a 40-hour workweek with time and one-half on Saturday. The Company was unwilling to accept the latter point, feeling that time and one-half should begin only after an employee had already worked 40 hours during the week. Subsequently the Union came up with a modified proposal to the effect that employees who, in following management schedules, were required to work on Saturday should be paid time and a half, but that time and a half would not apply where an employee had to work on Saturday because he had lost time for personal reasons during the regular workweek. The modified proposal, however, was not accepted by the Company.

(4) Another provision in the proposed Union contract related to leaves of absence to be granted to employees "with the consent of the Union and the Company." The Company squelched this proposal on the ground that it was not its practice to grant such leaves of absence. However, at the hearing before the trial examiner the Board introduced in evidence a Company "Book of Information for Employees" which included this sentence: "This [section relating to employee service credits] does not apply to cases where the Management has granted in writing permission for Leave of Absence."

(5) During the course of the negotiations the Union pointed out that at present employees who were on a piece-work basis received insufficient information to compute their incentive pay. The Union requested the Company so far as possible to supply each employee with a daily record of what he had done on that particular day similar to a method being used by other companies. Respondent rejected this suggestion, claiming that it was impossible for it to make these computations.

By October 31, since no agreement had been reached on even the most minor matters, both sides seemed to feel that the negotiations were at an impasse. Nevertheless, there were seven further meetings. On or about November 10 the Union submitted a final proposed contract which was complete except for a wage clause. On November 22 the Company, in turn, submitted its first and only proposed "contract", to which we shall make further reference subsequently. Neither of these documents served to bring the parties any closer to an agreement.

On December 4 respondent announced to its employees that a Christmas bonus would be paid to them "in recognition of their loyalty during the past year", with the expression of hope "that we shall be able to continue the payment for many years to come." On December 5 respondent posted a notice stating: "Based on certain decisions of the National Labor Relations Board, the Management is now permitted to put into effect immediately the 10¢ an hour increase previously offered to the factory employees in the National Labor Relations Board bargaining unit." This notice the Board regarded as another aspect of respondent's "lack of good faith in the bargaining negotiations with the Union." The Board also went on to add: "[We have] frequently had occasion to point out that the unilateral granting of a wage increase during the course of negotiations with the legally constituted bargaining representative . . . is a violation of the Act. Such action necessarily has the effect of undermining the representative status and prestige of the bargaining agent." While it was recognized that such a unilaterally announced wage increase might legally be made effective once the parties had reached, as a result of good faith bargaining, an impasse in the bargaining negotiations, it was the Board's view that the responsibility for the impasse here must be attributed to respondent's lack of good faith in the prior negotiations with the Union. It further found that "Respondent emphasized this bad faith by announcing the wage increase in such a way that the Union could not and did not in any way share the credit for it."

In the meantime the Union was becoming increasingly disturbed over what it called "the Company's bad faith" and the consequently decreasing likelihood of ever arriving at an agreement. On or about November 14 the Union reported to its membership that the Company was strongly against all the "basic provisions" suggested by the Union and that it appeared "that the Company is just stalling." Shortly thereafter the employees authorized a strike. At the December 27 meeting the Union advised the Company that there would be a strike at the plant effective January 2 "because they were not bargaining in good faith with the union." This strike was called, and was still in progress at the time of the hearing before the trial examiner.

Subsequently the federal and the Massachusetts conciliation services—which had come to play an active part in the negotiations—made several further, but unsuccessful, efforts to get the parties together. The Company told the conciliators that the parties were still bargaining and that it thought more progress could be made by direct negotiations between the Union and the Company, even though at the same time the Company admitted, as indeed it had to in order to sustain the validity of its unilateral announcement on December 5 of a wage increase, that the parties had reached an impasse. The conciliators suggested arbitration of the principal issues of disagreement, which proposal was accepted by the Union but not replied to by the Company. They also proposed various compromises, which the Company refused.

Shortly after the beginning of the strike, the Company initiated several back-to-work efforts. In this it was aided by one Donald Pierce, a Company stock expediter, who was entrusted with a Company car to furnish transportation to returning strikers. One employee testified that Pierce urged him to return to work "because Alden Reed [respondent's treasurer] is never going to sign a contract with the union" and told him that respondent "would rather sell the plant than sign a contract with the union." The admission of this testimony was strenuously objected to by respondent, but since Pierce was acting for the Company in these back-to-work activities, it seems clear that on ordinary agency principles the testimony as to Pierce's remark, which was uncontradicted, was properly let in as an admission by the Company.

Before us, respondent has sought to ascribe the undoubted stalemate to an adamant insistence by the Union upon acceptance of the basic provisions of its standard contract, submitted on a take-it-or-leave-it basis. As evidence of this, respondent relies upon certain expressions in a leaflet circulated by the Union negotiating committee to the employees, purporting to describe the bargaining meeting of November 14. But an examination of the record of the lengthy negotiations between the Company and the Union indicates that the Union's bargaining efforts were marked by a considerable flexibility of approach, for the Union negotiator at many important points submitted modifications of its proposals in an effort to meet Company objections. It even appears that the Union might have been willing to accept a contract with no union security provision or arbitration clause in it if the other provisions could have been worked out acceptably.

The plain fact is that after months of negotiations, as the Board observed, "practically all the Union could report to its membership in the way of progress was the 10-cent wage offer—freely given by the Respondent in an inflationary period of rising wages." Even in minor matters, such as the Union's request for use of the Company bulletin board, and the Union's request that the second proviso of § 9(a) of the Act be inserted in the recognition clause, the Company withheld assent. The Company's asserted justification for this is that it was "bargaining technique." But it may be wondered how the Company could in good faith ever expect to arrive at an agreement if the major proposals submitted by the Union are refused on principle and assent on the minor ones is withheld as a matter of bargaining technique.

In sustaining the Board's ultimate conclusion of lack of good faith, as deduced from the record as a whole and from the totality of respondent's conduct in its bargaining relations with the Union, we do not necessarily have to sustain the Board on each and every one of its subsidiary findings of fact. As stated in *N.L.R.B.* v. *Newport News Shipbuilding & Dry Dock Co.*, 1939, 308 U.S. 241, 247, 60 S.Ct. 203, 207, 84 L.Ed. 219: "We do not stop to consider these contentions, since, without such findings, there would still be a basis in the record for the Board's conclusions." As a matter of fact most of the underlying facts, certainly the more significant ones, are not in dispute.

Nor do we have to agree with the Board as to each and every one of the incidents which it specially emphasized in its decision as indicating a lack of good faith on the Company's part in the conduct of the bargaining negotiations. For instance, we are not inclined to agree with the Board that the Company's insistence, over the Union's strenuous objection, on having a stenotypist present at all the bargaining meetings to take down a verbatim transcript of the proceedings was evidence of the Company's bad faith. On the other hand, we think that the Board might well have lifted out from the record another item for special comment, as indicative of bad faith on the Company's part. We refer to the fact that, after discussion at several meetings of the Union's various proposals of items to be included in the contract, the Company on November 22 submitted its own proposal of a so-called contract. This was a brief two-page document containing a recognition clause which paraphrased the first proviso of § 9(a) of the Act but made no reference to the second proviso, and contained a provision as to hours of work substantially copied from its 1941 agreement, but had no provisions as to wages, grievance procedure, or the other major items which the Union had proposed for inclusion in the contract. It is difficult to believe that the Company with a straight face and in good faith could have supposed that this proposal had the slightest chance of acceptance by a self-respecting union, or even that it might advance the negotiations by affording a basis of discussion; rather, it looks more like a stalling tactic by a party bent upon maintaining the pretense of bargaining.

There may be cases where the ultimate finding of an administrative agency rests in part upon findings of subsidiary fact, or inferences therefrom, which a reviewing court deems insupportable, and where, because the court is in substantial doubt whether the administrative agency would have made the same ultimate finding with the erroneous findings or inferences removed from the picture, it may be appropriate for the court to remand the case to the administrative agency for further consideration. But in view of the record in its entirety, we are satisfied that this is not such a case.

After reviewing the facts and stating its conclusion on the record as a whole, the Board in its decision had this to say: "We have scrupulously avoided prejudging the Respondent because of its rather unsavory labor relations history, but the Board is not required by law to ignore this history. Accordingly, in evaluating the evidence in this case, we have given some weight to this factor." Respondent contends that the Board committed a glaring error in taking account of this factor and that for this reason the Board order should be set aside. We do not think it would be error, in a case like this, for the Board to take account of the prior history of the Company's labor relations, as disclosed in the prior record of which the Board might take judicial notice. The ultimate issue whether the Company conducted its bargaining negotiations in good faith involves a finding of motive or state of mind which can only be inferred from circumstantial evidence. It is similar to the inquiry whether an employer discharged an employee for union activity, or for some other reason, where the prior history of the employer's labor relations, whether good or bad, may be relevant. However, we do not stop to consider the contention at length, for in this case it is evident that the Board's reference to this factor was only as a make-weight, in support of a conclusion which the Board deemed inescapable from the present record—and a very light make-weight at that, for the Board went on to say that it was "not unmindful of the fact that from 1941 to 1945, as a result of the Court decree, the Respondent had contractual relations with the Union."

Finally, respondent contends that the trial examiner committed error in rejecting an offer of proof by counsel for respondent "that this strike has been prolonged by the violence of the union, and that had it not been for the violence of the union, the employees would have voted, through the union, to have returned to work." Of course such evidence would have had no bearing upon the issue of the alleged already accrued 8(a) (5) unfair labor practice which provoked the strike. Nor would the Union, at least in the absence of most extraordinary circumstances, thereby forfeit its status as the certified bargaining representative. Despite instances of violence in the course of such a strike, the Board would not be obliged to withhold an order upon respondent to bargain collectively with the Union, upon future request, as an appropriate remedial measure to undo the effect of the past unfair labor practice. Under the circumstances the Board had considerable discretion in the matter of inquiry into alleged incidents of Union violence during the strike. We do not find that the Board committed any abuse of discretion in excluding respondent's very generalized offer of proof.

A decree will be entered enforcing the order of the Board.

QUESTION

Consider the bargaining techniques used by the company entirely apart from what may be the statutory duty to bargain collectively. Do you believe that they were techniques which increased the possibility that the company would obtain an agreement on very favorable terms? Were they techniques which decreased the possibility of a strike? What objective or objectives do you believe the company was pursuing throughout the events described in the opinion?

NOTE

A detailed and very readable account of the events and negotiations connected with the 1978 strike which shut down the *New York Times* and the *Daily News* for three months and the *New York Post* for two months is presented in A. H. Raskin, *A Reporter at Large (Part I— Changes In the Balance of Power, Part II—Intrigue at the Summit)*, The New Yorker Magazine, January 22, 1979, p. 41, and January 29, 1979, p. 56.

GENERAL ELECTRIC COMPANY
150 NLRB 192, 57 LRRM 1491 (1964)

*Intermediate Report of Trial Examiner**

. . .

C. BACKGROUND OF 1960 NEGOTIATIONS

1. GE'S GENERAL APPROACH TO COLLECTIVE BARGAINING

As will later more fully appear, many of the specific events relating to the 1960 negotiations can be seen in true focus only if considered against the backdrop of GE's underlying policies relating to collective bargaining. It is therefore appropriate to examine such policies before undertaking a review of GE's specific conduct which is here under attack.

GE's present approach to employee and union relations was first conceived in 1947 and developed largely under the guidance of Lemuel R. Boulware, then and for many years later GE's vice president relations service. The approach has often been referred to as "Boulwareism," although GE itself abjures use of that term, claiming it has been misconstrued by outsiders to reflect a concept not actually GE's. It came into being as an aftermath of a lengthy companywide strike which the UE had conducted against GE in 1946. That strike was settled only after GE raised its wage offer from a prestrike 10 cents an hour to a poststrike 18½ cents an hour. As appears from one company report, GE's management regarded UE's "highly successful strike" as "little short of a debacle." Management had theretofore had a "feeling" of "security in the knowledge that the Company had been a good employer [which] had treated employees fairly, and had pioneered in the voluntary installation of many employee benefit program." Nevertheless, the strike had been "broadly supported" by employees. The realization that its earlier feeling of security had been a false one was a "somber event" for GE management.

The jolt of the 1946 strike led GE management to take a new look. GE sought to determine why it had failed (as it saw it) to achieve the same high degree of success and effectiveness in its employee relations as it had in other areas of its operations, such as, for example, in product development and marketing. Management concluded, *inter alia*, that to gain employee job satisfaction, loyalty, and support, it was not enough that the Company be a good employer. It was equally if not more important that the Company be *known* to its employees as a good employer. With regard to employee pay, benefits, and other terms and conditions of employment, as well as other elements entering into employee job satisfaction, the employees must be made to understand that it was the Company's aim "to do right voluntarily" and to allow its employees all that was fairly warranted, bearing in mind the "balanced best interests"

---

* Footnotes omitted.

of employees and all others having a stake in the Company's enterprise. Moreover, the employees must also be made to understand that, just as there was no need to drag reluctantly from the Company all that was fairly coming to them, so, too, there could be no profit in a show of force by a labor organization designed to extract more for the employees than the facts—as management evaluated them—justly warranted. This involved essentially a selling problem, or, as the Company termed it, one of "job marketing." If the Company was to achieve ultimately the same success in job marketing that it had accomplished in its highly successful marketing, it must assimilate to the latter what it had learned in the former about sound product planning and research, market development, and merchandising.

Application of this program necessitated a revision of the Company's approach to collective bargaining. The Company had theretofore engaged in the traditional type of bargaining, under which a union initially asks more than it expects to get and an employer offers less than it expects to give, and, through the process of compromise and give-and-take, both sides, if bargaining is successful, eventually arrive at a mutually acceptable middle ground. But that type of bargaining had to go if the Company was to establish its credibility with employees that it was putting into effect *voluntarily* and without need of outside pressures all that was warranted in the way of wage and benefit improvements.

Under GE's present approach to bargaining, as GE states it, the Company itself seeks through extensive year-round research into all pertinent facts to determine what is "right" for employees. Its research includes not only a study of business conditions, competitive factors, economic trends, and the like, but the gathering of its own information as to employee needs and desires through independent employee attitude surveys, comments made by employees at informative meetings, direct discussions by supervisors with employees, and statements in union publications. When bargaining begins, the Company, as part of its overall research, listens to the presentations made by all the unions with which it deals, and evaluates the unions' demands with the help of all the facts it has on hand, including those supplied by the unions.

On the basis of its study so made, GE makes its own determination of what is "right." GE then makes an offer which—as it declares to the unions and to its employees—includes *everything* it has found to be warranted, without anything held back for later trading or compromising. GE makes precisely the same basic offer to substantially all unions with which it is engaged in negotiations. Contrary to the assertion of the General Counsel, GE does not initially present its offer on an avowed "take-it-or-leave-it" basis. It professes a willingness to make prompt adjustments in its offer whenever (but only when) new information from any source or a significant change in facts indicates that its initial offer fell short of being right. But GE believes—or at least so declares—that if it has done its preliminary research into the facts accurately, no substantial reason for changing its offer should ever exist, save in the event of some new unforeseen development having an impact on the economy as a whole. And GE repeatedly emphasizes, especially to employees, that as a matter of policy it will not make any change it believes to be incorrect because of a strike or threat of strike and that it will "take" a strike of any duration to resist doing what it considers to be "wrong."

The Respondent extols its "fair and firm offer" approach as a straight-forward one that removes doubt from employees' minds as to precisely where it stands. It disparagingly refers to the "ask-and-bid" or "auction" form of bargaining as a "flea bitten eastern type of cunning and dis-honest but pointless haggling." Such bargaining, according to the Re-spondent's articulation, allows a union to *appear* to get more than an employer is willing to give, though that is often not the case, and this only serves, it says, to mislead employees into believing that union officials are useful in ways they are not, thus falsely enhancing the union's prestige while diminishing that of the employer and encouraging employee sup-port of union shows of strength. The Respondent's approach on the other hand, it says, makes it obvious to employees that the Company "is not being forced to be fair by the belligerent action of a labor union."

All that has been said above is tied to what clearly appears to be the keystone of Respondent's bargaining philosophy—the marketing of man-agement positions directly to employees so that the employees in turn may influence union acceptance. It is a stated policy of the Company to achieve maximum involvement and participation of employees in decisions affecting its business, including specifically though not limited to decisions relating to collective bargaining; to minimize opposition to steps management takes; and to build active employee support for management's goals and objectives. Toward that end GE has fashioned an elaborate employee communications system, making use of plant newspapers, daily news digests, employee bulletins, letters to employee's homes, television and radio broadcasts, and other media of mass com-munication, as well as personal contacts. Supervisors are instructed as to GE's views on controversial subjects and are expected to speak out to employees on such subjects and seek to gain employee confidence in the correctness of company decisions. The direct employee communi-cations—if 1960 may be considered as representative—are utilized on a most extensive scale both before and during negotiations to influence employee attitudes to a favorable reception of the Company's views and rejection of the Union's conflicting positions. After the Company's offer is presented to the unions, the flow of communications, directed toward that end, reaches flood proportions. At that time, the Company also discusses the terms of its offer at plant meetings; invites employees to take up individually with their supervisors or managerial officials any questions they may have about the offer; and seeks through direct con-tact of its supervisors with employees to sound out for its own guidance employee reactions to its offer. The avowed purpose of the communica-tions program is to equip employees to render their own independent judgment on matters commonly affecting their own interests and those of the Company. But, as related to bargaining issues, the record in this case, as will be seen, leaves no doubt that GE's more basic purpose is to compete with the bargaining representative for the allegiance and support of employees.

Another consideration which shapes the Respondent's approach to bargaining is its uniformity policy.

As noted above, GE deals with some 100-odd unions. With regard to wage and benefit improvements, it is GE's policy to see to it that no union gets more favored treatment than any other. GE justifies that policy on the basis of fair play, business realism, and as necessary to avoid whipsawing. In line with that policy, GE prepares and presents to substantially all unions with which it deals the same basic offer with regard to wage adjustments and benefit programs.

Moreover, as further noted above, about half of GE's employees are unrepresented. Representation elections frequently are held among different groups of such employees, and sometimes decertification elections among groups of employees previously represented. Where such elections are held, GE engages in preelection campaigning in which it makes no secret of its opposition to union organization. In urging its employees to vote against union representation, GE emphasizes, *inter alia*, that a union can obtain for them no benefits they would not otherwise receive. It points up the Company's policy to "do right voluntarily" and to put into effect for nonrepresented employees the same pay and benefit program it makes available to represented employees. In keeping with such assurances, GE applies in the case of its unrepresented employees the same principle of uniformity that it applies to represented groups. The terms of the basic offer made to unions are also put into effect for nonrepresented employees. Prior to 1960, GE invariably withheld such action until either the IUE contract had been settled or the anniversary date of the prior IUE contract had expired.

Theoretically, it is possible for company negotiators engaged in negotiations with a given union to improve as to that union the basic offer made by GE to unions generally, even though the offer has already been put into effect for other bargaining units or for unrepresented employees. But the company witness testifying on that point—Virgil B. Day, now vice president relations service—could recall only one instance where that was ever done. And that, as appears from his testimony, involved a situation squarely falling within the stated exception to GE's "fair and firm offer" approach, namely, that GE will change its offer where a new significant development has occurred to make that change "right." In one important area, however, the Company's negotiators have no flexibility whatever. As appears from Day's testimony, the Company insists for practical reasons on a single uniform pension plan covering all GE employees, and once an offer has been put in effect for other bargaining units or for nonrepresented employees, the freedom of negotiators to effect changes is foreclosed. The significance of what has been said will become more clear when the course of the 1960 negotiations is reported.

. . .

H. MEETINGS ON UNION'S GENERAL DEMANDS, PRIOR TO SUBMISSION OF GE OFFER, AUGUST 16 TO 25

Six meetings were held between August 16 and 25. The Union presented its justifications in support of its demands for a union shop, revisions of noneconomic terms in the national agreement, improvements in the pension and insurance plans, a general wage increase, improvements in vacations and holidays, and other proposed contract changes not covered at the early employment-security meetings. GE took the general position during these meetings that it was interested in ascertaining the facts on which to base its determination of what should appropriately be included in its offer. GE, however, did not decline to discuss the Union's demands. As to many of the demands, principally in the area of noneconomic contract changes, GE declared a position. It was almost invariably one of rejection. GE gave as its reasons for rejection, in the case of the union shop, that it was opposed to this on principle, and in the case of other changes, that they were either too costly, or would be too difficult to administer, or would deprive the Company of flexibility. As to other union demands, GE indicated that it was not satisfied with the Union's presentation and needed more facts and justifications. In a few instances, such as the Union's requests for weekly instead of biweekly dues deductions and for an added holiday, the Company stated that it would "give consideration" to the Union's proposals. The Company refused, however, to commit itself as to any of the demands, declaring that it did not engage in bargaining on an item-by-item basis, although it did regard itself as obliged to go through and consider the Union's demands *seriatim*.

During this period GE did not submit any proposals of its own. While leaving no doubt that the Union's economic demands were unacceptable to it, GE declined to give any indication of what it was *affirmatively* thinking on the subjects of wage increases, pensions, insurance, or other economic benefits, except to make clear that it intended to eliminate the cost-of-living escalator. GE stated that it was still attempting to assemble a common body of facts as a basis for negotiation and that its position on all issues would become known when its offer was eventually prepared and presented.

At various times, the Union asked GE to declare itself on how much it had available for its entire package so that the Union might suggest how it desired the available amount to be apportioned among the various economic benefits it sought. Although the Union indicated that it might be prepared to modify or rearrange its original demands accordingly, GE chose to ignore that request. GE, in turn, sought to have the Union declare itself on the order of priority it gave its various demands, but the Union refused to do so, stating at that point that all its demands were "musts."

On a number of occasions during this period the Union requested information. But its requests were either ignored or brushed aside. Thus, on August 18, during a discussion of the Union's proposal to eliminate certain deductibles from insurance benefits, Swire, the Union's pension and insurance expert, asked Willis, the Company's benefits specialist, the cost to the Company of eliminating the deductibles. Willis replied that he did not have the figures. When Swire asked Willis to confirm a figure of one-half cent per hour, which Willis had assertedly used in a speech, Willis stated, "I don't talk in figures." But later when the Union's pension proposals were being considered, Willis objected to them on the ground: "They will cost a lot." On August 24, during a discussion of the Union's proposal for a fourth week of vacation for employees with more than 20 years' service, the Union asked the Company for figures on the number of employees falling within that category. The Company stated that it did not have that information. In point of fact, as will later appear, that information could have been obtained by it. Again while the Union's sick leave proposal was the subject of the discussion, the Company termed the Union's demand an "expensive" one. But it made no reply when asked for its estimate of the cost.

At the end of the six bargaining sessions, the parties were no nearer agreement than at the beginning. The Union charged the Company with stalling. Declaring that it was not there for educational purposes and that negotiations did not really begin until the proposals of both sides were on the table, the Union urged the Company to come forward with its offer.

In the meantime, GE's plant communications program continued along the lines earlier stated, with constant reiteration of its arguments concerning competition, sales, and profits and the dependence of jobs on GE's ability to keep its costs down. In anticipation of the Company's forthcoming proposal, the communications now also restated GE's declared bargaining policy. They stressed the careful research and other practices that GE engaged in to assure that its offer would be "right," its fair, firm offer approach, its unwillingness to engage in haggling or horsetrading, and its refusal to make concessions beyond what it believed to be right because of a show of belligerence by union officials. The communications during this period also criticized the Union's demands and the Union's concept of collective bargaining. The Union was accused of being disinterested in facts. Its unwillingness to rank its bargaining demands in the order of their priority was particularly scored.

I. AUGUST 29 AND 30: GE PRESENTS ITS OFFER TO THE UNION

In the evening of August 29, Cary and Callahan met with Parker and Moore for a dinner meeting, at Moore's request. The purpose of the meeting was to give the IUE representatives a preview of the offer which Moore stated GE planned formally to present the next day to the IUE and to the UE and thereafter to some 100 other unions. Moore read a summary of the Company's offer from notes, stating that no written copy was then available. The offer which Moore outlined on August 29 was formally presented to the IUE in writing at a regular bargaining session the following day. The proposals provided in substance for the following:

1. *Contract duration:* October 2, 1960 to September 29, 1963.

2. *Wages:* 3% increase effective October 2, 1960; 4% increase, effective April 2, 1962; no cost-of-living escalator.

3. *Retraining and Reassignment:* Local management at its discretion may offer an employee having 3 years or more service a retraining or reassignment opportunity in another job at 95% of the job rate of his former job in order to equip the employee prior to any layoff for another job requiring other skills. The period of training would not exceed one week for each year of service. Disputes would not be subject to arbitration.

4. *Income Extension Aid:* This made available for an employee with 3 or more years service and not eligible for optional retirement a fund equal to one week's pay for each year service for use in the event of layoff or plant closing. The fund could be drawn upon under 4 options: (a) as payment for tuition while attending a recognized school during a period of layoff to train for another job; (b) as a lump sum payment available to the laid-off employee provided he elected within 60 days after his layoff to terminate his employment and forgo recall rights and service credits—but this option was available only if management determined the layoff would exceed 6 months; (c) as weekly income at the rate of 50% of normal pay if the laid-off employee remained unemployed after exhaustion of State unemployment compensation benefits; or (d) as a lump sum payment on plant closing—the last option modifying and superseding a provision for termination pay on plant closing contained in the 1955-1960 agreement.

5. *An Emergency Aid Plan:* Exclusively under management control, providing for loans or grants not to exceed $500 in serious emergencies. This plan was not to be effective at any IUE location until all existing local Relief and Loan plans were liquidated.

6. *Pension Plan improvements.*

7. *Insurance Plan improvements.*

8. *Contract changes:* The Company's proposal contained 3 items: (a) to allow local negotiations on the subject of weekly checkoff; (b) to allow local unions and local managements to negotiate to substitute a different holiday for any of the listed ones; (c) to allow death in family time and jury duty time to be considered as time worked for purposes of qualifying for holiday pay; and (d) to increase maximum leave for Union officials from 5 to 8 years.

At the August 29 informal meeting, Carey and Callahan expressed themselves immediately as being opposed to the company offer, protesting that it was not responsive to the Union's proposals. The union representatives voiced their strong disapproval, among other things, to the Company's elimination of the cost-of-living escalator provision, commenting that a 3-year contract without escalation and without opportunity to review wage trends was wholly unacceptable. Moore at once asked what they thought would be an adequate provision on that point. They wanted a continuation of the escalator clause; the union representatives replied. Moore then asked whether the Union would consider a wage reopener during the 3-year contract term, at the same time making it "plain," as appears from his testimony, that he "was not offering . . . [the reopener] at that meeting because it was not a bargaining session." The Union did not respond to that suggestion, expressing neither approval nor disapproval.

Carey asked the Company to refrain from presenting its offer to the IUE negotiating committee the next day, and also to withhold its release to other unions and the press. To do so, Carey said, would tend to "freeze" the Company's position and place it on a collision course. Carey urged that before the Company became publicly committed to its offer, there should be further discussion by those present to see what could be done about changing the Company's proposals to make them more acceptable as a basic for negotiations. The Company's representatives rejected Carey's request. They said they did not consider that meeting a proper place to discuss the Company's proposals, as it was not a formal negotiating session, only a courtesy preview meeting. The offer they had come up with, they said in substance, was the product of great effort, extensive research and surveys, and careful consideration of all relevant factors. The Company considered it the best offer it could make in the balanced best interests of employees and everyone else concerned, and one, moreover, that the union representatives could "sell." This was the offer the Company was going to make. And the plan to present it to the IUE and the UE the following day would not be altered. They would, however, withhold public announcement and presentation of the offer to other unions until the full IUE negotiating committee had had an opportunity to consider it and give the company negotiators some feel as to whether agreement was imminent.

At the negotiating meeting on August 30, the Company formally presented its offer to the IUE negotiating committee. Immediately following the reading, Moore announced that the Company was including in its offer an option to reopen the contract on April 1, 1962; for wage negotiations with no commitment for a further wage increase at that time, as an alternative to the proposed second phase wage increase effective that date.

Carey again described the Company's proposal as unresponsive. He proposed that the next 3 days be spent negotiating without the pressures and glare of publicity, with the company offer serving as a basis for discussion. And he again urged Moore not to publicize the offer and thereby freeze the Company's position. Moore responded that the Company had not held back anything, and that its proposal was not just the first of a series that would be put on the table. The Company, Moore stated, felt that the employees should know what was on the table. Moore stated, however, that if the Union wanted more time to consider the proposal, the Company would hold up its release until the following day.

At the opening of the session on August 31, the Company announced
that its offer was being released to the plants.

. . .

K. NEGOTIATING MEETINGS AUGUST 30 THROUGH SEPTEMBER 8

There were seven negotiating meetings between August 30 and September 8. The Union during this period indicated a willingness to
drop or scale down some of its demands, particularly in the areas of
contract changes, pensions, and insurance, but continued to press for
its major demands, including the union shop, a 3½-percent annual
wage increase (as opposed to the slightly more than 2 percent offered
by the Company), continuation of the cost-of-living escalator, SUB, an
added holiday, and an extra week's vacation for employees with more
than 20 years' service. The Union also sought revision of the Company's
retraining and reassignment proposal to assure the protection of employee
seniority rights. Even with respect to the foregoing stated demands,
however, the Union indicated near the close of this series of sessions
that its position was flexible.

The Company declared that it had a fixed position on cost-of-living
escalation, SUB, and the union shop, but that it viewed other union
demands as within the "areas of collective bargaining." At the same time,
the Company made it quite clear, however, that it was willing at most to
consider only such changes as were within the framework of its proposals.
On various occasions, the Company indicated that it had not granted
certain union demands because it had put such money as it had available
into improvements which it had determined from its own research would
best meet the employees' needs and desires. The Company summarily
rejected all union suggestions for revisions entailing added costs, frequently citing that consideration as the basis for its rejection.

The Union unsuccessfully sought to ascertain from the Company the
estimated cost of the company offer. It explained that it wanted the
information so that it might be able to tell the Company how it wanted
the available money allocated among different items. Moore stated
that the Union had no right to decide what was best for the employees,
and also said that he did not know the cost of the Company's proposal
"because it hasn't occurred yet." Asked more specifically whether the
Company's offer would cost less than 9 cents an hour, Moore said the
Company had not put a figure on its package. When the Union insisted
that the Company must have estimated the cost of its proposal before
submitting it, Moore denied having any such estimate. "GE works
on a level of benefits basis, not the cost per item," he declared. Actually,
as the record shows, the various items in the Company's proposal had all
been cost estimated by management representatives on a companywide
basis prior to its release.

The Company during this period similarly rejected, ignored, or brushed
aside union requests for cost or other information relating to specific

items in issue. Thus, for example, the Company resisted the Union's request for an added holiday and an extra week's vacation for employees with more than 20 years' service on the ground that it would add to the Company's costs. But when the Union asked for the number of employees who would be affected by the vacation proposal so that it might itself compute the costs, Moore, shifting ground, stated in effect that such data was irrelevant because the Company "discussed the level of benefits." The Company took a similar position with respect to the Union's request for cost information in the area of pensions and insurance. The Company likewise refused cost information relevant to the Union's revised SUB demand. When the Union on September 8 asked how many people would have benefited by income extension aid on the basis of the Company's layoff experience over the past 2 years, Moore responded, "Somewhere between zero and 100 percent." Later, however, when Carey persisted in his demand for this information, Moore told him to make the request in writing. As will later appear, the Union did thereafter submit such a written request, but the Company did not supply the Union with the information until after the strike was over when it no longer could do any good.

In other respects also, the Company registered impatience with the Union's efforts to have it justify bargaining positions it had taken. Thus, on September 6, after Moore summarily rejected the Union's principal justification for a 3½-percent annual productivity increase, declaring "there is no direct relationship of productivity to wages," Lasser for the Union asked Moore to state the factors that had influenced the Company's wage offer. Moore replied vaguely. "Many other factors, other settlements, competition, etc." But when asked for further explication, particularly with respect to a comparison of the Company's wage offer with those in other settlements, Moore evaded a direct reply. After lunch that day, Lasser asserted that the Company's offer was inferior to other settlements according to the Union's information. He asked Moore to disclose specific information with regard to the other settlements on which the Company relied. Moore declined to do so, stating that the information was in the "public domain" and that Lasser should have prepared himself before coming to the meeting. On the following day, when Lasser again sought to ascertain the Company's reasoning behind its wage offer, accusing Moore of having evaded an answer the preceding day, Moore again declined to be specific, stating, "The wage increase justified itself." He further declared, "We bargain on what is the appropriate thing to do and the level of benefits."

Throughout the period in question, the Company adhered firmly to its offer as presented to the Union on August 30, except for its clarification relating to retraining, noted above, and except also for the early signing bonus proposal to be referred to shortly below. Other than as stated, the Company, at the bargaining sessions here under consideration, indicated a disposition toward flexibility only in one regard—the substitution of holiday and vacation improvements for part of the proffered wage increase. The facts as to this will be related in the succeeding subsection of this report.

At the September 8 meeting, the Company announced that as a bonus for early acceptance it would make the 1960 wage increase effective on the Monday of the week the new agreement was signed instead of on October 2, 1960, as originally proposed. At the same time the Company pointed out that it was making the same bonus available for other unions. No such change in the Company's offer had ever been requested by the Union. When the offer was made, Moore indicated that he did not expect the Union to accept it because "you are going to the convention." One of the tacks thereafter taken in the Company's communication program was that the IUE leadership, by deliberately "stalling" negotiations because it assertedly wanted a strike, was depriving employees of the advantages of an early settlement.

The parties agreed when the IUE-GE negotiations were originally scheduled that there were to be no meetings between September 8 and 20 because of the conflicting IUE convention. Nevertheless, on September 8, the Company suggested the continuation of negotiating meetings during the convention period. In a "Dear Employee" letter teletyped that day for use by ERM's, as well as in subsequent employee communications, the Company made capital of the "cold reception" it received to its suggestion for continued meetings. Neither that letter nor earlier communications mentioned, however, that on August 31 the Union had asked for meetings 5 days a week but that the Company had then declined to modify the original schedule. Nor did the letter mention that on August 31, Callahan had suggested extra meetings beginning on September 19.

L. THE REVISION OF GE'S OFFER TO INCLUDE HOLIDAY-VACATION OPTIONS

After the Union made its offer, several members of the Union's negotiating committee from old-line plants mentioned the importance which employees at their locations attached to the Union's demand for an added holiday and for a fourth week of vacation for 20-year service employees. The Company indicated its interest in that demand from the outset and indicated a willingness to listen to any "within-the-framework" proposal the Union might have relating to vacations and holidays. The Union's negotiating committee, however, continued throughout this period to insist that the holiday and vacation improvements be *added* to the offer. In the meantime, the Company through its two-way employee communication channels began to get "feedbacks" of employee reactions to its offer. These indicated that among employees in old-line plants the holiday-vacation demand was a matter of special concern and that there was considerable interest among such employees in working out an eighth holiday and fourth week of vacation in lieu of part of the wage increase. On September 7, and again on September 8, the Company invited a proposal from the Union to have holiday and vacation improvements substituted for part of the wage increase. But the

Union stated bluntly that it was unwilling to consider any such substitution, explaining that it regarded the wage offer too low as it was. That was where the matter rested when negotiations suspended for the IUE convention on September 8.

. . .

On September 19, GE headquarters sent the ERM's a "Dear Employee" letter in Negotiation News format for release the following day when negotiations were to resume. The letter, subsequently used at plant locations, stated in part:

"At some locations it is reported that union officials are manufacturing a rumor that the Company can be persuaded to come up with some new proposal if employees will only show enough strike sentiment. It is doubtful that many employees will be misled into thinking that the Company would be indulging in last minute haggling. It is generally well understood by the union officials across the bargaining table that the Company is not holding anything back and that *the whole offer is now on the table*." [Emphasis supplied.]

When negotiations resumed on September 20, the Company advised the Union that its full offer was now on the table. "Come October 2, Thanksgiving, Christmas, and Easter, it won't be any different," declared Moore. At almost each negotiating meeting thereafter, the Company made statements of similar import. The finality of the position taken by the Company at the bargaining table was repeatedly reported to employees. One further example should suffice. The following is from a suggested employee letter in Negotiation News format, dated September 21, thereafter published at plant locations:

"We closed by saying again that everything that we are going to propose is on the bargaining table now, and there is simply nothing more to come. . . . It has become apparent that all the facts are in . . . and that we have gone as far as we can go without endangering the jobs of employees."

The repeated references to the finality of the offer, not only in written employee communications, but, as the record shows, also in oral communications by supervisors, were coupled throughout the remaining period of negotiations with declarations pointing up the inevitable futility of a strike, regardless of its duration, in the light of the Company's policy not to give more simply to avert a strike. Again one example should suffice. The general manager of the Bridgeport plant in a letter to employees, dated September 21, stated:

"Recently, a few questions have come to my attention as to why we modified our wage offer by offering an alternative extra holiday and fourth week of vacation. Actually, the optional proposal simply represents a rearrangement of our original offer and not something that was added to the Company offer. I mention this so that there can be no misunderstanding as to whether a strike threat, or a strike itself, will add more to the Company proposal than is now on the table. It never has in the past, and it won't now."

4. GE INTENSIFIES ITS ATTACK UPON THE MOTIVES OF IUE'S LEADERSHIP

As earlier noted, the Company in its communications to employees had suggested right along, beginning even before the start of negotiations, that the IUE top leadership, particularly Carey, was determined to strike GE in 1960 for reasons unrelated to the interests of the employees and regardless of the fairness of the Company's proposal. The employee communications began to concentrate sharply on this theme about the time the negotiations recessed for the convention. While the convention was in progress, and even more so after the announcement of the local votes, the Company's attacks upon Carey mounted in volume and vigor.

The employees were told, *inter alia*, that Carey never had any intent of reaching a peaceful settlement with the Company; that he was not sincerely concerned with the employees' interests but only with his personal and political ambition; that Carey, in furtherance of his ambition and in reckless disregard of employee interests, was determined to obtain a strike come what may; that to assure a strike he had come up with a "set of demands so fantastic—that no company could possibly agree to them without driving itself out of business and employees out of jobs"; that toward that end he had stalled negotiations, had deliberately avoided reaching an agreement, and had finally broken off negotiations completely to "attend a union convention in a plush Miami hotel"; that he had set in motion a "strike steamroller" at the IUE convention with the aid and support of delegates representing employees of competing companies whose employees would profit at the expense of GE employees' job security should a strike occur; that now he was trying to "sneak" through by a Sunday vote a quick "no contract—no work" vote which could only lead to a 156-day Westinghouse-type of strike doomed for failure; that he was willfully misleading employees into a false assumption that the Company was holding something back, that it might yield in a strike; that with Carey at the bargaining table there was no hope for any real attempt to reach agreement by the Union; that there was no more the Company could do to prevent a strike; and that only the employees themselves could prevent a long Carey-dictated strike.

5. GE MAKES ITS OFFER EFFECTIVE FOR NONREPRESENTED EMPLOYEES

Reference has earlier been made to the Company's practice under its uniformity policy of putting into effect for nonrepresented employees the wage and benefit improvements contained in its basic offer to unions. Prior to 1960, however, the Company had always withheld such action until either the effective date of its new agreement with the IUE or the terminal date of the old IUE contract, that is, the date that would correspond to October 2 in the instant case. In 1960, the Company at some of its locations, while presenting to nonrepresented employees the details of its proposal to the unions, had advised them that the program would be put into effect for them on October 2, with, as was stated at one plant, any modification that "may arise after further study."

Contrary to past practice, the Company in 1960 decided to accelerate the effective date for nonrepresented employees. The decision to do so was made after consultation with Moore about September 18 or 19. On September 20, GE headquarters by letter authorized operating managers to make effective for nonrepresented employees, as of September 12 if they desired, the 3-percent first-phase wage increase as provided for in the Company's offer to unions, and, in addition, to announce the changes in employee benefit plans which were to be effective October 2, 1960, including the improvements in the insurance plan and the new income extension aid plan. It was suggested, however, that changes in other benefits such as pensions, vacations, and holidays "be announced at a later date, when a clear picture emerges with respect to the application of the various options." Under the Company's proposal, the pension changes were not to be applicable until January 1, 1961. Nevertheless, on either September 22 or 23—only 2 days or so after suggesting that such announcement be withheld—the Company proceeded to announce that the pension changes were being put into effect for nonrepresented employees. Moore at the negotiating meeting of September 22 advised Carey of the Company's intention to make the announcement that day. The following colloquy then occurred:

CAREY: "Mr. Moore, don't you think that will inhibit you from making any modification to the arrangements that you proposed for us."

MOORE: "It is a factor that we have to take into consideration."

It will be recalled that GE Vice President Day testified in substance that once GE has put into effect a pension plan for other bargaining units or for nonrepresented employees, the freedom of negotiators to negotiate variances therein for other units is curbed.

Moore testified that his reasons for recommending that the wage and benefit improvements be put into effect at that time for nonrepresented employees were fourfold: (a) The Company's offer to the unions had been public knowledge for 3 weeks; (b) it seemed evident at that time that an agreement with the IUE was not imminent; (c) the Company was getting "a considerable amount of pressure from [its] operating people as to when they could be in a position to tell the nonrepresented employees what improvement in wages, benefits were in store for them and when they would be effective"; and (d) the Company had begun to receive acceptance of its proposal from other unions. (Actually, as the record shows, the Company up to then had received acceptances from only 9 local unions representing a total of 845 employees out of about 120,000 union-represented employees.)

. . .

O. NEGOTIATING MEETINGS BETWEEN SEPTEMBER 20 AND OCTOBER 1

Negotiating meetings resumed September 20, following the recess for the IUE convention. Under the schedule as originally agreed upon, negotiations were to continue through September unless an agreement was earlier reached. Ten formal negotiating meetings were held between September 20 and October 1, before the strike began. During that period, there were also three so-called "sidebar" (informal) meetings, to which more specific reference will be made below. Beginning on September 21, Federal mediators, who were called in at the request of the Union, attended the formal meetings.

As earlier noted, GE advised the Union on September 20 that its full offer was now on the table and would remain unchanged regardless of how long negotiations continued. Throughout the period now under consideration, the Company constantly reiterated that position.

The Company asserts that it nevertheless did in fact negotiate "changes in or additions to" its original offer during the period under consideration, and cites four in its brief. Two, however, did no more than provide for the furnishing of certain information relating to the operations of the GE pension and insurance plans. The information was of a kind that GE in the past had voluntarily furnished the Union and would have been legally required to furnish on request even in the absence of contractual covenant. The inclusion of the contractual requirement reflected simply an affirmation on an existing practice rather than a "change" through negotiation.

The third asserted change involved a reduction in the amount which GE employees on leave as union representatives had to pay to maintain their interest in the GE pension plan. Under the IUE-GE union representatives pension agreement, a collateral agreement, GE's entire cost of maintaining the union representatives pension plan interests was billed to the Union. The Union, in its detailed pension proposals submitted on August 18, had requested, *inter alia*, that GE modify the agreement so as to compute the cost to the Union on the basis of the current actuarial assumptions rather than on the basis of the higher 1955 assumptions. The Company's offer had made no reference to the union representatives pension agreement. Nor, so far as appears, was this matter considered in negotiations at any time prior to September 21, when it was collaterally raised during a discussion of another pension issue. At that time, Moore simply stated, "We reduced this [the cost of maintaining the union representatives interest] by one-third, you know." Later, Willis, the Company's benefits expert, made clear that the reduced amount was in line with the Company's "estimate" in rounded figures of what the *actual* cost would be during the new contract term. It would appear from all the evidence that this item did not involve a negotiated "change" or concession but simply an original declaration by the Company of its position.

The fourth asserted change relates to a provision in the insurance plan known as exclusion K, also sometimes referred to as the "spouse" provision.

. . .

Perhaps the clearest revelation of the Company's bargaining frame of mind came at the meeting on September 28. At the time there were still three scheduled negotiating meetings left before the contract was to expire. The Union had theretofore several times reduced its demand for SUB in an effort to meet company objections. Its last previous proposal had been rejected on the ground of costs. On September 28, Jandreau, the Schenectady delegate on the IUE negotiating committee, suggested as a possible solution "within the framework of the [Company's] costs" that the Company provide an additional option (presumably on a local-by-local basis). Under it 1 percent of the Company's proposed wage increase along with money available under income extension aid would be used to set up a fund upon which employees might draw to bring their unemployment compensation up to 50 percent of earnings. Jandreau made it clear that the plan he proposed working out along those lines was not to add to the costs of the Company's proposals. Jandreau's suggestion was rejected by the Company. Later at the meeting the following colloquy occurred:

JANDREAU: Mr. Moore, can I ask a question? Is it possible to change the company proposal one way or another? I ask this because you said to me and McManus that this is it. It is all on the table. Is there any chance of changing your position one iota?

MOORE: There are two things, Mr. Jandreau. After all our month of bargaining and after telling the employees *before they went to vote that this is it, we would look ridiculous to change it at this late date*; and secondly the answer is no. We aren't changing anything come a strike or high water. [Emphasis supplied.]

JANDREAU: There is no sense in being here.

MOORE: Unless there is anything you want us to hear. If you have something new or persuasive, persuade us.

CALLAHAN: You said you wouldn't change the proposal before, because of the employees.

MOORE: I said two things—one, that everything we think we should do is in the proposal and we told the employees that, and we would look ridiculous if we changed it.

Later, Hilbert adverted specifically to Jandreau's aforementioned suggestion for an additional option within the framework of the Company's costs, and declared:

"I think we are in the final stage of negotiations, and I think it is frivolous for the union to make proposals for changes at this time in the nature of Mr. Jandreau's. There would be three possible reasons why we would make a change at this time. First, if we had intentionally held something back and if we had done that and we revealed it now *we would look foolish in the eyes of employees and others.* . . . Secondly, if we made a serious error, an inadvertent error in the offer, and we have no such evidence of that, to warrant a change. Third, if we were so frightened of a strike that we would change the offer just to avoid it and *then we would look even more foolish in the eyes of our people and of the country.* We don't think any of the three apply to this case." [Emphasis supplied.]

Later:

JANDREAU: . . . I am not trying to build up a ratchet situation. I am trying to work within the proposal.

HILBERT: I am not sure you are saying that seriously, Leo.

JANDREAU: I am speaking seriously and I am seeing whether you are following Boulwareism or not.

HILBERT: What do you mean, Boulwareism?

JANDREAU: Your take it or leave it. Moore said that that is all and there isn't any more, and you have just backed him up with your three types of reasons.

HILBERT: What other reasons could there be?

JANDREAU: Option 4 we put forth.

HILBERT: That falls into reason 3.

The negotiating minutes and other evidence relating to this period do not bear out GE's representations to employees that Carey was determined to force a strike on GE, come what may. On the contrary, the record reflects that Carey, while unwilling to capitulate to the Company's position, was anxious to open up some other avenue that might possibly lead to a peaceful solution on terms more to his liking. The Company showed little inclination to aid him.

Carey had long complained—whether correctly or not is not in issue—that the Company's principal negotiator, Moore, lacked the requisite authority to deviate in any significant way from GE's offer. On a number of occasions, Carey unsuccessfully sought an opportunity to meet and confer with Vice President Parker, the GE officer having primary responsibility in the area of labor relations. On September 26, the mediators requested that such a meeting be arranged. In response, Moore stated that Parker would meet with Carey that evening "if Carey wanted to hear from Mr. Parker that that's all there was and that it [the full offer] was on the table." At the sidebar meeting that evening—attended by Carey, Callahan, and Fitzmaurice for the Union and by Parker, Ritter, and Moore for the Company—Parker declined to do any more than state what Moore had said he would state. When Carey sought to discuss with him some of the issues in dispute, Parker refused to be drawn into any such discussion, declaring that that was not a negotiating session. He told Carey that "as far as the Company is concerned, we have no more to offer, but if you want to talk about it at the bargaining table you go ahead and do it." Parker's assertion that the Company's offer would not be changed was thereafter broadly publicized by the Company to its employees as positive confirmation of the Company's earlier declarations that employees could hope to gain nothing further through strike action.

Also at the sidebar meeting on September 26, Carey specifically proposed that the six people then meeting should spend some time in an effort to hammer out some agreement in principle. Carey explained that it was his experience that a meeting of that nature was more conducive to the settlement of issues than larger meetings of the kind engaged in at formal negotiating meetings. The Company rejected Carey's request. Moore at the hearing testified that his stated and actual objection to Carey's proposal for a reduced bargaining committee was his "sincere belief" that:

". . . collective bargaining takes place across the bargaining table with the full committee and is not to take place at any sidebar meetings or with any side deals not in *full view of the public* and the negotiating committee on the union side." [Emphasis supplied.]

On September 26, Carey in a letter to Ralph J. Cordiner, chairman of the GE board, proposed that the issues between the parties be submitted to either (1) a factfinding board without authority to make binding recommendations, or (2) an arbitration board with power to make a binding award, the choice to be left to the Company. The matter was referred to Moore who rejected the request, stating numerous reasons. The reasons are not detailed here, because, contrary to the Union's contention, I do not consider the Company's rejection of third party intervention as having evidentiary value on the issue of whether the Company bargained in good faith. The Union's request for such intervention is cited here only because of its bearing on GE's representation to employees concerning Carey's strike motives.

Cordiner in his direct reply to Carey's letter of September 20, while reasserting that Moore had "full authority and responsibility" to represent the Company in its negotiations with the Union, told Carey that Parker "as the senior officer in this important area of responsibility" would continue to be "available for meetings outside the negotiations." On the strength of that statement Carey arranged further sidebar meetings with Parker—also attended by others on each side—on September 29 and October 1. These meetings took substantially the same course as the sidebar meeting of September 26.

During the last days of September, as the contract's expiration date neared, the Union sought an extension of the contract so that efforts to reach agreement might continue without a strike. Prior to September 29, all of the Union's extension proposals were tied to other requests, either that the Company arrange to have an officer participate in negotiations or that the Company consent to factfinding or arbitration. The Union's extension proposals were "categorically" rejected by the Company, primarily on the ground that it was the Union and not the Company that had elected to terminate the contract on its expiration date. The Company made it quite clear that it was opposed, even in the absence of conditions, to any contract extension, or, for that matter, to any "delay in settling the strike question—one way or another."

At the September 29 formal negotiating meetings, the mediators proposed that the parties continue to bargain without interruption of production and preserve the "status quo" (which they explained contemplated the extension of the contract) until a new agreement was reached. In a private session with the mediators the previous day, Carey had indicated his willingness to agree to an unconditional contract extension. Both he and the mediators believed, however, that the chances of a cordial reception by GE would be greater if the proposal came from the mediators rather than from the Union, and if the Union were to withhold formal acceptance until the Company replied. It had been arranged to proceed accordingly. When the mediators on September 29 made the proposal, Carey immediately responded that the union committee would withhold its reply until after it received the Company's answer and had reported to the Conference Board. The Company, however, after ascertaining that the proposal contemplated an extension of the contract, promptly declared that its answer had already been given. The Company's reference was to its "categorical" refusal at the bargaining session the day before to agree to any extension beyond the contract's expiration date. Though not so told at the meeting, it appears that the Company was aware that the mediators' proposal had the prior blessing of the Union.

Later in the session the Company formally declared its positions as follows:

". . .we must point out that on October 1 the IUE agreement will terminate as a result of notice given by the IUE to us several weeks ago. There will be no extension of the contract beyond that termination date . . . for 15 days, 10 days, for five days or even one day. *With that termination, the cost of living escalator arrangement will terminate. In addition such matters as union dues checkoff, pay to union officials for grievance time and superseniority for union officials and related matters will have to be considered and reconsidered by us as they will no longer be binding.* . . . The current pay, seniority, pension and insurance and other benefits will be continued in effect for all employees who report for work. . . ." [Emphasis supplied.]

At the opening of the September 30 session, Carey announced that the IUE-GE Conference Board had adopted the recommendations of its negotiating committee to reject GE's offer and to shut down GE plants on October 2 because of GE's refusal to continue the contract.

On October 2, the strike began as scheduled, with only the Schenectady local remaining at work.

. . .

Decision and Order of the NLRB*

. . .

The Trial Examiner found that Respondent had not bargained in good faith with the Union, thereby violating Section 8(a)(5) and (1) of the Act, as evidenced by:

(a) Its failure timely to furnish certain information requested by the Union during contract negotiations.

(b) Its attempts, while engaged in national negotiations with the Union, to deal separately with locals on matters which were properly the

---

* Footnotes omitted.

subject of national negotiations, and its solicitations of locals separately to abandon or refrain from supporting the strike.

(c) Its presentation of its personal accident insurance proposal to the Union on a take-it-or-leave-it basis.

(d) Its overall approach to and conduct of bargaining.

We agree with these findings of the Trial Examiner. Because Respondent's defense of its bargaining conduct raises a fundamental question as to the requirements of the statutory bargaining obligation, we have stated for more particular emphasis the reasons why we agree with the Trial Examiner that Respondent did not bargain in good faith with the Union.

In challenging the Trial Examiner's finding that it violated Section 8(a)(5), Respondent argues that an employer cannot be found guilty of having violated its statutory bargaining duty where it is desirous of entering into a collective-bargaining agreement, where it has met and conferred with the bargaining representative on all required subjects of bargaining as prescribed by statute and has not taken unlawful unilateral action, and where it has not demanded the inclusion in the collective-bargaining contract of any illegal clauses or insisted to an impasse upon any nonmandatory bargaining provisions. Given compliance with the above, Respondent further argues that an employer's technique of bargaining is not subject to approval or disapproval by the Board.

Respondent reads the statutory requirements for bargaining collectively too narrowly. It is true that an employer does violate Section 8(a)(5) where it enters into bargaining negotiations with a desire not to reach an agreement with the union, or has taken unilateral action with respect to a term or condition of employment, or has adamantly demanded the inclusion of illegal or nonmandatory clauses in the collective-bargaining contract. But, having refrained from any of the foregoing conduct, an employer may still have failed to discharge its statutory obligation to bargain in good faith. As the Supreme Court has said:

". . . the Board is authorized to order the cessation of behavior which is in effect a refusal to negotiate, *or* which directly obstructs or inhibits the actual process of discussion, *or* which reflects a cast of mind against reaching agreement." [Emphasis supplied.]

Thus, a party who enters into bargaining negotiations with a "take-it-or-leave-it" attitude violates its duty to bargain although it goes through the forms of bargaining, does not insist on any illegal or nonmandatory bargaining proposals, and wants to sign an agreement. For good-faith bargaining means more than "going through the motions of negotiating." ". . . the essential thing is rather the serious intent to adjust differences and to reach an acceptable common ground. . . ."

Good-faith bargaining thus involves both a procedure for meeting and negotiating, which may be called the externals of collective bargaining, and a bona fide intention, the presence or absence of which must be discerned from the record. It requires recognition by both parties, not merely formal but real, that "collective bargaining" is a shared process in which each party, labor union and employer, has the right to play an active role. On the part of the employer, it requires at a minimum recognition that the statutory representative is the one with whom it must deal in conducting bargaining negotiations, and that it can no longer bargain directly or indirectly with the employees. It is inconsistent with this obligation for an employer to mount a campaign, as Respondent did, both before and during negotiations, for the purpose of disparaging and discrediting the statutory representative in the eyes of its employee constituents, to seek to persuade the employees to exert pressure on the representative to submit to the will of the employer, and to create the impression that the employer rather than the union is the true protector of the employees' interests. As the Trial Examiner phrased it, "the employer's statutory obligation is to deal with the employees through the union, and not with the union through the employees."

We do not rely solely on Respondent's campaign among its employees for our finding that it did not deal in good faith with the Union. Respondent's policy of disparaging the Union by means of the communications campaign as fully detailed in the Trial Examiner's Intermediate Report, was implemented and furthered by its conduct at the bargaining table. Thus, the negotiations themselves, although maintaining the form of "collective bargaining," fell short, in a realistic sense, of the concept of meaningful and fruitful "negotiation" envisaged by the Act. As the record in the case reflects, Respondent regards itself as a sort of administrative body which has the unilateral responsibility for determining wages and working conditions for employees, and it regards the union's role as merely that of a kind of adviser for an interested group—the employees. Thus, according to its professed philosophy of "bargaining," Respondent, on the basis of its own research and evaluation of union demands, determines what is "right" for its employees, and then makes a "fair and firm offer" to the unions without holding anything back for later trading or compromising. It professes a willingness to make prompt adjustments in its offer, but only if new information or a change in facts indicates that its initial offer is no longer "right." It believes that if its research has been done properly there will be no need to change its offer unless something entirely unforeseen has developed in the meantime. Simultaneously, Respondent emphasizes, especially to employees, that as a matter of policy it will not be induced by a strike or a threat of a strike to make any change in its proposals which it believes to be "wrong." This "bargaining" approach undoubtedly eliminates the "ask-and-bid" or "auction" form of bargaining, but in the process devitalizes negotiations and collective bargaining and robs them of their commonly accepted meaning. "Collective bargaining" as thus practiced is tantamount to mere formality and serves to transform the role of the statutory representative from a joint participant in the bargaining process to that of an adviser. In practical effect, Respondent's "bargaining" position is akin to that of a party who enters into negotiations "with a predetermined resolve not to budge from an initial position," an attitude inconsistent with good-faith bargaining. In fact Respondent here went even further. It consciously placed itself in a position where it could not give unfettered consideration to the merits of any proposals the Union might offer. Thus, Respondent pointed out to the Union, after Respondent's communications to the employees and its "fair and firm offer" to the Union, that "everything we think we should do is in the proposal and we told our employees that, and we would look ridiculous if we changed now."

In short, both major facets of Respondent's 1960 "bargaining" technique, its campaign among the employees and its conduct at the bargaining table, complementing each other, were calculated to disparage the Union and to impose without substantial alteration Respondent's "fair and firm" proposal, rather than to satisfy the true standards of good-faith collective bargaining required by the statute. A course of conduct whose major purpose is so directed scarcely evinces a sincere desire to resolve differences and reach a common ground. For the above reasons, as well as those elaborated at greater length by the Trial Examiner in his Intermediate Report, we adopt his conclusion that Respondent did not bargain in good faith with the Union, thereby violating Section 8(a) (5) and (1) of the Act.

Our concurring colleague, Member Jenkins, who joins us in finding certain conduct of the Respondent inconsistent with its bargaining obligation under the statute, misreads the majority opinion and the Trial Examiner's Intermediate Report, which we affirm, in asserting that our decision is not based on an assessment of Respondent's conduct, but only on its approach to or techniques in bargaining.

On the contrary our determination is based upon our review of the Respondent's entire course of conduct, its failure to furnish relevant information, its attempts to deal separately with locals and to bypass the national bargaining representative, the manner of its presentation of the accident insurance proposal, the disparagement of the Union as bargaining representative by the communication program, its conduct of the negotiations themselves, and its attitude or approach as revealed by all these factors.

Nothing in our decision bans fact gathering or any specific methods of formulating proposals. We prescribe no timetable for negotiators. We lay down no rules as to any required substance or content of agreements. Our decision rests rather upon a consideration of the totality of Respondent's conduct.

In one central point of our colleague's comment, with all respect we believe he is in error. His strictures in relation to our interpretation of the law's restraints on "take-it-or-leave-it" bargaining were decisively answered by the Supreme Court in its review of the nature of the bargaining obligation in *Insurance Agents:*

". . . the legislative history [of Taft-Hartley] makes it plain that Congress was wary of the position of some unions, and wanted to ensure that they would approach the bargaining table with the same attitude of willingness to reach an agreement as had been enjoined on management earlier. It intended to prevent employee representatives from putting forth the same "take it or leave it" attitude that had been condemned in management."

And in Justice Frankfurter's opinion in *Truitt* upon which our colleague relies, the Justice also wrote:

". . . it [good faith] is inconsistent with a predetermined resolve not to budge from an initial position."

While we share his objective and that of our dissenting colleague of encouraging a maximum of freedom and experimentation in collective bargaining, when questions are raised under the law as construed by the courts and the Board concerning the conformity of a specific respondent's course of conduct with the requirements of the law, the Board must apply the law to the totality of that conduct in the interest of preserving and fostering collective bargaining itself. That is what we have sought to do here.

. . .

MEMBER JENKINS, concurring:

. . .

In effect I read the majority opinion to hold that the Act so regulates a party's choice of techniques in collective bargaining as to make unlawful an advance decision, and a frank communication of that decision, concerning the position from which a party is unwilling to retreat. The majority would apparently find that it is unlawful for a union to present a contract proposal on a take-it-or-leave-it basis since I assume the majority would not apply different standards to unions than to employers. The bargaining technique often employed by unions in support of "area standards" contracts is not significantly different from the technique described as the "firm, fair offer" by an employer. I would not find a lack of good-faith bargaining where either the employer or the union entered the negotiations with a fixed position from which it proposed not to retreat, engaged in hard bargaining to maintain or protect such position, and made no concessions from that position as a result of bargaining. As one member of the Supreme Court has pointed out, good faith is not necessarily incompatible with stubbornness or even with what to an outsider may seem unreasonableness.

The majority states frankly that the holding of a predetermined resolve not to budge from an initial position is incompatible with good-faith bargaining. That statement seems to ignore the language in Section 8(d) of the Act which makes it clear in unequivocal words that "such obligation does not compel either party to agree to a proposal or require the making of a concession." The opinion of my colleagues fails to distinguish between two important concepts; *viz*, the formulation of a settlement position and the techniques employed in reaching a settlement. The Act does not dictate the methods which a party may choose to utilize in formulating its bargaining position. Indeed, many unions and employers use surveys of one sort or another as a fact-gathering device in advance of bargaining. Moreover, both employers and unions are free from statutory regulation under this Act in formulating the kind of proposal or counterproposal which each will communicate to the other. I know of no decision of the Board which has sought to interpret the statute as requiring either unions or employers to follow a prescribed timetable in communicating the various shifts in position which seem desirable as a matter of self-interest. Thus, if either an employer or a union for reasons dictated by self-interest chooses to include in a proposal trading items which it is willing later to withdraw or conversely chooses to limit its proposal to items which it will never withdraw voluntarily, the choice is its and not the Board's.

To describe the foregoing in shorthand by evocative terms provides little guidance for either unions or employers. To condemn bargaining techniques as unlawful because of the utilization of what the majority describes as "take it or leave it" is to obfuscate the issue. Basically it is our purpose to examine industrial relations against the realities that exist. It is not our function to require the adoption of a particular technique or to condemn the use of a given technique as such. Under circumstances where the overall conduct is designed to destroy the bargaining relationship or to undermine the status of a bargaining representative, it is clear that good-faith bargaining has not occurred. This, however, does not flow from the adoption of a technique or from an effort to gain the supposed advantage of winning acceptance of one's own proposal. There is adequate evidence in this record to support a finding that the Respondent by its course of conduct sought to bypass the Union and deal directly with the employees, to discredit the collective-bargaining representative with which it was obligated to deal and carry on negotiations with others.

Some portions of my colleagues' opinion may be read as holding that the Act was violated because Respondent chose to decide in advance on the proposal which it was willing to make and from which it was unwilling to retreat unless forced to do so by economic pressure which it apparently regarded as a calculated risk. If such an inference be drawn I disavow it. If free collective bargaining is to survive, both employers and unions must remain free of governmental interference with their right to formulate independently the economic positions which each desires to take and to decide without governmental compulsion whether that position shall be conveyed to the other party at the outset, at some midpoint, or at the conclusion of negotiations. To do otherwise maximizes governmental construction of the bargaining and minimizes the free flow of independent economic judgment essential to a strong, independent trade union movement and a strong, independent entrepreneurial system, both of which are vital to the kind of economy envisaged by the Act which we administer.

MEMBER LEEDOM, dissenting in part:

. . .

Notwithstanding the foregoing, I cannot fully accept Respondent's view of the breadth of the bargaining obligation imposed by the Act, nor the limitation it believes the law places on those matters which can properly be considered where good- or bad-faith bargaining is in issue. In both regards its construction seems too rigid. I nevertheless believe that both the law and good policy require that this Board not be hyper-critical of what goes on at the bargaining table or in a developing situation. In order for collective bargaining to be free and to succeed, the parties themselves must with a minimum of exceptions have the right to resort to such tactics, and to take such positions, as they believe necessary or desirable in dealing with the matters before them. If at each step they must consider the effect of their specific words, actions, and proposals upon some distant tribunal unacquainted with the particular problems in dispute, and with that more subtle distinction, the personalities of the negotiators themselves, they surely lose the flexibility and spontaneity necessary for free, effective bargaining. Thus they are deprived of their right to determine, free of governmental intervention, the substantive terms of their agreement, should one be reached.

. . .

NOTE

The order of the NLRB was enforced in *NLRB* v. *General Electric Company*, 418 F.2d 736, 72 LRRM 2530 (2d Cir. 1969), Friendly, J., dissenting in part. The majority believed the Board was justified in finding a refusal to bargain on the basis of the overall conduct of GE, noting in particular the company's "take-it or leave-it" stance, its failure to provide information with respect to the cost of components of its offer, its insistence upon the use of a short-form memorandum to end the strike rather than agreed-upon contract language, and its use of publicity that froze its bargaining position. Judge Friendly, dissenting with respect to the conclusion that the overall conduct of the employer established a refusal to bargain, argued that the Board could not find a refusal to bargain absent evidence establishing a "desire not to reach an agreement," cf. *NLRB* v. *Reed & Prince*, p. 112. He noted that then Judge Burger had dissented in the only prior court decision approving a finding of bad faith where there was a desire to reach an agreement. *United Steelworkers of America* v. *NLRB*, 389 F.2d 295, 67 LRRM 2450 (D.C. Cir. 1967), *cert. denied*, 391 U.S. 904 (1968). Judge Friendly believed that Section 8(c) of the Act protected an employer's attempt to persuade his employees by speech that it would be unwise for them to strike.

The Supreme Court denied certiorari, 397 U.S. 965, 73 LRRM 2600 (1970), and later denied a petition for rehearing in which it was argued that the finding of a refusal to bargain in the General Electric case was inconsistent with the Supreme Court's holding in *H. K. Porter Co. v. NLRB,* 397 U.S. 99, 73 LRRM 2561 (1970), that the NLRB could not order an employer to agree to union proposal as a means of remedying a refusal to bargain.

Review the history of the GE negotiations described above, and consider, entirely aside from what is required by the National Labor Relations Act, the extent to which the bargaining tactics utilized by General Electric were well adapted either to obtaining a contract on the most favorable terms possible for the company or to avoiding a strike. Do you believe they may have been directed toward some objective other than obtaining a very favorable contract or avoiding a strike?

Normally, uncertainty is an important ingredient in negotiation, and its elimination may create obstacles to reaching agreement. For example, a person selling a house who knows both the maximum amount a prospective purchaser would be willing to pay and his initial low offer will see no reason to accept anything less than the maximum amount. If the prospective purchaser knows not only the asking price but the lowest price the seller will accept, he will see no reason to pay any more than the minimum amount. Negotiations are thus stalemated until some new development creates additional uncertainty. If the parties negotiate in ignorance of these limits they may by chance reach an agreement, never learning how much better terms they might have obtained if they were more determined. The GE formula for negotiation may thus be criticized for eliminating a factor which ordinarily is of considerable importance in reaching agreements.

Of course, the rationale for the GE formula was that it wanted to do what was "right." Assuming that there is such a thing as the "right" price for bread, eggs, milk, or butter and that marketing experts constantly attempt to set that price, can the process by which a customer decides whether or how much to buy of any of those commodities from a chain supermarket be considered a form of negotiation or bargaining? Would it constitute negotiation or bargaining if the supermarket had a well-established policy of immediately reducing its prices upon proof that a competitor sold at a lower price?

Perhaps an even greater difficulty for the GE formula lies in the question of whether the total package of wage and fringe benefits and working conditions can be meaningfully considered in terms of whether it is "right" or "wrong". As the trial examiner noted, General Electric decided to achieve the same degree of success in its employment relations that it had achieved in product development and marketing. It may make some sense to talk about the "right" way to make and market a light bulb, a refrigerator, or a television set. But does not the variety possible in establishing the arrangement of wage and fringe benefits and working conditions present an occasion for accommodating preferences and making value judgments that cannot be properly performed by conducting an investigation into what is "right"? GE's determination of what is "right" for the employment relationship made it, rather than the union, a spokesman for employee interests, and tended to reduce the role of the union to that of advisor to the company in determining what employees wanted. See Cooper, *Boulwareism and the Duty to Bargain in Good Faith,* 20 Rutg. L. Rev. 653, at 675-676 (1966).

As the report of the GE negotiations makes apparent, the company's publicizing of its offer had the effect of freezing its position, which reduced the possibility that agreement would be reached. Thus, even though a revision of the terms proposed might not have been of great significance to the company though it was of great value to the union, the company could not "lose face" by making that adjustment. However, reduction of the possibility that agreement would be reached does not mean that the possibilities of reaching agreement on terms most favorable to the company were likewise reduced. The union knew that the company had so incapacitated itself, making it clear to the union that the alternatives available were acceptance of the company proposal or a strike. By eliminating the uncertainties concerning how much contract terms could be improved, the company succeeded in directing the union's attention to the uncertainties of how long the strike would last and how well the union members could stand its economic deprivations.

If an employer is to be denied the opportunity to establish its commitment to an offer in this manner, should a union bargaining with a single employer be permitted to argue that its proposal must be accepted because it has negotiations pending with other employers? A "parity clause" is one by which a party to an agreement promises to extend to the other party any more favorable terms which might subsequently be negotiated with another employer or union. The New York Public Employment Relations Board has held that a "parity clause" binding a public employer is a prohibited and unenforceable provision of a collective bargaining agreement because it will so diminish the right to negotiate of employees represented by another union. 10 PERB ¶ 10-3003 (1977). How does a parity clause differ in effect upon negotiations from a union's reliance upon its pending negotiations with other employers?"

In his famous essay on bargaining, *infra,* p. 237, Professor Thomas Schelling demonstrates that a party may generate bargaining power by establishing that a commitment to a proposal is irrevocable because the party has put it beyond his power to change position. Is this such a dangerous negotiation technique that it should be denied to parties in collective bargaining relationships?

In a book which is particularly valuable because of its theoretical and analytical treatment of collective bargaining, STRATEGY AND COLLECTIVE BARGAINING NEGOTIATION (1963), Professor Carl M. Stevens refers to the use of the "large-demand rule" in collective bargaining, by which he means that the initial bargaining demand and counterdemand are in excess of the least favorable terms upon which each party is willing to settle. He states that the only rule for beginning really consonant with subsequent negotiation is the initial large demand. He then makes the following observations concerning "Boulwareism":

STEVENS, STRATEGY AND COLLECTIVE BARGAINING NEGOTIATION*

THE MINIMUM DEMAND OR MAXIMUM OFFER ("BOULWAREISM")

The major alternative to the large demand as a tactic for beginning negotiation is the "minimum" demand or "maximum" offer, that is, an initial bargaining proposal which is (virtually) identical with the least favorable terms to himself upon which a party is willing to settle. A prominent case in point is the approach to collective bargaining commonly termed "Boulwareism" (after a chief proponent of the technique, Lemuel Boulware of the General Electric Company).

The central feature of this approach is to meet the union's initial bargaining demand with a single counterproposal to which the company intends to adhere. That is, the union is told that it can accept or reject the company proposal, but come what may, the company does not intend to move from its announced position. With the Boulware approach, the single counterproposal is carefully researched in an effort to come up with an offer which is "right" by any reasonable standard, which is "fair," and which will be considered fair by the employees. Once the proposal is formulated, the technique is to stick to it, not to "haggle" about it.

Although emphasis has been put upon the negotiation implications of the Boulware approach, it is important to recognize that this approach is much more than simply a negotiation technique. Actually, it is a whole "philosophy" of labor-management relations. It involves not only carefully researched proposals, but also continuing, year-round efforts to keep lines of communication with employees open to insure that they are adequately apprised of the "fairness" of the proposals.

In large measure, the maximum offer (or minimum demand) is not just another way to begin a game of negotiation. It is a technique for converting a would-be negotiation game into one of take-it-or-leave-it. It may be argued that the maximum offer is basically inconsistent with the collective bargaining relationship underlying negotiation. It may be interpreted as an attempt to deny the function of the union as an organization which "gets something" for its members. It is, in a sense, an appeal directly to the employees. The latter are told that they will get what is "right" and "fair" because the company has decided to give it to them,

---

* From STRATEGY AND COLLECTIVE BARGAINING NEGOTIATION by Stevens. Copyright © 1963 by McGraw-Hill, Inc. Used by permission of McGraw-Hill Book Company. Footnotes omitted.

not because the union has extracted it from the company. Kerr has noted that "to insist to the end on the original proposal is almost an unfair labor practice, under the rules of the game, for it denies the other party the opportunity of forcing some concession and thus claiming a victory of sorts." Peters, having pointed out that "prestige is an inexorable regulator of the practices of collective bargaining, and will not be denied," noted that the prestige factor will not permit the parties to forego at least the semblance of bargaining. The difficulty is that if either side accepts a "one-shot" demand or proposal, in the eyes of the employees it might appear as if that side had surrendered. A bargaining technique which completely denies "victories" will invite interminable prestige fights. It is this basic nonconsonance of the minimum demand with the negotiation game and with the bargaining relationship underlying negotiation which suggests treatment of the large demand as rule for play—rather than just as a tactic used during the early stages of negotiation.

It should be noted that not all evaluation of the Boulware approach is negative. For example, R. W. McMurray, having expressed the view that the key to power in labor relations is to be found in the allegiances of the workers, advises that management demonstrate by actions that it can be depended upon, without constant prodding by the union, to be concerned with the welfare of its employees. From this point of view, he feels that Boulwareism is "basically more realistic" than more conciliatory techniques, although he does note that Boulwareism may be "unnecessarily provocative."

Further it may be contended that, in a bargaining situation such as that between the General Electric Company and the IUE, the union could develop an acceptable position (other than striking) in the face of what may be a reasonable, albeit take-it-or-leave-it offer. For example, if the union officials believe the offer to be reasonable, they might attempt to take credit for it by contending that the only reason the offer is satisfactory is because of pressure by the union.

THE "COMMITMENT"

Closely related to the maximum-offer approach to negotiation is a class of negotiation tactics to which T. C. Schelling has drawn attention, tactics which he considers "peculiarly appropriate to the logic of indeterminate situations." The essence of these tactics is somewhat voluntary but irreversible sacrifice of freedom of choice. By an indeterminate situation in this context is meant a bargaining situation featuring a manifest contract zone—a range of positions each of which is preferred by both parties to "no agreement," and both know this. He terms this class of tactics the "commitment." The essential thrust of this tactic is that it enables a player to convert the bargaining choice confronted by his adversary into one of the take-it-or-leave-it variety. For example, player A contrives to so bind himself to a position that B is convinced that A will not (cannot) make any concession. (A, having asserted that he will not remain up a tree, may issue irrevocable instructions to an accomplice to start sawing off the limb upon which he is sitting.) As we shall see, tactics such as bluff, notbluff, and threat, all involve a problem of (at least apparent) commitment—and means to such commitment will be discussed in conjunction with those tactics. The commitment itself, as a tactical entity, is to be distinguished as "a means of gaining first move in a game in which first move carries an advantage." This is in contrast to the threat which, although it involves a problem of commitment, is a commitment to a strategy for second move. The maximum-offer tactic characteristic of the Boulware approach may not be literally considered a commitment in the sense that the company has made an "irreversible" sacrifice of freedom of choice. However, it may be argued that this approach is virtually auto-committing. It has been pointed out with respect to this approach that: "Failure is disastrous. . . . If a company can be made to back down from what is originally announced as an unalterable position, future unalterable positions will not be taken seriously. A substantial gamble is involved, and the penalty for losing is heavy—the loss of the ears and minds of the 'job customers.' " In a continuing relationship such as collective bargaining in which negotiation occurs regularly, the minimum demand is autocommitting, that is, no special device is needed to bind the party to its position insofar as insuring its own performance is concerned.

Although Schelling has included wage negotiations among the economic interactions with which the subject of his bargaining essay is concerned, we should not expect the commitment tactic, as a way to seize first move, to be of prime importance in many collective bargaining negotiations. We have seen that the structure of the choice situation created by the bargaining relationship underlying collective bargaining negotiation is such that the parties are impelled to choose to negotiate rather than to play take-it-or-leave-it. In consequence it would not seem plausible that a primary negotiation tactic should be an attempt immediately to convert the game negotiation into one of the take-it-or-leave-it variety. As pointed out, in some collective bargaining negotiation (Boulwareism, for example) what amounts to the commitment has played a significant role. Further tactical implications of this move will be discussed later.

[For a spirited defense of Boulwareism by one who participated in the administration of GE's employee relations policies, see Northrup, BOULWAREISM (1964).]

NOTE

The importance of uncertainty to negotiation and collective bargaining has been noted with respect to legislative proposals for dealing with emergency disputes. The national emergency provisions of the Taft-Hartley Act, 29 U.S.C. §§ 176-180, provide for the issuance of an injunction against strikes or lockouts affecting an entire industry and imperiling the national health or safety. The injunction will be discharged, however, within 80 days even if the parties have not reached agreement. The provisions have worked fairly well in some cases, but in other circumstances they have been criticized for failure to create uncertainties which encourage collective bargaining. The course of events is predictable and therefore it may be used by one of the parties to put off serious negotiations. It has been suggested that instead the President should have an arsenal of procedures available—such as compulsory arbitration, mediation, and plant seizures, as well as injunction—to the end that the uncertainty about which will be used will eliminate the certainty of advantage to one party or the other from invocation of the emergency provisions. Bargaining might be stimulated because of the uncertainty about who might be disadvantaged from use of one of the procedures. A. Cox, LAW AND THE NATIONAL LABOR POLICY 53-58 (1960); Cullen, NATIONAL EMERGENCY STRIKES 92-96 (1968); Wirtz, "The 'Choice of Procedure' Approach to National Emergency Disputes," in EMERGENCY DISPUTES AND NATIONAL POLICY (I. Bernstein, H. Emerson & R. Fleming, eds., 1955).

While uncertainty may be an important factor in successful collective bargaining negotiations, knowledge is likewise an important factor. Unless both parties know enough about the matters under consideration to be able to discuss them sensibly, any agreement which they may reach is more properly viewed as the product of a lottery or game of chance than the product of negotiation. To put it another way, one must know enough about the subject to be able to appreciate the uncertainties of the situation and negotiate the way to agreement. Flipping coins is a game of chance. Poker, at least when played by a person who knows the value of his cards and the probabilities that one of the other players has a better combination, becomes in the long run a game of skill. The obligation of an employer to furnish a bargaining representative with information concerning individual earnings, job rates and classifications, and the fringe benefits of employees in the unit is well established. See, e.g., *J. I. Case Co.* v. *NLRB,* 253 F.2d 149, 41 LRRM 2679 (7th Cir. 1958). Making that information available permits negotiation to proceed; if that information could legally be withheld, economic force would be required to cause its production, and meaningful negotiation could take place only after it had been produced.

One of the leading cases concerning an employer's duty under the National Labor Relations Act to furnish information is *NLRB* v. *Truitt Manufacturing Co.,* 351 U.S. 149, 38 LRRM 2042 (1956). In that case the employer claimed during negotiations that it could not afford to pay the wage increase requested by the union, but it refused to furnish substantiating information or permit the union access to its books and financial records. The U.S. Supreme Court agreed with the NLRB that refusal to attempt to support a claim of inability to pay increased wages may support a finding of a failure to bargain in good faith. In his opinion for the Court, Justice Black specifically disavowed any holding that every such refusal constituted a violation of the duty to bargain. However, the decision has been subjected to severe criticism as a step in the direction of substituting objective criteria of what are good bargaining practices for the subjective test of willingness to enter into an agreement as the measure of what is required by the National Labor Relations Act. Cox, *The Duty to Bargain in Good Faith,* 71 Harv. L. Rev. 1401, 1430-1435 (1958).

Of particular relevance to this discussion is Justice Black's statement, "Good-faith bargaining necessarily requires that claims made by either bargainer should be honest claims." 351 U.S. at 152. Can this test be applied to the union negotiator whose straw poll has led him to conclude that the membership will vote down a strike proposal? If he threatens an employer with strike action or if he responds to a management inquiry by asserting solidarity among the membership in backing union demands with strike action if necessary, has he violated the union's duty to bargain? Can the test be applied to the employer representative who responds to a strike threat by asserting falsely that there has been such a decline in orders that future business can be handled out of inventory for a long time? As Professor Cox pointed out, a management's refusal to "open the books" might have been based upon fear that release of the information would impair its credit standing, leak confidential data to competitors, or in other ways harm company objectives, and not upon an unwillingness to enter into agreement. Indeed, the assertion that a company cannot afford to meet a union's demands creates only a variation in the uncertainties which a company may lawfully create by asserting a willingness to accept a long strike, conducting operations with the supervisory force until such time as replacements may be hired.

If collective bargaining is a reasoned search for what is "right" in the employment relationship, full disclosure of the financial condition of the employer would appear to be appropriate even when the employer does not plead inability to pay. If, however, as seems to be the case, the primary forces operating to bring about agreement are the respective fears that the alternatives to agreement will entail greater economic losses than acceptance of the agreement, such disclosure may have the effect of changing the balance of power, but it will not facilitate the process of negotiation unless it substitutes one set of uncertainties for another. Of course, if the data irresistibly lead to but one conclusion, this may produce a certainty which reduces the negotiation process to something like that practiced when customers make purchases at chain supermarkets.

Another of the Supreme Court's decisions which has received criticism for its lack of realism about the negotiation process is *NLRB* v. *Wooster Division of Borg-Warner,* 356 U.S. 342, 42 LRRM 2034 (1958). See Cox, *Labor Decisions of the Supreme Court at the October Term, 1957,* 44 Va.

L. Rev. 1057, 1074-1086 (1958); Feinsinger, *The NLRA and Collective Bargaining*, 57 Mich. L. Rev. 807, 826-830 (1959). In *Borg-Warner* the Court established the categories of permissive and mandatory subjects of collective bargaining, holding that an employer violated its duty to bargain by insisting among other things upon a ballot clause calling for a prestrike vote of employees on the employer's last offer on any nonarbitrable dispute which might arise during the term of the contract. That subject was viewed by the majority of the Supreme Court as a permissive subject for bargaining, but not one upon which the employer could insist to the point of refusing to conclude agreement upon the subjects of "rates of pay, wages, hours of employment, or other conditions of employment" mentioned in Section 8(d) of the Act. Said the Court, "This does not mean that bargaining is to be confined to the statutory subjects. Each of the two controversial clauses is lawful in itself. Each would be enforceable if agreed to by the unions. But it does not follow that, because the company may propose these clauses, it can lawfully insist upon them as a condition to any agreement." 356 U.S. at 349.

The Court thus suggests that real bargaining may take place without the presence of the forces which operate to produce agreement. This might be so if collective bargaining negotiations were a joint, reasoned effort to determine what is "right" for the employment relationship, but collective bargaining does not seem to lend itself to that characterization. The Court's view of the bargaining process is likewise to be criticized for its failure to acknowledge that it is the acceptability of the "total package" to both parties that brings about agreement, rather than acceptabiliy of proposals on those items considered to be mandatory subjects of bargaining. Reaching agreement will depend upon whether it contains enough of much-desired provisions, regardless of whether they are characterized as permissive or mandatory subjects of bargaining. Indeed, one result of the *Borg-Warner* decision may be to produce more extreme demands on mandatory subjects which are relaxed only when the message gets through that it is the granting of the permissive matter that will produce agreement. This inhibition of direct and forthright communication can hardly be expected to improve the chances that parties will reach agreement. Moreover, the variations which exist between industries as to what are important and relevant matters for unions or employers make it very possible that the Board will label permissive in a case involving one industry what is a very important and relevant matter in the relations between employers and unions in another industry. Indeed, as Feinsinger points out, if the Board applies a waiver doctrine in situations in which one of the parties permits discussion of a permissive subject raised by the other, the end result may be that one party does not want to insist upon what is of most concern to it, and the other may be unwilling to discuss it for fear that it will have converted it into a bargainable matter.

The Supreme Court has not always dealt with collective bargaining in terms suggesting that it can operate without a possibility of resort to economic force. Thus *NLRB* v. *Insurance Agents' International Union,* 361 U.S. 477, 45 LRRM 2705 (1960), involved collective bargaining negotiations which were accompanied by a union-inspired program of harrassing tactics, such as refusals to solicit new business, to comply with reporting procedures, or to perform customary duties at the offices during "sit-in" mornings. Assuming that these and other objectionable conduct of employees were not protected concerted activities and that employees might therefore have been disciplined or discharged for utilizing those tactics, the Supreme Court refused to approve the NLRB's conclusion that the union had violated its duty to bargain. Said the Court, 361 U.S. at 488-489:

"It must be realized that collective bargaining, under a system where the Government does not attempt to control the results of negotiations, cannot be equated with an academic collective search for truth—or even with what might be thought to be the ideal of one. The parties—even granting modification of views that may come from a realization of economic interdependence—still proceed from contrary and to an extent antagonistic viewpoints and concepts of self-interest. The system has not reached the ideal of the philosophic notion that perfect understanding among people would lead to perfect agreement among them on values. The presence of economic weapons in reserve, and their actual exercise on occasion by the parties, is part and parcel of the system that the Wagner and Taft-Hartley Acts have recognized."

The court saw nothing inconsistent between the use of unprotected economic weapons and the duty to bargain in good faith. Nor did the Court believe that the Board should supplement the employer's right to self-help to combat the harrassing tactics by declaring the use of those tactics in connection with collective bargaining an unfair labor practice.

A comparable rejection of the NLRB's power to regulate the use of economic weapons during the course of collective bargaining is found in *American Ship Building Co.* v. *NLRB,* 380 U.S. 300, 58 LRRM 2672 (1965). The employer was engaged in the highly seasonal business of repairing ships on the Great Lakes. When negotiations during the first part of the summer failed to produce agreement, the employer shut down its operations, thereby anticipating by several months the possibility of a strike during the winter months, when most repair work ordinarily is done. Noting that the NLRB had not found that the lockout thus accomplished was based upon either hostility toward the union or a desire to avoid bargaining obligations, the Court concluded that its use in support of a legitimate bargaining position did not conflict with the employees' right to bargain collectively or to strike.

The parties in *American Ship Building* had bargained to impasse before the employer shut down its operations, and the holding might have been limited to such situations. However, in *Darling & Co.*, 171 NLRB No. 95, 68 LRRM 1133 (1968), affirmed 418 F.2d 1208 (D.C. Cir. 1969), the NLRB found no violation of the Act when an employer locked out his employees before an impasse had occurred. In the Board's view *American Ship Building* obliterated any distinction between defensive and offensive lockouts, and the absence of an impasse is only one of the factors to be considered in determining whether a lockout is legal. A consequence of the decision is that a union no longer has exclusive power to determine when the economic pressure produced by terminating operations can be called into play, and this consequence may be of tremendous significance with respect to the bargaining power of the parties in seasonal industries. Employers may thus be able to move bargaining into the stage at which there is a threat of immediate application of economic sanctions if agreement is not reached, which is of course a much more intense period of bargaining than that which occurs during the exploratory stage when it is ordinarily understood that operations will not be terminated until a previously established "deadline" has been reached.

It is apparent from the NLRB's decision in *General Electric* that a stenographic record was made of the negotiation sessions between the employer and the union. That record was used by the Board for the purpose of reconstructing the course which the negotiations had followed and provided some evidence which was relied on to support the conclusion that the company had not bargained in good faith. The decision of the court of appeals in *Reed & Prince*, pp. 119-120, indicates that in that case the NLRB had concluded that the company's insistence, over strenuous objections of the union, upon the presence of a stenotypist to take down a verbatim record of the proceedings was evidence of bad faith. The court of appeals did not agree with that conclusion.

More recently, in *Bartlett-Collins Co.*, 237 NLRB No. 106, 99 LRRM 1034 (1978), the NLRB held that an employer had violated its duty to bargain when it insisted to the point of impasse that a certified court reporter be present to prepare a transcript of the negotiations. The employer's case was strengthened by the facts that it previously had been found guilty of a refusal to bargain and that it desired a record of negotiations so that what was said and done by the parties during negotiations could be established without resort to credibility determinations if another unfair labor practice charge were filed. Moreover, the employer agreed that it would bear the entire expense involved. The Board decided, however, that a demand for a reporter to record negotiations is not a mandatory subject of bargaining and hence not one upon which the employer could insist if the union refused to bargain with a reporter present.

Earlier, the general counsel for the NLRB had given a more functional analysis of the adverse effects of recording collective bargaining negotiations. In a report on case handling developments for the last quarter of 1977, he made the following statement as a partial explanation of his decision to issue a complaint against an employer that insisted that a stenographic reporter be present to take verbatim transcriptions of the bargaining sessions with no "off the record" discussion:

"Expert opinion in the field of labor relations is nearly unanimous in condemning the practice of recording bargaining sessions. See, for example, Commonwealth of Massachusetts, REPORT OF THE GOVERNOR'S LABOR MANAGEMENT COMMISSION (H. Doc. 1875, March 14, 1947); CAUSES OF INDUSTRIAL PEACE (National Planning Association, 1953); Slicter, Healing, Livernash, THE IMPACT OF COLLECTIVE BARGAINING ON MANAGEMENT (The Brookings Institute, 1960). According to a study conducted by Walton and McKersie, reported in A BEHAVIORAL THEORY OF LABOR RELATIONS (McGraw Hill, 1951), if they are to be free to communicate, the parties in collective bargaining negotiations need to know that what they say will not be turned against them. Imposing a stenographer upon a negotiator who objects to the presence of a stenographer may raise suspicions as to the ultimate use for which the transcript is to be put and, thereby, inject into the bargaining relationship an added basis for mistrust and contention. See Commonwealth of Massachusetts, REPORT OF GOVERNOR'S LABOR MANAGEMENT COMMISSION, *supra,* at p. 14. For example, a union which recognizes that employee work practices are deficient might be reticent to discuss this problem frankly in bargaining if negotiations were recorded, for fear that the employer would seek to capitalize on the hostility that would be engendered between the employees and the union's representatives when the employees read the transcribed remarks of the representatives. Experts have also pointed out that the use of verbatim transcripts tends to make the parties to negotiations 'talk for the record' rather than for the purpose of advancing negotiations toward settlement. . . .

"While generally disapproving of the use of stenographers during negotiations, experts have noted that the inhibiting effect of such a procedure may be lessened to some extent by a liberal policy of going 'off the record'. . . . However, the Employer in the case under discussion had taken the position that nothing said during negotiations would be 'off the record.' In these circumstances, it was considered particularly likely that the use of a stenographer to take a verbatim account of negotiations would inhibit the free and frank discussion among the parties which is necessary for meaningful bargaining and would foster an attitude of distrust between the parties." "Reports on Case Handling Developments at NLRB," reprinted in LABOR RELATIONS YEARBOOK—1978 at 277 (BNA Books, 1979).

Another aspect of the process of collective bargaining which deserves notice is what Professor Stevens has called the "agenda rule." His analysis of the subject is set out in the following excerpt from his book.

STEVENS, STRATEGY AND COLLECTIVE
BARGAINING NEGOTIATION *

THE AGENDA RULE—AGENDA SET BY INITIAL DEMAND
AND COUNTERPROPOSAL

Characteristically in collective bargaining the initial demand and counterproposal set the agenda for each periodic agreement conference. That is, there is no systematic negotiation of the agenda prior to the beginning of substantive contract negotiations.

As with other rules for play of the negotiation game, there are possible alternatives to the agenda rule. In some international negotiations, for example, it is customary to decide upon the agenda itself by negotiation before the beginning of substantive negotiation. In some collective bargaining relationships there are preagreement-conference procedures which tend in the direction of agenda negotiation.

The problem of the tactical significance of agenda composition is related to the institution of the "large demand" since the agenda is brought into being by the bargaining demand and counterproposal. Nevertheless, these phenomena ought to be distinguished. Suppose that "n" items are to be negotiated by the parties in one or more plays—that is, in one or more separate forums. The tactics of agenda design are concerned with the distribution of these n items among the one or more plays. The large demand institution is more concerned with the number n itself. The above supposed demand would have been larger, for example, if we had supposed that n + 1 items were to be negotiated by the parties in one or more plays (but this need not affect the composition of the agenda pertaining to other than one play). Since the agenda for each play is brought into being by demand and counterdemand, a decision to increase the magnitude of a demand will alter the composition of the agenda pertaining to that play. However, in this case the alteration of the composition of the agenda is essentially a by-product of the initial bargaining demand decision, the latter made on grounds not peculiarly concerned with the tactics of agenda composition.

Interest in the agenda rule for collective bargaining negotiation inheres in the possibility that agenda composition has tactical significance. There is no *prima facie* case that agenda composition has significant tactical implications in collective bargaining negotiation. Nevertheless, this possibility should be explored. Schelling has expressed the opinion that whether two or more items are negotiated simultaneously or in separate forums may affect the outcome. For example, negotiating items simultaneously may facilitate the use of threat, by bringing to bear on one proposition the threat of adverse action on others. Also, multi-item nego-

* From STRATEGY AND COLLECTIVE BARGAINING NEGOTIATION by Stevens. Copyright ©
1963 by McGraw Hill, Inc. Used by permission of McGraw-Hill Book Company. Footnotes omitted.

tiations may play a generally enabling role in cases where the principal means of compensation available to the parties is concession on some other item. In such a case, if two simultaneous negotiations can be brought into a contingent relationship, a means of compensation may be made available, where otherwise none might exist. These suggestions are aspects of the proposition frequently encountered in the literature on collective bargaining that items may be included in bargaining demands because of their trading value.

It is sometimes suggested that in a bilateral-conflict relationship such as collective bargaining there may be a tactical advantage attached to "first move," especially if this can be seized by commitment. However, the above considerations suggest that there may be an offsetting asymmetry of tactical advantage stemming from agenda composition inherent in any procedure in which the demand and counterproposal are not presented simultaneously. For example, in a nonsimultaneous procedure, the party with "first move" may "waste" a potentially useful threat by attempting to exploit it in circumstances which turn out to be inappropriate in the light of the counterproposition. Suppose that a union, aiming for a substantial wage increase, thinks that the company will offer little or nothing. The union might include a union security demand in the agenda for this forum, hoping to trade it for a tolerable wage increase. If, however, the company's "real" position on the wage increase is much more generous than the union had expected (a fact which might have been inferred had the company made the initial proposal), the union security demand "turns out to have been" used in a context in which its trading value significance was not tactically required. The party with "second move" may be able to avoid such waste. Moreover, the party with "second move" (the counterproposer) can judiciously avail himself of means to compensation and, thus perhaps induce agreements which would not otherwise be possible. A company, wishing to eliminate an objectionable clause from the collective agreement, might attach this demand to an agenda which contained union demands on which it is willing to make a concession. Thus, the company, in making its demand, does so in a context known to contain at least potential means of compensation. Were the demand and counterproposal proocedure simultaneous, the company might attach its demand to an agenda which contained no other union propositions it was willing to concede and which therefore contained no means (agreeable to the company) for compensating the union for accepting its own demand.

Why do the parties to collective bargaining negotiation not engage in prenegotiation agenda negotiation rather than simply accept whatever agenda eventuates from the initial demand and counterproposal? One answer to this lies in the nature of the political relationship between the negotiators and their constituents, especially on the union side, a matter to be discussed subsequently. Another answer probably lies in the nature of those sanctions available to the parties which underlie their bargaining relationship; namely, the strike or lockout. Just as A's refusal to accept a given B demand may be backed if necessary by the strike, so A's refusal to admit a given B item to the agenda may be backed by the strike or lockout if this be necessary. What is to be gained by striking an opponent during prenegotiation if he may be struck as well during the course of substantive negotiations?

Another answer is that the continuing nature of the collective bargaining relationship may greatly attenuate the tactical implications of agenda composition. In a continuing relationship such as collective bargaining it may not be possible to achieve *de facto* isolation of the agenda for one play from the (anticipated) agendas for subsequent plays. Indeed, and this is another explanation of large initial bargaining proposals, some demands may be included in this year's agenda largely for "educational" purposes; that is, included not so much with the intention of obtaining them this year as with the intention of familiarizing the bargaining opponent with demands to be pursued in earnest at a future date. A recent case in point has been the guaranteed annual wage (GAW) demand. For many years before the UAW finally negotiated a GAW plan with the automobile industry in 1955, many major CIO unions made demands for the GAW, only to drop these in favor of other benefits more directly felt by their members. Hence, in the years just prior to 1955, a question existed as to the "seriousness" of the GAW demand.

More generally, many demands and counterdemands tend to be in the air before they make a formal appearance at the bargaining table. The mere exclusion of a pension demand, for example, from this year's agenda may not keep the expectation of such a demand on next year's agenda from having a strong influence upon this year's negotiation. Even if the agenda pertaining to any one play of the collective bargaining game is not neutral with respect to the outcome of that play, it would not be of great significance in collective bargaining if the agendas pertaining to a succession of plays were collectively neutral with respect to the grand total outcome. However, since some significance attaches to the order in which items are negotiated, nonneutrality of the agenda *vis-à-vis* the whole series of plays seems probable.

. . .

ADDITIONS TO INITIAL DEMANDS

Another aspect of agenda composition is the proscription that, generally speaking, a party to collective bargaining negotiation does not during the course of negotiation make demands in excess of those contained in his initial proposal. This proscription applies both to increasing the magnitude of a given item and to adding additional items to those contained in the initial proposal.

Since negotiation sessions are frequent and the initial bargaining demands can be "large" in any event, there is no general necessity to provide for subsequent increases in demands. Moreover, the practice of adding to demands during the course of negotiation is not compatible with the negotiation process. How can a party really begin to negotiate until he knows what his opponent's maximum asking price will be? Certainly the basic bargaining processes of changing position, rewarding by concession, threatening by adherence, and so on, could scarcely begin until the total demands to be served during a given play of the negotiation game were on the table.

The above considerations do not rule out the possibility that certain special functions might be served by such subsequent changes in position. One such function, for example, would be the exploitation of information about one's opponent gained during the course of negotiations. The fact that negotiation sessions are frequent greatly reduces the importance of serving this function *vis-à-vis* any particular contract negotiations; that is, it can be served during the next contract negotiations. One legitimate aspect of this function *vis-à-vis* a particular set of negotiations is the case in which the initial demander gets new ideas from the counterproposal— ideas which suggest that some redesign of the initial demand would facilitate agreement.

Much more dubious is the practice whereby a party attempts during the final stages of negotiation to exploit the fact of near agreement by tacking a last-minute demand, as a sort of "rider," onto a virtually wrapped-up package. Such an attempt, even if successful, would surely degenerate the atmosphere prevailing during subsequent negotiations sessions. However, Peters, discussing "bad faith" on the part of negotiators, cites the case of a union negotiator who habitually uses this tactic. Peters classifies this tactic as, while not perhaps properly considered bad faith, a borderline case—certainly to be regarded as bad practice.

"PACKAGE" SETTLEMENTS (TENTATIVE PROPOSALS) RULE

The outcome of collective bargaining negotiation is by agreement. Characteristically, such agreement must be upon all the items comprising the agenda. Agreement upon all items is defined as mutual assent to a disposition for each of the agenda items. This may involve overt agreement in the sense of settling upon a wage rate somewhere between the initial demands of the parties. But it may also involve other kinds of disposition such as covert agreement in the sense of the parties' refraining from further mention of an agenda item. Or it may be agreement by the parties to submit a disputed item to arbitration. Such a provision for package settlements is fairly straightforward. The items comprising a package are to a considerable extent commensurable in terms of cost, and, to a considerable extent, it is the total cost of the package that matters. In consequence, agreement on all the items is what matters.

Discussion of the package settlement provision, relating as it does to termination of negotiations, should perhaps have been delayed till the end of this chapter (where we will deal more generally with the rule for termination). Nevertheless, an aspect of the package settlement relating to tentative proposals during the course of negotiation is involved with the matter of agenda composition, and, in consequence, it facilitates matters to bring it into the discussion at this juncture.

The agenda-related point of interest is that even though a number of items are on the "same" agenda, they may in a sense be accorded separate "forums." In some collective bargaining negotiation, a division is made between "cost" and "noncost" items, and an effort is made to get the latter out of the way first. The union in particular is apt to favor seriatim treatment in an effort to wrap up fringe items before attention is given subjects of major importance. According to Peters, the motivation for this is the union's knowledge that the employer is aware that a strike is unlikely over subordinate differences. However, so long as the major issues have not been settled, the union exerts strike pressure in the negotiations.

The significance of the attempt to distribute items on the "same" agenda among separate forums by pressing for seriatim treatment is conditioned by a provision strongly implied by the package settlement rule: Any agreements or proposals relating to individual items made during the course of negotiations are understood to be provisional and may be withdrawn (without prejudice) if final agreement upon all items in dispute is not reached prior to a strike or lockout. This tentative-proposals provision is not quite a necessary consequence of package settlements. Even with package settlements, it could be understood that all interim agreements and concessions were binding in the sense that they would comprise part of the final agreement if and when such was achieved.

Perhaps the most interesting aspect of the tentative-proposals provision is its ambiguous status as a "rule." Dunlop and Healy have observed that withdrawal of an offer is more a matter of ritual than of fact in the sense that, barring serious defeat of one side or the other in a strike or lockout, offers already made are seldom effectively withdrawn. The ambiguous status of this "rule" would seem to reflect a basic institutional ambiguity in the negotiation situation. On the one hand, such a rule is very understandable. Agreements and concessions during the course of negotiations are expected to induce mutual agreement. These are made as "promises" against a *quid pro quo*—namely, concessions and agreement by the opposite number. If agreement is not reached prior to strike or lockout, earlier concessions have not served their function. They become essentially gratuitous. In such circumstances, it seems reasonable that they be withdrawn.

On the other hand, free withdrawal without prejudice of prior agreements and proposals in the event of strike or lockout would seem to decrease the efficiency of the negotiation process. If the parties characteristically returned to their initial positions in the event of a strike or lockout, whatever function the prestrike negotiations had served in bringing the "real" positions of the parties closer would be nullified; that is, the efficiency of the negotiation process as a whole will be enhanced if strike negotiations are concerned with settling a residual difference between the parties inherited from the prestrike negotiations, rather than with settling the entire initial difference between the parties.

D. PUBLIC SECTOR COLLECTIVE BARGAINING

Statutes in Alaska, Hawaii, Pennsylvania, Vermont, and Oregon permit strikes by government employees under certain limited conditions.[1] Generally, however, statutes and judicially developed law prohibit strikes by government employees. Accordingly, the force field for producing agreement in public sector collective bargaining differs significantly from that found in private sector relationships. With the explosive growth of collective bargaining in the public sector since the 1960s, efforts have been made to provide substitutes for the strike that motivate the parties toward reaching agreements.

One frequently used procedure is that of statutorily mandated fact-finding by neutral persons. The theory is that the fact finder will hear and weigh evidence concerning the positions taken by the parties and issue a report that will inform the public of the issues involved. An informed public will then know which party should be supported on the various issues, and the force of that public opinion will move the parties to agreement. Experience indicates, however, that the public pays little attention to the findings or even the recommendations of fact finders; the report therefore generates little force toward producing agreement. When "fact-finding" has been successful it most likely has been that the fact finder actually served as a mediator and brought the parties together. Simkin, "Fact-Finding, Its Values and Limitations," in ARBITRATION AND THE EXPANDING ROLE OF NEUTRALS, Proceedings of the Twenty-Third Annual Meeting, National Academy of Arbitrators 165-172 (G. Somers ed. 1970); Aaron (Chrmn.), FINAL REPORT OF THE ASSEMBLY ADVISORY COUNCIL ON PUBLIC EMPLOYEE RELATIONS, 206-214 (March 15, 1973).

Interest arbitration is also used with considerable frequency in public sector collective bargaining disputes. A traditional objection to making such arbitration compulsory is that it inhibits the collective bargaining process. The fear is that the weaker party will prefer arbitration to a negotiated result, believing that it is likely to get an arbitrated result halfway between its proposal and the proposal of the other party. To avoid this and to provide incentive to reach agreement, statutes have provided for what is referred to as final-offer arbitration, pursuant to which the arbitrator is limited to acceptance of the last offer of one of

[1] Alaska Stat. Sec. 23.40.200 (1972); Hawaii Rev. Stat. Sec. 89-12 (Supp. 1972); Pa. Stat. Ann. tit. 43, Sec. 1101.1001 (Supp. 1972-73); Vt. Stat., tit. 21, Sec. 1703 (Supp. 1978) (*state* employees are denied the right to strike in tit. 3, Sec. 903 (b)); Oregon Rev. Stat. Sec. 243.726 (1973).

the parties. A variant form of final-offer arbitration permits the arbitrator to select, issue by issue, the last offer of one or the other party. The theory is that both sides will formulate final offers so close to what they believe the arbitrator will accept that the differences between them become negligible and agreement is reached. Whether or not agreement is reached without arbitration proceedings obviously is affected by the requirement of when final offers must be exchanged, because if no time limit is fixed, a party may make a last offer at the conclusion of the hearing or just prior to decision. There are some indications that the parties find the arbitration process to be so expensive, time consuming, and burdensome that the process itself provides an incentive for reaching agreement. For discussions of final-offer arbitration, see Stevens, *The Management of Labor Disputes in the Public Sector,* 51 Ore. L. Rev. 191, at 194-199 (1971); E. Ellman, "Legislated Arbitration in Michigan— A Lateral Glance" and J. Loihl, "Final-Offer Plus: Interest Arbitration in Iowa," Truth, Lie Detectors, and Other Problems In Labor Arbitration, Proceedings of the Thirty-First Annual Meeting, National Academy of Arbitrators 291, 317 (1978).

E. Miscellaneous Interest Relationships

Negotiation is a part of the process of producing an accommodation of miscellaneous conflicting interests for which standardized procedures do not exist. For example, at political conventions, protagonists of an interest group often must negotiate for acceptance and inclusion of their objectives in the party's platform and do so by agreeing to support or oppose other interest groups engaged in framing that platform. A candidate for office, seeking a political convention's endorsement or nomination, likewise must negotiate with interest groups concerning programs which he will support or oppose. "Logrolling" in the legislative process is another type of negotiation. Confrontations which occurred between students, faculties, and university administrations in the late 1960s and early 1970s presented occasions for negotiations which followed no previously established procedures. See, e.g., the Cox Commission Report, Crisis at Columbia, and the Report of the Fact-Finding Commission Appointed to Investigate the Disturbances at Columbia University in April and May 1968. More recently, terrorist groups and hijackers have used violence and threats of violence to negotiate for political and economic purposes.

Tenant unions, utilizing tenant rent strikes, engage in another form of negotiation, with a noticeable similarity to negotiation of collective bargaining agreements between employers and labor organizations. The withholding of rent, or payment of rent into escrow, creates a bargaining power comparable to that of labor unions in withholding labor. However, if the rent is finally paid to the landlord he does not suffer a loss of the use of his investment comparable to that of an employer whose plant has been closed by a strike. And, so long as they remain in possession, tenants do not suffer a loss comparable to the wage loss of striking employees. Tenants do have a significant bargaining power in their ability to offer and provide protection to landlords from vandalism and destruction of property. As with collective bargaining agreements, the establishment of a system of speedy and inexpensive arbitration for disputes is an important feature of a landlord-tenant union agreement.

A comment, *Tenant Unions: Collective Bargaining and the Low-Income Tenant,* 77 Yale L.J. 1368 (1968), makes the following statements: *

"C. *The Collective Bargaining Agreement*

"The final negotiation of a collective agreement with the landlord represents the fruition of the tenant union's efforts. The contracts vary widely in sophistication, specific terms, and the number of buildings covered. The typical agreement contains the following provisions:

"*Substantive promises:*
- a union commitment to encourage and oversee tenant efforts in responsible apartment maintenance;
- a landlord commitment to make certain initial repairs and to meet basic maintenance standards thereafter;
- a maximum rent scale for the life of the contract;
- a union commitment not to strike;

"*Enforcement provisions:*
- machinery for the regular transmission of tenant complaints and demands to the landlord;
- an arbitration board to resolve disputes over grievances with power to compel repairs;
- a procedure for rent withholding if the landlord fails to comply with the agreement;

"*Landlord-union relations:*
- landlord recognition of the union as exclusive bargaining agent;
- a landlord commitment not to discriminate against union members;
- a requirement that the landlord inform the tenant union of the addresses of all buildings owned and managed by him, and of the names of all new tenants as they move in.

"Increasingly, collective bargaining agreements provide for a dues check-off by the landlord."

* Reprinted by permission of the Yale Law Journal Company and Fred B. Rothman & Company from *The Yale Law Journal,* Vol. 77, pp. 1395-96.

3. The Relationship of Negotiation to Other Processes

A. Counseling and Negotiation

BERGSTROM v. BERGSTROM *

VISITATION RIGHTS OF A DIVORCED FATHER

In March 1965, Carl Bergstrom retained Leonard Sanders as his attorney to represent him in a dispute which had arisen when his former wife, Astrid, had filed a petition for the modification of their divorce decree substantially curtailing Carl's rights of visitation with his children. Sanders had met Bergstrom in connection with a real estate transaction with which they both had been involved. Sanders replaced Thor Johnson, who had been Carl Bergstrom's attorney in the original divorce proceeding. Johnson had asked to be relieved of the case because of Carl's apparent belief that Johnson was not sufficiently vigilant in the defense of the case.

The file which Sanders put together from the papers forwarded to him by Johnson and letters and copies of letters exchanged between Carl and Astrid Bergstrom indicated the following.

Carl and Astrid Bergstrom were married in 1948, and had since lived immediately to the north of the Ballard section of Seattle, Wash. The Ballard section has a very high proportion of residents of Scandinavian birth or descent. They had four children at the time of the divorce: two girls, Hilda and Catherine, age 13 and 10, respectively, and two boys, Paul and Eric, aged 7 and 6, respectively. Carl was a real estate broker and in the years before his divorce had earned between $15,000 and $18,000 a year, though at the time of the divorce his income had dropped to a little over $800 a month.

In September 1963, Astrid Bergstrom obtained a divorce from Carl upon the grounds of adultery. Specifically, Carl had had an affair with Britt Peterson, who had been one of Astrid's close friends and the mother of four children. She had given birth to a fifth child, of which Carl was agreed to be the father. Britt's former husband had divorced her, likewise on grounds of adultery. Subsequently Carl and Britt had married, and in 1965 lived together with the four Peterson boys, of whom Britt had retained custody, and their own child. Britt's former

---

* Reproduced by permission of the copyright holders, Robert L. Fletcher and Cornelius J. Peck.

166

husband had liberal visitation privileges, and usually took his children with him for weekends.

The Bergstrom divorce decree awarded Astrid $150 per month as alimony and $100 per month for the support of the four Bergstrom children. The Bergstrom house, valued at over $40,000, had been awarded to Astrid, who also had a fair amount of separate property. Carl was required to take out insurance policies on his life for the benefit of each of his children. Astrid was given custody of the children, provided that Carl was to have reasonable rights of visitation, not less than every Wednesday from 7:00 p.m. until bedtime and every Sunday from noon until bedtime. In addition, he was to be allowed to visit with them on alternate single-day school holidays and to share their vacation time.

By November 1963, disputes had arisen between Carl and Astrid over Carl's right to see the children in places other than the former Bergstrom house and at times other than those specified in the decree. Carl's tardy payment of the November installment of alimony brought a warning letter from Lon Carlin, Astrid's attorney, warning that any attempt to enlarge upon the visitation rights by withholding of alimony payments would promptly result in the institution of contempt proceedings. The letter continued, suggesting that relations had become unnecessarily acrimonious, and that both should attempt to avoid disputes in the interest of the children.

In April 1964, by an exchange of letters, Carl and Astrid had agreed that Carl could have the two boys with him from 6:00 p.m. on Saturday evening until 8:00 p.m. Sunday evening. He was to have the two girls with him from 9:30 Sunday morning until 8:00 p.m. Sunday evenings, and on Saturday afternoons if the girls wished to be with him. Matters proceeded with some disagreements, but generally without significant controversy until near the end of August 1964.

At that time Astrid wrote to Carl in preparation for the coming school year, informing him that he was not to visit the children on week days during the school year because it interfered too much with their homework and rest. She also told him that he would be allowed to have the children with him on the Labor Day weekend on either Saturday and Sunday, or Sunday and Labor Day, but not all three days. Looking forward she announced her intention to keep the children with her on Thanksgiving Day and Christmas, and to allow Carl to have them with him on November 11, a state holiday, and on New Year's Day.

Carl responded, sending copies of his letter to attorneys Johnson and Carlin. He said that Astrid's concern for her children was admirable and expected, but that he thought that he deserved consideration and credit, if not admiration, for his concern for the welfare of his children. He closed by stating that he expected Astrid to conform generally to the divorce decree and that he would not accept any unilateral action on her part with respect to his right to visit with the children.

Astrid's immediate response was a letter stating that she had meant exactly what she had said, and that in eliminating the weekday visits she had thought only of the welfare of the children.

Early in September 1964, Carl wrote to his attorney, Thor Johnson, stating that his wife was not living up to the agreement they had made concerning his visitation rights. He believed that Astrid made an issue of his adultery in discussions with the two girls, so as to degrade him in their eyes and make visits to his home with Britt unacceptable to them. He thought she also had discussed the matter with the boys, who were then seven and eight years of age. He requested Johnson to arrange a more specific schedule for visits with his children. In particular he wanted it made clear that:

1. There was no need to tell Astrid where he was taking the children when they left with him;

2. Astrid was not to make plans for the children which were inconsistent with the scheduled visits;

3. Twice a month the two boys were to stay with him on weekends; and

4. Vacations of three weeks length for the girls and the boys were to be spent with him, either concurrently or consecutively as he desired.

Near the middle of October 1964, Carl wrote to Astrid suggesting that she, as he did, always remember that the things they arranged concerning the children should be in the best interests of the children. Specifically, he requested Astrid not to show any displeasure with Catherine because her slip of the tongue in a telephone conversation had revealed that they recently had not gone to school one day when the teachers had a workshop, creating a school holiday to which he was entitled under the decree.

At the first of November 1964, Astrid filed the previously mentioned petition for modification of the divorce decree. The petition requested the court to make specific and determinable in advance all visitation periods between the children and Carl, to establish a limitation upon the number of telephone calls to the children he might make per week, and to restrain Carl from using the children as messengers in his attempt to negotiate with Astrid concerning his rights of visitation. As is customary, the petition ended with a prayer that Carl be required to pay Astrid's attorney's fees in connection with the petition for modification.

Three days later Carl wrote a letter to Astrid, expressing his surprise that upon telephoning he had found that Astrid had left the house in charge of Catherine, and suggesting that a child of 11 was not sufficiently mature to serve as a baby sitter for her two younger brothers. Two weeks later he wrote to Astrid informing her that he had managed to get an extra ticket to the last of the University of Washington football games and that from his telephone conversations with the girls he knew they both would like to go, but that he thought that Hilda, the older, was the one who would enjoy it most. He did not believe either of the boys could sustain an interest throughout the game. He requested that she inform him which of the girls could go, and whether he should pick her up at the house or elsewhere.

Near the end of November 1964, Carl wrote to Johnson saying that he believed that what Astrid wanted to achieve by her petition was a return to the original decree, but that she could not be expected to cooperate in a sensible interpretation of that arrangement. He mentioned that she had refused to allow either of the girls to go to the last football game of the University of Washington season, and that this was consistent with what appeared to be her lack of concern for the children. Specifically, he wanted Johnson to be aware that Astrid had had the children with her on Thanksgiving Day in 1963 and 1964, and that she was currently planning to have the children with her on both Christmas and New Year's Day, giving him the less desirable half of the Christmas holidays. This, he concluded, was typical of her gamesmanship.

Discussions between Johnson and Carlin relating to the hearing on the petition for modification of the decree led to their suggesting to their clients that the parties enter into a stipulation that a social worker of the domestic relations department of the King County Superior Court be requested to investigate the question of custody and visitation rights and report thereon, with recommendations, by which Carl and Astrid agreed to be bound. After some discussion, both agreed, and such a stipulation was filed with the court in January 1965.

Near the end of January 1965, the social worker filed her report. In it she noted that Carl and Astrid had been married in 1948 and that both had been well known in the Swedish community of Seattle and in particular in the Ballard Lutheran Church. She reported that the two girls had considerable hostility toward their stepmother, and that at first they had refused to go to Carl's house on Sundays, although they had agreed to visit and had had dinner there in September 1964. Hilda had indicated to the social worker that she did not want to spend as much time with her father as he desired, but instead preferred to have free time at home or with her friends. In particular, she disliked going to the Ballard Lutheran Church with her father, as they had done several times, because everyone there knew what had happened in her family and it embarrassed her. Catherine, the younger girl, was not as communicative as Hilda, but the social worker concluded that she did not think of Britt as her stepmother and that she did not want to stay overnight with her father. Paul, aged 8, was generally uncommunicative, but likewise appeared to be uncomfortable in staying overnight with his father and Britt. Eric, the younger boy, being of a cheerful disposition, did not object to staying with his father, and indeed, enjoyed it if some of his stepbrothers were present at the time.

The social worker had visited both houses, and reported them to be in the upper-middle class category. The house in which Carl and Britt lived was certainly adequate for housing Carl's children on weekends if the Peterson children were away with their father. If not, accommodations became crowded, which the social worker considered to be unsatisfactory for teen-age girls, particularly since the older two of the Peterson boys were aged 16 and 15.

The social worker concluded that Carl was greatly influenced in his conduct by guilt feelings, for which he wanted to compensate by spending the maximum amount of time with his children, and that he sought to do so without being aware of the effect it was having upon the children, particularly the two girls. She recommended the following:

1. All midweek visitations end.

2. Carl was to have the children with him on Sundays from 2:00 p.m. until 9:00 p.m.

3. Schedules were to be established for national and State holidays, Thanksgiving, Christmas, New Year's, and Easter, alternating visists with Carl and remaining with Astrid for even and odd numbered years so that within a two-year period the children would have spent each particular holiday with one parent or the other. Holidays with Carl were to begin at 9:00 a.m. and end at 9:00 p.m. Mother's Day and Fathers' Day were not to be considered holidays.

4. Short school vacations were to be divided equally between Carl and Astrid. However, single-day vacations, such as those resulting from a teachers' workshop, were not to be considered holidays or vacations.

5. Carl was to have all four children with him for a three-week vacation sometime between the end of the school year and the beginning of the next.

6. Carl was not to telephone the children more than twice a week, provided, however, that if when he did call one of the children to whom he wanted to speak was not there, that child would be requested to return his call.

7. Carl was to be prohibited from using the children as messengers with regard to any visitation problems, but instead was to discuss such matters only with Astrid directly.

Copies of the social worker's report and recommendations were furnished to Johnson and Carlin, who in turn forwarded copies to their clients. Four days later Carl sent to Johnson a five-page, single-spaced letter commenting upon the social worker's report and recommendations. He took vigorous exception to her findings that the two girls did not like to spend the night at his house, questioning the adequacy of the investigation upon which she based these conclusions. He suggested that whatever truth there was in the statements came from Astrid's indoctrination, and that the report should have included a recommendation that Astrid cease making degrading comments about Carl and Britt.

His conclusion was that the findings did not reflect the whole and true picture, in support of which he reported in question and answer form his discussion of the subject with Hilda, ending with her denial that she had told the social worker she did like to visit her father. He recognized that it might have been better not to engage Hilda in such a conversation, but thought the matter sufficiently important to justify what he had done.

Specifically, he noted that the recommendations failed to deal with the problem whether he was to have the children from 9:00 a.m. or 2:00 p.m. when holidays fell on a Sunday, or whether, if such a holiday were observed on the following Monday he was to have the children on that Monday. He felt aggrieved by the holiday schedule as it applied to Christmas and New Year's, pointing out that the social worker's recommendation left the children with Astrid on every Christmas Eve and every New Year's Eve. He was willing to have Mothers' Day treated as a holiday if Astrid would agree that Fathers' Day receive like treatment. He questioned whether the children's Thanksgiving vacation was to be considered a short vacation, divided between him and Astrid, or a single-day vacation, pointing out that except for the holiday the children missed only one day of school. He believed the provision relating to vacations was defective, because Astrid knew that he could not take all of the children at the same time if Britt's children were also in the house, and she would so schedule their vacation unless otherwise prevented from doing so.

He suggested that he be allowed to have the children with him for three weeks in the summer between July 1 and August 15, at which time Britt's former husband had the Peterson children with him, and that he be permitted to have the four children together or to have the girls and the boys in separate consecutive three-week periods. He thought provision should be made as to whether if the scheduled vacation began or ended on a weekend, the Sunday involved would be treated as a regular Sunday visit or as a part of the vacation and hence not subject to the Sunday time limits. He also requested that the provision governing telephone calls be changed to provide that he could telephone the children *an average* of twice a week. He urged Johnson to get in touch with the social worker and bring about the requested changes in her report and recommendations.

Early in February Johnson and Carlin had met to discuss the case and to work out the details of a modified order in terminology more precise than that used by the social worker. Carlin agreed that he would recommend to Astrid that a single three-week vacation be scheduled sometime between July 1 and August 10 of each year, provided that Carl agree that Astrid be permitted to take the children out of the city for a long summer vacation without the necessity of returning them for the Sunday visits with their father. Dealing with the matters which Carl had raised in his letter to Johnson, they agreed that the holiday hour schedule would be followed if a holiday fell on a Sunday; that the Thanksgiving holiday be considered a short vacation to be divided between Astrid and Carl; and that the three-week vacation periods would begin on a Saturday morning at 9:00 a.m., and end at 9:00 p.m. on the fourth Sunday thereafter. Johnson informed Carl accordingly by letter, enclosing a draft modification of the custody portion of the divorce

decree incorporating these features. The variations from the social worker's recommendations were to be discussed with her prior to presentation
of the modification order for approval of the judge.

Two days later Carl replied in a two-and-one-half-page single-spaced
letter. Briefly, he thought it unfair that Carlin had used the social
worker's obvious mistake in not scheduling the vacation period when
the Peterson boys were not in the house to obtain additional advantages
for Astrid. Some other concession should have been obtained by Johnson
if he were to agree to the long vacation proposal. He believed that the
decree was defective in that it failed to require Astrid to refrain from
making degrading remarks concerning Britt and himself. In particular,
he noted that Johnon had failed to obtain an agreement that if the
Monday following a holiday which fell on Sunday were observed as a
holiday, the holiday visitation schedule was to apply to that Monday and
that no concession had been made with respect to either Christmas Eve
or New Year's Eve. He also noted that the proposed order did not provide
for *an average* of two telephone calls per week. He concluded by asking,
"If I can't depend on you, Thor, to protect me in these things, to whom
can I turn?"

Mr. Johnson replied by letter, stating that the only maters he thought
could be discussed with any chance of success with the social worker
were those upon which he and Carlin had reached agreement. He said
he was willing to attempt to have included a provision requiring both
Carl and Astrid to refrain from making remarks to the children which
might reflect adversely upon the other. If this was not satisfactory to
Carl, Johnson wished to be relieved of responsibility for the case.

It was then that Carl Bergstrom decided to retain Leonard Sanders
and brought the case to him.

QUESTIONS

1. Should Leonard Sanders have agreed to take over the representation
of Carl Bergstrom? Why or why not?
2. Do you think that Mr. Johnson had represented Carl adequately?
What criticism, if any, would you make about his handling of the case?
3. Would you have stipulated to be bound by a social worker's report?
4. What do you think the effect of the events described above have
been upon the Bergstrom children and their relationships with their
parents?

DENOUEMENT

After the initial and somewhat prolonged interview, Sanders thought
the case looked like a tough one. A consoling feature was that he couldn't

lose much. The social worker's report and recommendations had, in his opinion, devastated Carl, and in fact gave him less in the way of visitation rights with his children than Astrid had been willing to give when seeking a modification of the divorce decree. This was the bottom as far as Carl was concerned, and if any change was made it would almost certainly have to be an improvement.

Sanders telephoned Carlin, whom he had previously known from professional contacts, and suggested that they meet to discuss the case. He had confidence in Carlin as an attorney with whom the strength and weakness of a case such as this could be discussed in the attempt to get a clearer picture of the position of the parties and without fear that the frankness of the discussion would be used later to advance the other's case. He expressed to Carlin the view that Carl had been and still was heavily ridden by feelings of guilt; that he was attempting to spend every bit of time possible with the children as compensation for having created the situation which brought about their separation; that he had hoped to prove through his attention to the children that he was not as bad a man as some people might think; and that the social worker's report was to Carl another official pronouncement that he was an s.o.b. He also suggested that Astrid, who had not remarried, still felt the necessity of hurting Carl in retaliation for what he had done and that she had found interference with the visitation rights, in which Carl manifested such interest, a wonderful means for accomplishing this. He thought also that one of the reasons for her requesting the modification of the divorce decree was that she wanted another judicial declaration that Carl was not a decent or fit man. He doubted that either Carl or Astrid really had the best interests of the children in mind when they disagreed on visitation matters, but instead used these disagreements as a means of getting at each other or establishing their positions as the wronged or not-so-wrong-doing party. Carlin agreed that this was probably the case—and in this respect not unlike a number of others which he had handled. Sanders suggested that he would take the social worker's report and work out a visitation schedule which conformed to most of the social worker's recommendations, but gave Carl some of the things which he thought most important. He would submit this to Carlin for review and possibly further discussion.

Sanders then prepared a visitation schedule which provided for overnight visits by the children on every other weekend, or twice a month in lieu of a visitation every Sunday. He proposed that the summer vacation period be cut from three weeks to two weeks, and that only Christmas, New Year's, Easter, the Fourth of July, and Thanksgiving be treated as holidays for visitation purposes, with a special provision including Christmas Eve from 6:00 p.m. on December 24 as a part of that holiday. He prepared the following schedules to show the differences between what the social worker's recommendations would allow and what he proposed.

SOCIAL WORKER'S RECOMMENDATIONS

	Overnights	Separate Contacts
Sundays (less three for vacation with Astrid)	0	49
Holidays	0	9
Vacations	22	1
Totals	22	59

SANDER'S PROPOSAL

	Overnights	Separate Contacts
Sundays (two per month, less three-week vacation with Astrid)	21	21
Holidays (Christmas Eve, every other year)	½	5
Vacations	15	1
Totals	36½	27

Sanders then undertook to "sell" this proposal to Carl, in what turned out to be a prolonged discussion ranging into many aspects of the marriage relationship. He urged upon Carl the view that the important thing in the relationship with his children was not the frequency of contact or even the total amount of time spent with them, but instead the quality of the experiences they had together. Thus, a schedule which provided for fewer separate contacts and even for less total time together was preferable if the contacts for which it did provide made possible some meaningful relationship. In addition, he suggested that Astrid still felt aggrieved and wanted to punish Carl. She could do this by obtaining another judicial declaration that he was not an admirable man by having his visitation rights curtailed, as she was seeking to do. She could also hurt him by interfering with what remained of those rights as occasions permitted, and a schedule which provided for frequent contacts provided frequent opportunities for doing just this in small but irritating ways. A slight delay with respect to a substantial visitation period would not prove to be as irritating as one associated with a visitation period of as little as the seven-hour Sunday periods provided for in the social worker's report. Sanders discussed at length the psychological motivations of Astrid's behavior with respect to Carl's visitation rights. He stressed the possibility that while she may not have consciously recognized it, her actions were controlled, not by concern for the welfare of the children, but by the feelings engendered by the divorce in general and the adultery in particular. He told Carl several times that Astrid wanted another judicial declaration that he was an s.o.b. He did not expressly say to Carl that the same was true of Carl's behavior, and that Carl wanted a judicial declaration that he was not so bad after all. But Sanders believed that, being an intelligent man, Carl eventually came to understand that this might have played too great a part in the position he had taken with respect to visitation rights. In any event, he eventually agreed that Sanders could submit the proposal to Carlin for the purpose of getting Astrid's approval.

Sanders sent the proposed order incorporating his proposal to Carlin, and later telephoned him to be sure that the purposes he was attempting to achieve were understood. A number of the technical refinements which Carl had suggested to Johnson were also included in the order, such as that holiday hours apply to a holiday falling on Sunday, vacations might be scheduled between July 1 and August 10, and that the limitation on phone calls be *an average* of two per week. Also included was a provision requiring both Carl and Astrid to encourage in their children an attitude of respect for the other and a desire to achieve a desirable parent-child relationship. Carlin agreed to take the proposed order up with Astrid in the near future, noting that the scheduled hearing date on the petition for modification was rapidly approaching.

A week later Carlin telephoned Sanders to inform him that Astrid would not agree to his proposal, but instead insisted that an order be entered incorporating the recommendations of the social worker. Sanders commented that this was unfortunate, because it would solve no problems but instead provide the basis for further and more exacerbated arguments. Carlin agreed that this was probably the case. Sanders then suggested that he submit his proposed order to the social worker and that the social worker be requested to review the situation to determine whether the proposed order, or portions of it, might not be incorporated in her recommendations. Carlin said he would go along with the proposal because he wanted a solution to the matter.

Sanders then sent a copy of his proposed order to the social worker, and Carlin joined him in the request that she review the situation. The social worker agreed to do this and in fact again visited the two households and interviewed Carl, Astrid, and the children. Apparently because he had been persuaded by Sanders, Carl's attitude toward visitation rights and the relationship with his children had undergone a change. In any event, the social worker believed she could note a change in attitude, and filed a second report stating that this was the case. However, her second report did not explicitly state whether her recommendations had changed or whether she thought any part of Sanders' proposed order should be incorporated in her recommendations.

On April 16, 1965, the scheduled hearing was held on Astrid's petition to modify the visitation provisions of the divorce decree. Sanders agreed that his client Bergstrom was bound by the stipulation which he had made to accept the recommendations of the social worker, but he pointed out that neither parent could make a stipulation which would bind the children. The question before the court remained that of determining how the interests of the children could best be served. Ultimately the judge decided that he would not be bound by the stipulation, and advised counsel to set the case for a hearing on the merits.

On April 20, 1965, Carlin wrote to Sanders saying that after a great deal of discussion and much shedding of tears, Astrid had finally agreed to his proposed order, provided that certain changes were made. First, she wanted additional language making it clear that if a particular month had five weekends, Carl was to have the children for only two of the weekends—the first and the third of each month. She also wanted to add a proviso that in the event that either of the girls had social engagements for Saturday night, the required visit would be one limited to 9:00 a.m. to 9:00 p.m. on Sunday. If Carl would not agree to these changes, Carlin prophesied that they were in for a long and very emotional hearing.

Sanders then obtained Carl's agreement that these changes be made. On April 26, 1965, an order was entered by agreement, incorporating Sanders' proposal with the provisos demanded by Astrid. On April 28, 1965, Sanders sent a copy of the order to Carl expressing the hope that this would bring an end to the difficult situation which had prevailed. He said, however, that he believed that in a very short time a change would occur in Astrid's behavior because of the deprivation of the more frequent opportunities to interfere with Carl's visitations. He suggested that the interferences would become more substantial, and that Astrid would more aggressively attempt to provoke arguments. He urged Carl to refrain from responding at any time in anger, but instead calmly insist that matters be done as provided for in the modified decree.

Approximately two weeks later Sanders began to receive telephone calls from Carl who was obviously in a state of excitement and anger because of what he considered violations of the modified order—in particular, he resented the frequency with which the children requested that departures be made from the schedule established, saying that Astrid had suggested they discuss it with their father. When he objected to Astrid that this constituted a violation of the provision prohibiting both from using the children as means of communication concerning visitation problems, she would reply in angry and provocative language. This in turn angered Carl tremendously.

In the conversations concerning these growing problems Sanders suggested to Carl that one of the reasons why he in turn became so angry was that he thought he was entitled to a certain standard of behavior from Astrid—that she ought to do things in the prescribed way. He further suggested that perhaps there was no reason why he was entitled to expect decent behavior from Astrid, but that, if he could bring himself to look at it as she did, he was entitled to nothing and the only "oughtness" of conforming to the modified decree was that it was what the judge had required. In any event, whether he was "entitled" or she "ought," the only realistic way to look at the matter was to recognize that in fact she was not going to behave differently for some time. There is no sense in getting angry about facts, and her expectable conduct is a fact he emphasized.

Nevertheless, the disagreeable exchanges increased in frequency and intensity so that on June 9, 1965, Sanders filed a motion to hold Astrid in contempt for failure to comply with the modified decree, in particular by involving the children in discussions of problems with the visitation schedule, by failing to encourage the children to abide by the visitation program, by failing to give prime consideration to the welfare of the children, and by affirmatively arranging social events for the girls on the first and third Saturdays of each month. He telephoned Carlin and informed him that he hoped that they would be able to get both Carl and Astrid before one of the judges who could deliver to them a good lecture on the necessity of complying with the decree. Carlin objected that this was premature and would do no good. In fact, when the hearing was held on the motion to hold in contempt on July 7, 1965, the judge went even further, and besides delivering a stern lecture required both of them to take a tour of the county jail so that they could see where he would send them—and he promised that he certainly would send them there—if they did not comply.

The lecture seemed to have worked, and there were no more incidents, or at least incidents reported to either Sanders or Carlin through April 1966. At that time, however, Britt Bergstrom came to Sanders for help. It appeared that her former husband wanted to rearrange the summer vacation schedule so that he would have the children from the end of school through the Fourth of July and from August 16 through Labor Day.

QUESTIONS

1. Do you think that Sanders performed what is appropriately the work of a lawyer? Why or why not?

For differing views of the counseling role of lawyers in marriage dissolutions, see J. Elkins, *A Counseling Model for Lawyering in Divorce Cases,* 53 Notre Dame Law. 229 (1977); B. Callner, *Boundaries of the Divorce Lawyer's Role,* 10 Family L.Q. 389 (1977).

2. Do you believe he properly analyzed the motivations underlying the actions of Carl and Astrid?

3. Why didn't Sanders expressly tell Carl that his behavior was motivated more by concern for proving himself than by his concern for the children and their welfare? Would you have done so?

4. How important was it that Sanders held such a favorable opinion of Carlin and trusted him to the extent of expressing what might have been taken as statements against the interest of his client? Was it proper for him to do so?

5. Do you think the program Sanders arranged will be better for the children in the long run than the one proposed by the social worker? Could you suggest a still better program?

6. Was it proper for Carlin to agree that the social worker reconsider her report?

7. Do you have any suspicions about the reasons why Mr. Peterson wanted to change the summer visitation schedule for his four boys?

ADDITIONAL READINGS

Goode, AFTER DIVORCE (1956), particularly pp. 307-330.

Despert, CHILDREN OF DIVORCE (1953) (popularized).

Children of Divorced Parents, 10 Law and Contemp. Prob. 697-864 (11 separate articles).

H. Freeman and H. Weihofen, CLINICAL LAW TRAINING: INTERVIEWING AND COUNSELING, 169-240 (1972).

A. Watson, THE LAWYER IN THE INTERVIEWING AND COUNSELING PROCESS (1976).

THE CASE OF THE FRUSTRATED PRESIDENT *

For many years we have represented the client whom I will identify as "Sidney." He is now about 55 years old. About 30 years ago—I am not sure of this date—he started a manufacturing business which became prosperous. Approximately ten years ago, he felt that he wanted to sell his business. From time to time he consulted our law office and occasionally came up with a possible deal. First he suggested a sale to a charitable organization. He had expected to be able to dispose of his business without capital gain but upon being advised of the tax consequences the deal did not progress. On a subsequent occasion, about three years ago, another arrangement was presented to us and, again, it did not materialize, apparently for tax reasons.

Over the past few years our client has discussed with us the notion that he would very much like to dispose of his business to some larger organization and that he was interested in becoming a part of a larger enterprise. About two years ago he commenced negotiations with a larger company which had some publicly issued stock. The company was in approximately the same line of business as his, was much larger, was headquartered in another State and, so far as he knew, generally had a good reputation. Our client made the initial contact and developed negotiations up to a point. He then brought us as his lawyers into the picture and negotiations continued.

---

* Reprinted by permission from Freeman, LEGAL INTERVIEWING AND COUNSELING 170-172, copyright 1964 by West Publishing Co., St. Paul, Minn.

Our client had for many years been his own "boss." On more than one occasion during the course of the negotiations we pointed out to him in private conversations that his notion of being a part of a larger organization would put him in a different position from that of being his own boss. Just exactly how this would work out we could not foretell. It depended largely on the kind of organization that was acquiring his business. We tried to outline the psychological difference between being "boss" and being employed, between owning or controlling and merely investing, between self decision and board or committee decision. We also advised against a fifty year old man as active as he was thinking he could retire. We urged him not to allow money considerations nor expectations of added power from being part of a larger company or a concept that his small business had "graduated" to hide the problem involved in the new arrangement.

The transaction was somewhat complicated, from a technical legal and tax point of view, but these were left to us and we worked them out. Our client was most interested in disposing of his business in such a way that he would have no taxable gain on the disposition of his own manufacturing business. We succeeded in negotiating a so-called B reorganization and obtained a ruling from Internal Revenue Service.

The contract of purchase-and-sale was made, on the basis of our client's accounting records and data. Between the time when the contract was made and the closing date after the ruling was received, it so happened that our client's business took something of a turn for the worse, perhaps because of some general business conditions or some lack of management or some uncontrollable other factors. As a consequence of this turn of events, the buyers sought to renegotiate the transaction. In one intense day of negotiation, the transaction was renegotiated and our client received approximately 10% less than the original deal contemplated. It brought the deal up-to-date and afforded both parties the opportunity to reconsider whether they would go forward. We again pointed out to our client what we had said before and that the purchasing company's attitude showed some evidence of close dealing and lack of concern for individuals. They decided to go forward and the deal was finally completed and closed.

As a rule, we lawyers do not negotiate management positions. Sidney had discussions with the top management of the purchasing company and orally agreed to some management position not too heavy in its demands, a salary the general limits of which were fixed and membership on the Board of Directors. He had informed us from time to time that he was satisfied about making the deal and the position in which he would find himself after the deal was made.

Thereafter our client discovered that the major public company not only was acquiring his company but two other companies in this vicinity. Our client became almost immediately unhappy. He found that there were others who were put over his head. He found that he could no longer run the business as he had anticipated. Although he had had some expectation that the publicly-held corporation would help in connection with manufacturing processes and other business matters, he found on the contrary that the policies of the publicly-held company conflicted pretty seriously with his own ideas of how a business ought to be run. He found that being a member of the Board of Directors did not give him too much authority, and that the business was run somewhat by an executive committee. Although upon his insistence he was given an appointment thereon he discovered that the executive committee itself is a group with some prearranged notions and run by a subgroup. In his own division, he found himself in a position of a consultant and something of a kind of director of research, and that people do not listen to him. More seriously, the company which he had built up continues to have a loss and the loss is an ever-increasing one. One of the persons who had previously been his competitor as the president of another company acquired by the publicly-held company, now has become his superior.

It would seem, looking at this picture from the outside, that our client made an excellent deal. He sold his business for more than it is presently worth. He holds shares of stock in a publicly-held company. The stock of the publicly-held company seems to have maintained itself reasonably well. He has assets worth in the neighborhood of $3 million, whereas formerly, when he was running his own business, he seemed always to have been fighting a weak cash position. He has no complaint of that sort at the present time. He is basically free to do as he wishes. Certainly as I observe the situation, he is financially secure.

But he is basically an unhappy man. His unhappiness came to light in a very interesting fashion. He has endeavored to commence some discussions with the publicly-held company to see whether he could buy back his company. In my humble opinion he needs his old business "like he needs a hole in the head." In a recent conversation I pressed the point as politely as I could to inquire why it was that he was really interested in reacquiring his old business. I pointed out to him that his other interests, which would include operation of some ranches and other small business, could be sufficient to occupy his time and attention. I questioned him to inquire why it was that he was really interested in reacquiring his old business, especially now that it is operating at a loss and a rather severe one. The best explanation he can give, and the best explanation I can give, is that his old business is one that he had built up from the start and it's like a child that is dying or has died. A parent just does not like to see this sort of thing happen. So he is extremely unhappy about it and would like to "revive" his own creation, but realizes this is futile. At a recent meeting of the board of the publicly-held corporation, the board voted to liquidate the business and even our client had to vote along with the rest of the board members. No plans for such liquidation have been spelled out so far.

His present unhappiness in connection with his business status cannot be explained on financial grounds. It can only be explained in terms of his own psychological makeup.

I honestly do not know very much about our client's personal life. He is married and has two children, both of whom are adopted. I have never met his wife, although I have talked to her on the telephone on a few occasions. They have been married many years. Generally speaking our client is in reasonably good health, is a good-looking man in his middle fifties and, so far as I know, his only hobby is playing golf. I believe he has rarely, if ever, taken any interest in collateral activities of a community sort or of a charitable nature. His contributions to charity (I have seen his tax returns!) are extremely meager. He is a pleasant person to talk to, a reasonably intelligent businessman aware of business conditions, and appears on the whole to have good business skills and good business judgment.

At this writing I cannot say that there is anything different that we as lawyers could have done in guiding our client, nor is there anything different that we should have done. I am not at all sure that anybody should have done anything differently. I am not at all sure that he should have retained his business. In fact, I now believe that if he had retained his business, his business would probably be suffering something of a loss, although perhaps not nearly as great a loss as it is now suffering, and he would find it much more difficult to make the kind of a dream deal that he had had in mind at one time.

I think his unhappiness is occasioned by other factors. I believe such a person would be a happier individual if during his lifetime he had developed some hobbies, some interests in outside activities, some attachment to community organizations and the like, toward which he could now devote time and attention. I must, however, agree with his basic feeling that he is unhappy because he built up a business which has now deteriorated considerably. I must agree that one just does not like to see his business brainchild come to such an unfortunate ending. Certainly this is an interesting study in the attachment which an individual can have to a business that he did develop. I am sure, however, that this is not an unusual kind of attachment and that there are many men in our society who have a similar attachment. But, can a counselor solve this problem?

NOTE AND QUESTIONS

For the comments of a professor of law and a practicing psychologist upon this case, see Freeman, LEGAL INTERVIEWING AND COUNSELING 173-176 (1964).

1. Is the counseling function which is called for in this case properly viewed as the function of a lawyer?

2. If it is a proper function of a legal counselor, was it performed properly in this case? If not, how should it be performed?

3. Does the informant's statement, "As a rule, we lawyers do not negotiate management positions," reflect a defensive attitude for having failed to protect the client with a properly drafted contract of sale? If lawyers don't involve themselves in negotiation of management positions, how will such matters be handled to ensure that expectations are stated and guaranteed?

4. If you believe that the counseling function which might have been performed in the case is not the function of a lawyer, by whom do you think it should be performed, and how would you get the client to accept such counseling?

B. Creating the Fact Pattern for the Negotiations

The note, pages 155-156, concerning the Supreme Court's decision in *American Shipbuilding* v. *NLRB,* pointed out that the time of the year at which collective bargaining is undertaken and a strike or lockout deadline passes may drastically affect the balance of power in a bargaining relationship. In that case, it was the seasonal nature of ship-repair activities which made it of such importance whether an impasse was reached during the winter or summer. The bargaining power of the United Auto Workers is much less during the summer months and prior to the annual model changes than it is during the fall months when new models of cars have begun to appear. That union accordingly has attempted to have bargaining take place so that a strike poses the threat of interruption of sales of new models. The Retail Clerks generally would prefer to have collective bargaining agreements expire so that a strike threat could be imposed shortly before the Thanksgiving-to-Christmas shopping rush develops, whereas department store managers would prefer to have collective bargaining agreements expire so that a strike threat would most likely have to be made at a time of greatly reduced business activity. School teachers have more bargaining power in the fall than they do late in the spring. Many other bargaining relationships are affected by seasonal changes in the bargaining power of the parties.

A union which represents the employees at only one of an employer's plants, each of which is capable of producing the same product, can obviously enhance its bargaining power if common agreement can be reached with other unions as to the date for expiration of all collective bargaining agreements. Otherwise, as it was once put, a strike may be no more effective than an attempt to bail water with a sieve. As a general proposition, employees are probably more willing to stay on strike during summer months than during the winter months. Careful analysis of the factors affecting the power structure in a bargaining relationship may reveal unexpected tactical advantages to one party or the other: even the manufacture of coffins has a seasonal variation. Fixing the expiration date of one collective bargaining agreement is therefore of great significance for the power structure of the negotiation of the next agreement.

Even where seasonal factors do not provide any significant advantage, it is sometimes possible to take action in anticipation of negotiations which will affect the balance of power in forthcoming negotiations. Thus, as appears to have been the case with the 1959 steel strike, management can do much to strengthen its bargaining position by building up inventories and persuading customers to build up inventories in anticipation of a strike. A union counterpart is that of building a strike-assistance fund of substantial proportions in anticipation of its need to maintain morale during a prolonged strike.

This ability to affect the course of negotiations by creating a favorable fact pattern in anticipation of the actual negotiations is not, of course, limited to collective bargaining. A lawyer handling a personal-injury case may similarly build a favorable fact pattern by giving careful attention to the evidentiary matters and developing the proof of what he will be able to present through expert witnesses if trial becomes necessary. Or, as is demonstrated by the plea-bargaining case at pages 47-51, by planning what appears to be a hopeful program of rehabilitation, or, demonstrating that the client has had a sufficient exposure to jail to ensure that the deterrent effect of detention has had an opportunity to work, a lawyer may greatly enhance the client's prospects of successfully arranging a plea to a lesser charge. EEOC representatives themselves created much of the bargaining power with which they obtained the Newport News and the AT&T agreements.

There follows a case history detailing a young attorney's efforts to build a favorable fact pattern in what might be considered a small and unimportant case.

A CHARMING HOUSE ALL COVERED WITH LIENS*

The following account is drawn from the files of the first case which came to Edward McDuff after his admission to the bar. His clients, Mr. and Mrs. George Waters, came to him on May 11, 1960, upon the recommendation of a mutual friend and, it might be added, without a thorough understanding of how serious was their problem.

Mr. and Mrs. Waters had made a contract for the construction of their new house with Moss Construction Co., which was in fact the sole proprietorship of Charles Moss. In a loosely drawn contract, he had agreed to construct a house for them in accordance with specified plans for a total contract price of $24,591. Extra items which the Waters subsequently

---

* Reprinted by permission of the copyright holders, Robert L. Fletcher and Cornelius J. Peck.

decided they wanted resulted in additional charges of $448. Trouble developed early in May, when John Jackson, attorney for four of Moss' employees, filed a lien against the house for unpaid wages, giving notice thereof by letter to the Waters. It seemed quite likely that Moss had fallen behind in payments to his suppliers and was in fact using the money received as work progressed with one house to pay the bills for houses previously completed. As of that time, materials and subcontracted services supplied to Moss, but not paid for by him, apparently amounted to $5,424. Additional materials and services valued at $5,119 would be required to complete the construction. Thus, if the Waters were to pay both these sums, they would require a total of $10,543, but, in fact, the payments they had made to Moss had reduced the remainder which they could draw down under the construction loan they had arranged to only $6,011. Unless they could avoid responsibility for some of the unpaid bills, it seemed quite likely that they would lose their entire investment in the uncompleted house. After discussion of the matter with the Waters and review of the various invoices and bills which they brought with them, as well as a rather extensive review of the Washington law of liens, McDuff wrote the following letter to his new clients.

"Dear Mr. and Mrs. Waters:

"The basic problem is how to keep your total payments for your home down to a sum equal to the original contract price of the house plus extras less credits. Assuming the contractor is unable to pay all the materialmen, laborers, and subcontractors on the job, the only way to keep your payments at or below the contract price is to refuse to pay some of the bills of the materialmen, subs, and laborers.

"Basically, you are legally obligated to pay only for items you or an agent contracted to purchase. The law, however, provides that persons supplying materials and labor on a construction project may exert a lien on the structure on which the materials or labor were used. Once the lien is properly placed on the property, the lien holder may sue the owner of the property for the amount claimed under the lien. Should the owner of the property fail to pay the lien holder, the court may order a sale of the property upon which the lien was placed.

"As a practical matter, therefore, it will be necessary for you to pay all persons who have supplied material or labor on the job who have a potentially lienable claim. All those who do not have a lienable claim should not be paid.

"There are about forty different statutory liens, two of which particularly concern us—(1) materialman's lien and (2) labor lien. In order to exert either of these liens, the materialman or laborer must file his lien claim within 90 days of the cessation of the performance of his labor or furnishing materials. In addition, a materialman must give the owner of the project notice of intention to claim a lien not later than 10 days after the date of the *first* delivery of materials or supplies. If a materialman gives late notice, he may only claim a lien for the value of the materials supplied after the notice was given.

"For the purpose of the lien statute, a person may be both a materialman and a laborer. For example, Stuart's Cabinets contracted to build and install cabinets for your home. If the contract were to build the cabinets and deliver them to the job, Stuart's would be materialmen only and would not have a lienable claim if they failed to give notice of an intention to file the lien within 10 days after the first delivery. The contract, however, called for installation on the job. To this extent, they are laborers and fall within the labor lien statute. The courts have held in a case of this nature that if the contractors file a lien within 90 days in accordance with the labor lien statute, he may recover only for the value of the labor expended on the job. In the case of the Stuart's Cabinets, this would be but a small portion of the total bill.

"What happens when one who is both a materialman and laborer has received partial payment which equals the value of the labor? This is not particularly clear. The court may hold that a partial payment shall be considered made for both labor and materials in the same ratio as each bears to the full contract price. For the time being, I think we should take the position that where a partial payment has been made, no lien may be claimed unless the value of the labor exceeds the partial payment.

"Listed below is a breakdown of current and future bills into (A) bills which are not lienable, (B) bills potentially lienable in part, and (C) bills potentially lienable in their entirety.

. . .

[The listings which followed indicated that $1,154 of the bills were not lienable, in McDuff's opinion; that $4,307 of the bills were potentially lienable in part; and that $525 of the bills were potentially lienable in full. He concluded his letter in the following manner:]

"Some items of labor and materials yet to be supplied are not mentioned above. Whether they will be lienable depends upon the factors mentioned above. Some items such as the side sewer and sewer hookup are necessary in order to make your home habitable. You will undoubtedly want to complete these items regardless of their potentially lienable nature. As to other items, you have a choice of stopping the contractor or allowing the contractor to continue ordering the materials and work and running the risk of a lien. You may want to substitute a less expensive item in place of the one originally desired. The following items, not mentioned above, remain to be completed:

1.	Finish hardware	$ 75.00
2.	Bulldozing	30.00
3.	Acoustical tile (basement)	60.00
4.	Vinyl tile (basement)	54.00
5.	Appliances	?

6. Terrazzo (Entry & Hearth)—Formica (Kitchen & Bathroom)—
   Corlon (Kitchen & Bathroom)—   700.00
7. Blacktop driveway   200.00
8. Lumber   200.00
9. Labor   ?

"In addition, we should obtain more information about the water hookup charge. If it is a water district charge, it is lienable.

"This should clarify each of the bills so far mentioned. Remember that all potentially lienable bills become liens only if a lien is filed within 90 days after the cessation of the lien claimant's work. Because of this, it may be wise to refrain from paying any bills until a lien has actually been filed with the hope that some potential lien holders will fail to file a lien within the required time period.

"Very truly yours,

"Edward McDuff"

McDuff also advised the Waters by telephone to tell any subcontractors or materialmen who might inquire about getting payment to discuss the matter with Moss, who was the person with whom they had contracted. In particular, he cautioned them to make no promises to subcontractors or materialmen that the bills would be paid. He specifically instructed them not to mention that they had consulted an attorney lest that lead the subcontractors and materialmen to take action to perfect their liens. When Mountain Glass, the subcontractor supplying windows, refused to deliver a substantial number of the windows unless paid the balance due on their account, he directed the Waters to obtain the windows from another supplier rather than do anything which would indicate that the Waters were parties to the contract with Mountain Glass.

All construction at the Waters' new house was completed on June 14, 1960. On July 1, 1960, Tiles and Tiles, Inc. filed a lien against the house in the amount of $512.46 for tile installation work performed on May 31 and June 1, 1960. This was followed by the filing of three liens by the law firm of Short and Legis on behalf of Northwest Lumber Co. for $879, for Stuart's Cabinets in the amount of $735, and for Susser Sheet Metal for $285. However, these three lien notices mistakenly contained the legal description of the property on which the Waters' old house was located and where they were living while their new house was being built. Other subcontractors and suppliers began to make contact with the Waters, requesting payment, so that by July 27, 1960, McDuff was able to prepare the following letter summarizing their position.

"Dear Mr. and Mrs. Waters:

"I have reviewed the outstanding claims and made an effort to evaluate them so that you might be able to make the necessary financial plans. I am sure you understand that estimated ultimate payments are plainly "estimates." In some instances, we really have inadequate factual information to make a proper estimate. Most estimates are on the pessimistic side on the theory that you will not want to be placed in a position to obtain funds twice.

CLAIMANT	UNPAID AMT. OF CONTRACT OR INVOICE	ESTM. MINIM. PMNT.	ESTM. ULTIMATE PMNT.	ACTUAL PMNT.
NORTHWEST LUMBER	$879.00	$00.00	$792.00	
SUSSER SHEET METAL	285.00	00.00	225.00	
STUART'S CABINETS	735.00	00.00	180.00	
PIRE OIL	100.00		100.00	
ADE SD. & GRAVEL	100.00	00.00	00.00	
M. S. DRY WALL *				
LAIR HEATING	1103.44	299.67	375.00	
FOX ORN. IRON	200.00	00.00	00.00	
GALLE ROOFING	524.16	00.00	00.00	
STEVE QUARTO	210.60	60.00	90.00	
MOUNTAIN GLASS **				
PACIFIC PLUMBING	440.00+			
	wtr. hook up	405.00	415.00	415.00
FOX & GEORGE	45.00	00.00	00.00	
COOPER S. PETERS	1931.28	00.00	850.00	
URLET et al.	220.00	197.60	197.60	197.60
TILES & TILES	490.00	230.00	285.00	
PETERSON	219.00	219.00	219.00	219.00
DUCTS	60.00	estimated cost to obtain same		
DRIVEWAY	550.00	estimated cost to obtain same		
TOTALS	$8092.48	$1411.27	$3728.60	

Totals do not include MOUNTAIN GLASS, BURR PAINT and M. S. DRY WALL

* Need amount of bid to make estimate.
** Future events will determine. Maximum should be reasonable value of glass left to be installed plus a few dollars for value of labor spent on job site to date. It would be a good idea if you would call in several glass suppliers and installers and get a bid on supplying and installing remaining Thermopane as long as Mountain Glass would not learn of your actions.

BURR PAINT: If they follow course indicated in their letter, may be $00.00. Otherwise there will be a dispute over effectiveness of their notice of an intention to file a lien.

"I hope the above information is satisfactory. I would be happy to prepare a memorandum for the bank if you desire. In addition, I shall be glad to accompany you on a visit to the bank to discuss the feasibility and amount of the loan.

"Very truly yours,

"Edward McDuff"

As various subcontractors and suppliers filed liens, McDuff would respond to them in the following fashion. If the lien were for materials and labor supplied and a notice had been given to the Waters within 10 days after the materials were first delivered, he would have the Waters pay the bill in full. If a timely notice had not been filed, he would indicate a willingness to pay the amount of the labor charges attributable to the claim made but requested proof of how many hours of labor had actually been performed at the job site, insisting that he would not recognize the validity of a lien for labor performed elsewhere, including labor charges in connection with the making of deliveries to the construction site. When the time for filing all lien claims had passed, there were only eight liens which had been protected by the filing of the requisite notices.

It became appropriate to consider what defenses might be asserted to the liens for which the required notices had been filed. McDuff first turned his attention to the three lien claims filed by Short and Legis. He summarized his views on the matter in the following letter to his clients.

"Dear Mr. and Mrs. Waters:

"I have completed my research on the impact of a misdescription of property on a lien claim. Unfortunately, the research failed to disclose a definitive answer.

"The statute requires that description sufficient for the purposes of identification be included in the lien claim. However, it also provides that the claim may be amended on leave of court, provided the interests of third parties are not adversely affected. My research has disclosed two major issues arising from our set of facts. The first is whether the amendment portion of the statute applies when there is an 'unambiguous erroneous description.' The second is whether subsequent lien claimants are third parties within the definition of the statute, and if so, whether their interests would be adversely affected by allowing the subject three lien claims.

"The early Washington cases interpreting a statute with the same language as the present statute all held that a property description could not be amended. The latest case on the point (1915) departed from the earlier cases. The court held that where the property description was ambiguous and contained a partially correct description which could be practically corrected by striking the erroneous part, the description could be amended absent proof of injurious effect on third parties. As you can see, this latter case would not control the facts in our case. However, it does show a general attitude on the part of the court to be more liberal in the matter of technical errors. This attitude of liberality has been expressed frequently on other issues by the current members of the appellate court. I checked a few cases in other states that have statutes similar to ours. I did find two states that have held that an unambiguous erroneous description containing no elements of the proper description cannot be amended. However, several other states were discovered which apparently held that such a description might be amended. In conclusion,

I think we would have approximately two chances in five of being successful on this issue.

"Surprisingly enough, there are few Washington cases which discuss the issue as to who is a third party and what constitutes an 'injurious effect.' The only case with any relevant discussion indicated that only those persons who acquired some interest or claimed interest after that claimed by the lien claimant with an erroneous description in his claim were third parties within the terms of the statute. This means that the only possible third parties are those who filed liens after the subject lien claimants. Five lien claimants fall into this category. The total amount claimed for the five is $2,775.

"If these claimants are third parties, would allowing the subject claimants' liens injuriously affect them? Again, we have no Washington cases to guide us on this isuue and little from other jurisdictions. It is clear that, in fact, allowing the subject claimants' claim would decrease the value (sales value) of the property upon which subsequent claimants rely for satisfaction of their claim. However, where the total value of the property exceeds the total value of all claims, is the decreased security meaningful? If so, does it make any difference if the owner of the property has settled subsequently filed claims and obtained and filed lien satisfaction notices? If it does, should we attempt to proceed slowly in effecting a settlement of subsequently filed claims?

"These are but a few of the questions one has to consider. In my judgment, if the court holds that an unambiguous erroneous description can be amended, there would be only about one chance in four of its holding that the facts of our case showed third parties would be injuriously affected by allowing the amendment.

"From a purely academic standpoint, all of the questions are fascinating and ones which might be argued with the greatest degree of conviction. However, as I need not emphasize to you, we are not dealing with an academic question. The practical matter of who is going to pay concerns us.

"We have two methods of raising the issues discussed above. We may refrain from disclosing to the attorney for the subject claimants the fact of the erroneous description and refuse to pay. This would force them to file a foreclosure action and presumably describe the wrong property in their complaint. We would then answer by denying that work was performed on the property and deny that you were the owners at the time the work was allegedly performed. We would, at the same time, file a Request for Admission on these matters of fact. They would have no choice but to admit them. We would then request a judgment based on the pleadings and admissions. At the hearing on this request, the points of law would be argued. If the court held in our favor, that would end it unless an appeal were taken. If the court held in favor of the claimants, we would then set the case for trial and be in the same stage of the game as we are now with Cooper and Peters. We might also at this point make a settlement offer in order to attempt to protect you from possible responsibility for paying the opposing claimants' attorney fees.

"The other method is to bring the issue to the attention of counsel for the subject claimants and use it in an effort to effect a better settlement. If this failed, the issue might also be raised by proper pleadings before trial. However, it could not be raised so directly and might possibly be avoided until trial by skilled pleadings prepared by counsel now aware of the potential pitfall.

"In my judgment, our argument is not going to be too persuasive as a settlement club, though it will undoubtedly be of some help. Any settlement should and almost of necessity does involve complete agreement to the settlement by the client. What has apparently occurred in our controversy is an attorney error compounded by lack of diligence in bringing the controversy to a speedy head. It is not going to be easy for the attorney to explain this to his client. Consequently, he is apt to refrain from disclosing to his client that any serious or potentially serious error has been made. Therefore, if the attorney wanted to settle the matter, he would probably use some other reason to convince his client of the need to settle. The question is, at this late stage, has the attorney discussed the issues with his client and committed himself on all plausible settlement arguments? If he has, he may feel he has no choice but to proceed to trial on the hope that the judgment will be favorable, thus avoiding the necessity of bringing up the unpleasant possibility of a serious error. In my own mind, the only course counsel has is to inform his client of his error and the possible consequences so that the client may be fully informed and make a reasonable decision as to the wisdom of a settlement. What will happen is anybody's guess.

"The decision as to which of the two methods of raising the issue you wish to follow is yours. It is safe to say that any settlement that is made would be acceptable only if it were more than a token settlement. I would say that under the most favorable conditions, the best we could expect would be approximately as follows:

NORTHWEST LUMBER	$ 700.00
SUSSER SHEET METAL	145.00
STUART'S CABINETS	300.00
TOTAL	$1,145.00

"I doubt that the attorney for the subject claimants could justify a lesser amount.

"If we were successful at a trial or pretrial motion for summary judgment, your total cash outlay would be nothing. You would, of course, have slightly higher attorney fees, because of the additional time a trial would require. However, a summary judgment proceeding would probably require little if any more time than preliminary negotiations.

"My personal opinion is that the best course to follow would be a combination of the two. I would negotiate from the standpoint that we are not convinced their claims are valid (without emphasizing this point or stating the reason), but even if they were they would only be valid to a certain extent (labor in the case of Stuart and Susser). If it appeared that a reasonable settlement might be reached, the erroneous property description might then be interjected to clinch the settlement. This does run the risk of allowing the attorney time to further commit himself to the client.

"I hope that the above information serves the purpose of informing you of the potential consequences of your decision, insofar as the law and facts make this possible.

"Very truly yours,

"Edward McDuff"

Mr. and Mrs. Waters accepted McDuff's recommendation that disclosure of the error in the property description be withheld and on September 3, 1960, McDuff wrote to Short and Legis to elicit a settlement offer. He noted that Stuart's Cabinets had failed to give the required written notice of an intention to file a lien, and that for this reason only the claim for labor actually performed on the job site was lienable. With regard to Northwest Lumber, he noted that there was no certainty that the lumber which was covered by the invoices on which Northwest relied had actually gone to the Waters' house instead of some of the other houses upon which Moss was then doing work. In addition, he noted that some of the prices charged for the lumber were considerably in excess of ordinary retail prices, and hence substantially in excess of the price usually charged to contractors. Susser Sheet Metal's claim was substantially like that of Stuart's Cabinets, with only the labor performed at the job site being lienable.

At the same time he affirmatively sought offers in compromise from other lienors who had filed liens with proper legal descriptions, but whose liens, because of their failure to give the required notices, were likewise limited to labor performed at the job site. On September 19, 1960, McDuff summarized the situation for his clients in the following letter.

"Dear Mr. and Mrs. Waters:

"I am now in the process of arranging with Mr. Denton of S.S.S. Loan Company to release the reserve fund so that you may complete the house and have some leftover for satisfaction of liens. I should have definite information on the procedure that must be followed within one to two days.

"I talked with the collection agent for Fashion Painters. They indicated that they would refrain from taking any action to collect this account and from bothering you with any further correspondence. Should you hear from them in the future, please advise me immediately so that I may take appropriate steps to eliminate future bothersome occurrences.

"The time for filing liens on your home has now expired. Any person who has not filed a lien by this time may collect money from you only by establishing the existence of a contract between yourself and that particular person. On the basis of our past conversations I would doubt that there are any persons who could establish the existence of such contract. Consequently we are able at this time to compile a fairly satisfactory resumé of your potential responsibility by virtue of filed liens. The liens filed to date, together with the amounts, are as follows:

(a)	Northwest Lumber Company	$	879.00
(b)	Susser Sheet Metal		285.00
(c)	Stuart's Cabinets		735.00
(d)	M. S. Dry Wall		386.00
(e)	Lair Heating		596.00
(f)	Steve Quarto		210.60
(g)	Mountain Glass		1,167.92
(h)	Fox & George		308.19
(i)	Cooper & Peters		1,931.28
(j)	Tiles & Tiles		512.00
	Total Amount Claimed		$7,010.99

"Based on the information you have given me, my estimate would be that the total amount of money required to pay these lien claims will be somewhere between $1,300 and $4,623. The exact amount, of course, depends upon the resolution of some fairly complicated hitherto undecided legal questions and disputed matters of fact.

"The total amount of money paid out which has gone through my hands is as follows:

(a)	Pacific Plumbing	$415.00
(b)	Urlet *et al.*	197.60
	Total Paid Out	$612.60

"In addition to the above, you, of course, paid out a considerable sum for work which should have been included in your contract with Moss Construction. I assume that you are keeping accurate records of these payments.

"To date we have managed to exclude the following unpaid claims from individuals or firms who have performed work on your house. The amounts in some instances are estimated:

(a)	Ade Sand & Gravel	$	100.00
(b)	Lair Heating		607.44
	(Contract price was $1,103.44, lien claim is for $596.00 because of attorney's agreement with my contention that labor only was lienable.)		
(c)	Fox Ornamental Iron Works		200.00

(d)	Galle Roofing Company	524.16
(e)	Pacific Plumbing	25.00
(f)	Urlet *et al.*	26.40
(g)	Burr Paint approximately	500.00
(h)	Fashion Painters	164.32
	Total amount excluded to date	$2,147.32

"You are also probably concerned about the number of hours I have spent on this matter to date. I note from the records that the last resumé I gave you of my time covered the period from our initial interview up through June 30. I have attached an itemized statement indicating the time that I have spent from that date up through August 31. You will notice on the statement a column marked "costs advanced," a total to date of $12.50. I would appreciate receiving a small deposit to cover past and future costs. My prior statement with respect to postponing payment of my fee until completion of several of these matters still stands.

"I hope that by this time you have made some satisfactory arrangement for the installation of the remaining portion of the glass work on your home. I think that it will be wise for you to do everything in your power to complete your home as soon as possible. The current trial docket is running about six months behind schedule, consequently any of these matters that may proceed to trial will not be determined until at least six months after service of the complaint. Of course we hope that we may reach a satisfactory settlement of all of these matters and avoid the expenses and time of the trial. However, in view of the potential long delay it would probably be advisable for you to not postpone completing work on the house until completion of all of the outstanding controversies.

"Thank you for your past cooperation.

> "Very truly yours,
>
> "Edward McDuff"

The attempt to elicit an offer from Short and Legis failed, and on September 29, 1960, they filed actions against the Waters seeking to foreclose on the liens of Northwest Lumber, Stuart's Cabinets and Susser Sheet Metal. On October 21, 1960, McDuff filed answers denying all the material allegations of the complaints and in addition motions for summary judgment based upon the inaccurate legal descriptions of the lien notices actually filed. He also prepared an extensive memorandum in support of the motion. The motion was to have been argued on November 3, 1960, but three days before the hearing Short and Legis telephoned McDuff to concede the propriety of the motion. An agreed order was entered dismissing the action to foreclose the lien, but reserving the right of the claimants to file suit as on an open account. Complaints based on this theory were filed on December 14.

Negotiations with several other lien claimants—M. S. Dry Wall, Lair Heating, and Steve Quarto—had produced settlements based upon the value of the labor performed at the job site. However, on January 3, 1961, McDuff wrote to his clients, reminding them that suit must be filed within eight calendar months after the filing of a lien claim, and suggesting that they not press dormant claims any further in the hope that the statutory time period might elapse without action being taken. He also suggested that they wait to let Northwest Lumber, Stuart's Cabinets, and Susser Sheet Metal make the first settlement offer.

Not all of the lien claimants slept on their rights, and before the end of January 1961 three actions to enforce liens had been filed against the Waters. Among them was the very substantial claim of Mountain Glass for $1,167.92, the balance due on its account, and the claim of Cooper and Peters in the amount of $1,931.28 for masonry work. Another substantial claim was that of Galle Roofing Company for $524.16, but, although asserted in the form of a suit to foreclose a lien, the claim clearly had to be on a contract basis because the notice of the lien had not been filed until October 1960.

What was more troublesome was that Mountain Glass sought to join all other parties who had filed lien notices, asserting that their claims were inferior to Mountain's. This threatened, of course, to upset McDuff's plan to allow time to run to bar the lien foreclosure actions. He succeeded in obtaining an order which limited the power of Mountain Glass to join additional parties to those lien claimants who instituted independent lien foreclosure suits or who sought to join in the Mountain Glass case. Moreover, their attorney informed McDuff that Mountain's office manager and his secretary were both willing to testify that Mr. Waters had agreed to be personally responsible for all the bills covering glass shipped to his house. This supposedly occurred when Mr. Waters delivered a check in part payment of the bill for glass delivered and Mountain's manager indicated that he would make no further deliveries because he did not believe Moss Construction to be financially reliable.

McDuff questioned his clients about this, pointing out that it would make a considerable difference in the value he would attribute to Mountain's claim for settlement purposes. Mr. Waters vigorously denied having made any such promise and, in fact, questioned whether he had ever gone to the Mountain Glass office. A search of the accumulated papers revealed that the check with which the payment in question had been made was drawn by Mrs. Waters and not Mr. Waters. Mrs. Waters remembered taking the check to the Mountain Glass office, but likewise denied making any promise to be personally responsible for all the bills covering glass shipped to their house. Thereafter there was an exchange of interrogatories directed at establishing the number of man-hours of work actually performed at the construction site, as well as the manner in which Mountain Glass had credited partial payments to its bill. It developed that in fact Mountain Glass had applied the partial payments to its ledger account for labor charges.

After a similar exchange of interrogatories related to the claim of Cooper and Peters for masonry work, the two cases came to trial. The manager of Mountain Glass testified as had been indicated. By doubting his ability to remember the visit of a particular customer, McDuff succeeded in having the manager repeat several times that Mr. Waters had made the promise upon the date the particular payment had been made. He then presented the cancelled check to the manager, asking if in fact it had not been Mrs. Waters who had delivered the check. Later, Mrs. Waters testified that it was she who had delivered it.

The result in the cases was a judgment entered on June 21, 1961, for Cooper and Peters in the amount of $969 (or approximately $90 more than the Waters had offered to pay in August 1960) and a judgment for Mountain Glass in the amount of $92.40 (or $230 less than the Waters had offered prior to trial). It was apparent that the trial judge had refused to credit the testimony of Mountain's manager and that he had held Mountain to the application of the partial payments which it had in fact made upon its ledger accounts. The plaintiffs also recovered attorneys' fees of $150 for Cooper and Peters and $75 for Mountain Glass.

As McDuff had predicted, suit was not commenced with respect to one claim—the $512 claim of Tiles and Tiles. Strangely enough, on the date when the suit should have been filed, he received from the attorney for Tiles and Tiles an offer to settle the claim for $322.25. Pursuant to McDuff's advice, the Waters rejected that settlement offer. The result was that within a month suit was filed on the theory that the Waters were liable on an open account. McDuff's answer denied all the allegations of the complaint, and in addition raised the defense that the alleged contract was to stand good for the debts of another and hence was barred by the Statute of Frauds because it was not in writing. Nothing further developed in the case during 1961.

At this point it became appropriate to close out the construction loan and establish the mortgage loan on the house. This, it developed, was not a very difficult matter to accomplish because the title insurance company's legal department determined that the mortgage which the company granting the construction loan had taken was superior to all lien claims, and hence the loan could easily be transferred to a bank and thereafter serviced as a typical mortgage loan.

Again matters entered a period of inactivity. But by January 1962 the three claims of Northwest Lumber, Stuart's Cabinets and Susser Sheet Metal had reached the stage at which the taking of depositions was scheduled and trial dates in March had been set. At this point, Short and Legis made the following offer: The Northwest Lumber case, in which $879 was claimed, could be settled for $400; the Stuart's Cabinets claim, which was for $735, could be settled for $365; and the Susser Sheet Metal claim, which was for $285, could be settled for $200. McDuff advised the Waters of the settlement offers, but suggested to them that, despite the inevitable risk of loss in any trial, a settlement should not greatly exceed the amount of the attorneys' fees they would have to pay to defend the cases. He suggested to them counteroffers of $100 on Northwest Lumber; $150 on Susser Sheet Metal; and between $200 and $250 on Stuart's Cabinets.

The Waters approved, and McDuff wrote to Short and Legis, informing them that his clients had reluctantly agreed to make an offer "to get rid of the cases" in the manner he had suggested to the Waters, with the exception that the $50 margin he had suggested to the Waters was made available for distribution among the three claims as Short and Legis thought appropriate if all three claims were settled. He concluded by saying that he could guarantee immediate payment if settlement were arranged on these terms, because the Waters could obtain the money if not forced to trial, whereas obtaining satisfaction of any judgment might be considerably more difficult. He concluded with the comment that the Waters also had lost a considerable amount because of the insolvency of Moss Construction Co. The counteroffer was accepted immediately.

Near the end of January 1962, McDuff wrote to the attorney representing Tiles and Tiles. He reminded him that he had offered to settle the case for $322.25 at a time when Tiles and Tiles had a valid lien claim. McDuff said that the value of the claim was now considerably less, but that, in order to avoid the cost of litigation, the Waters would offer to settle the case by payment of $250. The month of February passed without response, but early in March the offer made by the Waters was accepted, and an order dismissing the Tiles and Tiles suit was entered by agreement.

There remained only the claim of Galle Roofing for $524.16, against which McDuff had filed a counterclaim for $1000 based on the theory that the lien claim was without merit and an abuse of legal process designed to coerce payment. The case was noted for trial in June 1962, but in April Galle's attorney indicated that a compromise payment of $250 would be acceptable. A check in this amount, together with forms for satisfaction of the lien, was promptly sent to him, but it was not until four months later and an additional prodding letter that the check was cashed and the satisfaction of the lien returned.

QUESTIONS

1. To what extent was McDuff able to "make" the facts of this case?
2. Do you believe he explained too much to his clients? Should he have told them he had to research the various legal questions? Did he allow them to make decisions which he, as attorney, should have made? Why or why not?
3. Was there any impropriety or unethical conduct in allowing companies which had not yet performed work to do so in reliance upon the credit of Moss Construction Co. alone?

4. Was there any impropriety or unethical conduct in delaying the payment of bills until after the time for filing a lien had expired?

5. Are there as many uncertainties in the lien law of Washington as McDuff indicated? If so, can you offer an explanation of why this should be?

6. Would you have discussed with the Waters the error made by Short and Legis and the possible effect it might have upon the advice given their clients? Do you think McDuff's analysis of this aspect of the case is correct? What was his concern about the lawyers committing themselves to their clients?

7. How would you evaluate the threat posed by the statement that the manager of Mountain Glass and his secretary would testify that Mr. Waters had agreed to be personally responsible for all the bills covering glass shipped to his house, assuming that Mr. Waters denied doing so?

8. Was the $50 extra in case all three claims of Northwest, Stuart's Cabinets and Susser were settled in the nature of a bonus for Short and Legis if they could get settlement on all? What problems do you see in leaving it for opposing counsel to decide how to distribute a settlement offer among his several clients?

9. Do you think that Galle Roofing and Tiles and Tiles received more than they would have if they had pursued their claims vigorously? That is, do you think that by being the last two claimants they were able to profit from the desire of the Waters to conclude the entire course of litigation and negotiation?

10. What advantage was possessed by McDuff which was not possessed by any single attorney for the various lien claimants? How was it used by McDuff? Do you believe McDuff spent more time on this case than its efficient handling required?

C. The Relationship Between Litigation and Negotiation

HERMANN, BETTER SETTLEMENTS THROUGH LEVERAGE *

THE CRITERIA OF COMPETENCY

What are the criteria which govern the selection of a trial lawyer who will most effectively represent, and exert the strongest settlement leverage in behalf of, his client, whether plaintiff, defendant, or defendant's insurer? First, he should be a man who is still in *active trial practice.* This doesn't necessarily mean that he must be continually engaged in trying lawsuits; many first-rate trial lawyers are so successful in settlement

* Chapter 7, "The Professional Competency of Trial Counsel—Another Important Lever," pp. 240-245 (1965). Reproduced by permission of the copyright holder, The Lawyers Co-Operative Publishing Co., Rochester, N. Y.

negotiations that they may go for years without finding it necessary to employ their skills in the courtroom.

The second criterion is that the attorney chosen have a *fine trial record* (and one good source of information as to his record is a reliable verdict reporting service, of the kind now in existence in many areas, which includes in its reports of local verdicts the names of counsel involved). The trial record over a number of years should be examined––today, there are very few attorneys who try, to verdict, more than 10 cases annually—in fact, most are lucky to bring 2 or 3 cases through verdict in the course of a year. Indeed, in view of the large number of cases that are disposed of through settlement prior to verdict, the trial, to verdict, of even one case may represent a total of 10 to 20 times that number that were prepared for trial.

The trial record should not be examined merely to count the number of big verdicts secured by plaintiff's lawyers, or the number of defense verdicts achieved by defense counsel. Accurate assessment of the talent of the attorney in question requires a qualitative evaluation of the cases he tried. Thus, many first-rate defense lawyers try cases, not because they feel there is any chance of avoiding liability entirely, but because they believe the settlement demand is too high. Similarly, a plaintiff's lawyer, handling a case involving serious injuries, may go to trial even though he knows the chances of establishing liability are slim.

To the extent that an attorney's trial record should be judged on a quantitative basis, judgment should be made by comparing what the attorney has accomplished with the record of attorneys throughout the nation—and this record shows that, in cases that go to verdict, approximately 60 percent result in verdicts for the plaintiff, and 40 percent result in verdicts for the defense. Better still, the attorney's trial record should be compared with figures showing general verdict experience in the locality in question.[2]

In measuring the trial record of a plaintiff's or defendant's lawyer, the verdicts returned in the cases in which the attorney has appeared should be assessed in the light of final settlement offers and demands made in the case. Thus, if plaintiffs' verdicts are for amounts considerably less than the plaintiffs' final settlement demands, it is reasonable to conclude that at least some of the difference is a product of defense counsel's skill. Similarly, it is reasonable to question the ability of the defense lawyer whose efforts in trying cases often result in verdicts far in excess of the plaintiffs' final settlement demands. And a record of verdicts which are consistently lower than the defense's final settlement offer may, of course, be taken as an indication of special skill on the part of defense counsel.

In assessing the competency of a trial lawyer the verdicts returned in the cases in which he has served should, as has been pointed out, be

---

[2] [Footnotes numbered as in original—Ed.] This information is available in 3 PERSONAL INJURY VALUATION HANDBOOKS AND VERDICT SURVEY FOR THE AREA (Jury Verdict Research, Cleveland, Ohio) .

evaluated statistically. Such an evaluation should be made with respect to the nature of the verdicts—whether for plaintiff or defense. To the extent that the attorney's record varies from the statistically established probability of recovery in a case of the kind in question, his skill, or lack of skill, is indicated.[3] Thus, for example, statistics show that, on a national basis, 73 percent of the verdicts in rear-end collision cases are for the plaintiff; a top-flight plaintiff's lawyer should, of course, do better. On the other hand, a truly skillful defense lawyer should achieve defense verdicts in considerably more than 27 percent of the rear-end collision cases he tries.

Available statistical information as to verdict size[4] makes it possible to judge the skills of a trial lawyer by comparing sizes of verdicts in the cases in which he has appeared with the statistically demonstrated verdict expectancy. A record, in terms of verdict size, which is in substantial excess of the established expectancy indicates, in the case of a plaintiff's lawyer, substantial effectiveness; and, in the case of a defendant's lawyer, the same record raises serious doubt as to his skill. But it is again wise to take into consideration the relationship between the size of each verdict and the final settlement offers and demands made in the case in which the verdict was returned.

Another way of determining a lawyer's trial skills is to talk to the trial judges before whom he has frequently appeared. A trial judge has a unique opportunity to see lawyers in action, and to observe their strong points and weaknesses. And trial judges can ordinarily be counted on for relatively unbiased opinions.

Consultation with trial judges is, obviously, a special problem for insurance companies, which lack regular contact with the Bench. But there is nothing to stop a representative of an insurance company from actually visiting the courts, and talking to the judges. Trial judges will usually find time for such interviews, and will manifest a cooperative attitude.

Ability on the part of a trial lawyer can be expected to earn him the respect of those lawyers who have appeared as his adversaries in the courtroom. In this connection, it is important to distinguish between respect and popularity. A lawyer may be popular with his trial adversaries, not because he is skilled, but, on the contrary, because he is a pushover at the settlement table. On the other hand, a trial lawyer may be decidedly unpopular precisely because of his ability to apply settlement leverages effectively.

It should be borne in mind that it is difficult to determine whether the talents of a particular lawyer are viewed with respect by asking a

---

[3] For statistics as to probability of establishing liability in particular types of cases, see 3 PERSONAL INJURY VALUATION HANDBOOKS (Jury Verdict Research, Cleveland, Ohio).

[4] See 1, 2, and 2A PERSONAL INJURY VALUATION HANDBOOKS (Jury Verdict Research, Cleveland, Ohio).

brother lawyer who ordinarily tries the same kind of cases and on behalf of the same side of the controversy. Thus, one plaintiff's lawyer is not likely to give an accurate evaluation of the respect the abilities another plaintiff's lawyer have earned, if only for the reason that every lawyer suffers from the human failing of reluctance to state that someone else is his equal or superior.

The trial lawyer's professional library is a not insignificant index of his competency. Today, a good personal injury lawyer often owns more medical books than many a doctor, and, of course, he also has the latest and best texts and services covering substantive law, procedure, and trial practice.

There are additional guides that are helpful in discovering talented trial lawyers. Has he published treatises, or law review articles? Law publishers and law journals seek out only the best men to write for them, and it is only the first-rate attorney who so matches the fast pace of his practice with efficiency in his accomplishments that has time to engage in this extracurricular writing.

Look into the attorney's activities in bar association and other professional organizations. This kind of activity is characteristic of the capable lawyer who looks forward to attendance at local and national meetings for the opportunity to learn—and impart learning—that they afford.

It is obvious that not all of the sources of information as to a trial lawyer's competency is available in every instance. But it is rare that none of them is available, and securing maximum settlement leverage requires that as many as are available be made use of. Time expended in the investigation will be more than paid for in settlement dollars.

NOTE

At p. 24 we noted a correlation between the amounts recovered on personal-injury claims and the frequency with which suit is filed, suits being filed much more frequently upon larger claims. A similar correlation exists between the amounts recovered and the frequency with which the suits go to trial, trial being begun more frequently in the case of large recoveries. That correlation does not exist with respect to suits that go to verdict, and once in trial large suits are no more likely to go to verdict than other suits. See Rosenberg and Sovern, *Delay and the Dynamics of Personal Injury Litigation,* 59 Colum. L. Rev. 1115, 1126-1137 (1959). A number of factors appear to produce these results. As Rosenberg and Sovern suggest, for small claims the expense of litigation may make both parties more willing to compromise because trial would result in victory for neither party. When large claims are involved, the parties may prefer the uncertainties of waiting to the certainty of surrendering a large sum. To put it another way, they may not want to make a difficult decision until the last moment possible. A large case does not get the careful and deliberate attention which will be required for compromise until the pressure of an impending trial forces a realistic appraisal of the case.

The pressure of trial provides an occasion for educating the opposite party and his attorney with respect to the weaknesses in his case and the strengths in the case against him. At that time, even if he has not done so earlier, the attorney will most likely give careful attention to what his opponent has prepared for use at trial through depositions, interrogatories, and other discovery techniques. Possibly the opponent will have furnished copies of medical reports which he plans to use at trial, and the attorney can compare them with those he has obtained. The taking of depositions provided a preview of how prospective witnesses perform under questioning, and it may be possible to predict how their testimony will affect the jury. Assignment to a particular judge and selection of the jury eliminate more of the chance factors of litigation. Both sides are now in a better position to make a judgment about how the trial probably will go if pursued to verdict. They now know enough about what they are discussing to be able to engage in realistic negotiations.

Of course, the negotiations are realistic only if one has done enough to educate his opponent about the case. Unless this has been done, he may be thinking about an entirely different case from the one which can and will be presented absent settlement, and the divergence of views may make agreement impossible. Upon occasion, it may be desirable to withhold information about a case from the opponent, relying upon surprise or some version of trial by ambush to produce a better result than that which could be agreed upon. Generally speaking, however, the lawyer who wishes to protect his client from the unavoidable chance elements of a litigated result must educate his opponent, both as to the law and the facts, and to do so he must have made effective use of discovery procedures. Indeed, he may have used them primarily for the purpose of education rather than for the purpose of obtaining information. Because the same procedures are so important to cases which do go to verdict and judgment, it is not surprising that effectiveness as a litigant makes a lawyer effective as a negotiator in dispute settlements.

D. Negotiating From Weakness

Ordinarily, a party who has little or no negotiating power must capitulate to the demands of his stronger bargaining partner. This is not necessarily the case, however, and one with little or no bargaining power may succeed by appealing to either the noble or the ignoble traits of his bargaining partner. As Professor Edwards and White pointed out in THE LAWYER AS A NEGOTIATOR (1977), Brer Rabbit succeeded in getting what he wanted by pleading with his captor that he not be thrown into the briar patch. The soldier who throws down his gun and advances with hands in the air usually is successful in negotiating for at least the preservation of his life. Sickly Asian beggars, sometimes carrying sightless children, turn their weakness into a bargaining power for the alms they seek simply by remaining in one's presence. A child sometimes gets what he wants by holding his breath. An appeal to the bargaining opposite's view of the better side of himself, particularly if reinforced with a modicum of publicity, may succeed in producing a much more favorable result than could be obtained with full use of a limited bargaining power.

The following case history presents an opportunity to observe how a weakness may, paradoxically, serve as bargaining power.

GEORGE NIVENS' CASE

or

AN EMBEZZLER'S LIFE IS NOT AN EASY ONE*

In March 1962, George Nivens, an accountant by training and the credit manager of Friendly Finance Co., Seattle, Wash., informed his immediate supervisors that within the last 11 months he had embezzled $63,000. He had lost all of it in gambling, primarily betting on horses. His technique, simply explained, was to establish false loans for which he established a repayment schedule from a continuing series of false loans. He had hoped to repay the amount he had taken out of winnings before completion of the annual audit then taking place, but was unable to do so.

He was arrested, charged with statutory larceny, pleaded guilty, and was sentenced to imprisonment for not more than 15 years, with a recommended minimum sentence of two years. The Board of Prison Terms and Paroles accepted the recommendation. Receiving one-third time off for good behavior, Nivens in fact served only 15 months at the Walla Walla penitentiary and was released in July 1963.

At the time of his arrest Nivens was 36 years old, married, and the father of three girls, the oldest of whom was 13. He was earning $450 a month and considered his work "okay," but boring. His wife, Helen, who was employed at the time, continued to support the family during his term in prison and took him into their home upon his release. She had known nothing of his embezzlements while they took place, and in fact, because she had established a budget and kept the records of household expenses, it would have been impossible for him to make any contributions to family living expenses without arousing her suspicions.

Nivens spent the remainder of the summer of 1963 at work as a laborer maintaining the grounds at the University of Washington. In fall of 1963 he responded to an advertisement of Bellingham Lumber and Supply, Inc., seeking the services of a qualified accountant to serve as their office manager. He made full disclosure of his prison record. Impressed by his otherwise perfect record as well as his abilities as an

* Reproduced by permission of the copyright holders, Robert L. Fletcher and Cornelius J. Peck.

accountant, the management of Bellingham Lumber and Supply gave him the job, taking a few extra precautions, such as the requirement of two signatures on all checks. The management of the Bellingham First National Bank, at which the supply company keeps its account, the supply company's auditors, and its two major suppliers were confidentially informed of his background, but otherwise the matter remained unknown in the community. His salary was fixed at $7,200 per year, or $600 per month. His work proved to be excellent, and at the beginning of 1965 his salary had been increased to $8,400 per year or $700 per month.

In December 1964, however, he was visited by a representative of Rockport Accident and Indemnity Co., which had paid to Friendly Finance Company the sum of $65,000 in satisfaction of its obligations under the bond it had issued covering his work as credit manager. The matter had been reactivated by the bonding company when in the course of a routine check of the persons for whom it stood as surety with Bellingham Lumber and Supply, it had discovered that he was the George Nivens formerly employed by Friendly Finance. The representative had stressed the importance of establishing a repayment schedule. Nivens readily agreed that it was his obligation to repay the sum, but had asked for additional time because personal bills which had accumulated during his time in prison still had not been paid. In addition, he urged the Rockport representative to help him keep the matter quiet because he did not know what would happen if his prison record became generally known in Bellingham. The Rockport representative told him then, "Rockport won't persecute you if you are reasonable."

However, on January 11, 1965, Nivens was served at home with a summons and complaint prepared by the Seattle law firm of DeForest, Porter, and Rudd demanding judgment in the sum of $65,000 with interest at 6 percent per annum from April 15, 1962. The complaint was a tremendous emotional shock to Mrs. Nivens, who found particularly objectionable the formal allegations of the complaint to the effect that Nivens and his wife were husband and wife, ". . . and that all acts herein alleged done by them were done for and on behalf of the marital community composed of them." In fact, the complaint made no mention of embezzlement, but instead alleged merely that within the three-year period preceding the filing of the complaint the defendants became indebted to Friendly Finance Co. of Seattle in the sum of $65,000, which had not been paid, and that the claim against the defendants had been transferred to Rockport for a valuable consideration.

The next day Nivens telephoned Alfred White, the attorney who had signed the complaint to discuss the matter, and then wrote a letter to him containing the following:

"Dear Mr. White:
"I want to repeat what I said during our telephone conversation—I've never denied the debt and I've never refused to pay it. Mr. Geraghty's file should bear me out. I was approached but one time. When R. J.

Geraghty left our house, I had the understanding that Rockport would allow me a period of time, but that I would again be contacted. I can't remember his exact words, but he said 'Rockport won't persecute you if you are reasonable.' Obviously, they haven't, and my appreciation can't be put on paper. But I've never forgotten the obligation.

"We were both shocked by the summons, but my wife is an emotional wreck. I know that civil action would destroy her and ruin our future.

"It's ironic that the summons came at this time because I was going to Rockport next week and talk to someone about a fidelity bond. And, I was going to see Mr. Geraghty to discuss a repayment plan. The company covering our comprehensive here at Bellingham Lumber & Supply is Rockport. What will be my status when I apply for a fidelity bond? This question is very important now.

"Specifically, you wanted me to outline a repayment plan. What can I tell you beyond that I will sign a note, and state I'll repay you a fixed amount each month for as long as I work, or until the note is paid? Will you accept 5 percent of my gross earnings each month?

"Our assets are few. We have a newer home, with an equity of about $400. We own two cars. A few weeks ago the 1953 Plymouth was totalled out while parked in front of our home. With the $165 release money we've purchased a 1956 Studebaker. The other car is a 1948 Studebaker. We have the usual furnisings and negligible savings.

"I realize that this is a big loss for Rockport. I know they can't file it and forget it. In view of all this though, I hope they will permit me to 'move ahead.' Through the kindness of my employers I've done very well here. I've worked hard and I've worked seven days a week making up for my past. And I've got a good job now. Financial reward will come, too. And as it comes, my debt will reduce more. But as I look at possible court action, I can't be blessed again to overcome that obstacle too.

"With the past now passed, I've got a good future. I'll do anything within reason to cooperate with Rockport. I've been given a real chance, I don't know if I'll ever get another.

"Mr. White, call me, please, at FE 3-3333 or HI 4-4444.

"Sincerely,

"George Nivens"

After another telephone conversation, Mr. White replied by letter stating the following:

"Dear Mr. Nivens:

"Pursuant to our telephone conversation, we are enclosing a Demand Promissory Note for $65,000, payable to the order of Rockport Accident and Indemnity Co. You and your wife will both have to sign this Note and have your signatures acknowledged in front of a Notary Public and then return the Note to this office. Upon receipt of the signed Note, Rockport will discontinue action on the lawsuit which has been commenced against you.

"As I explained to you by telephone, we expect you to arrange a payment program to Rockport in as substantial amounts as possible, taking into consideration minimum personal needs to support your family. Payments should commence February 1965, and continue thereafter on a monthly payment basis. We request that you prepare a financial statement detailing your income and minimum needs and estimating your future potential income which you can reasonably expect to achieve. Upon the basis of this statement you must allow for maximum monthly payments to Rockport. We request that Rockport be supplied with a copy of this statement.

"Giving the Promissory Note to Rockport does not reduce or lessen in any way your obligations to make restitution to Rockport, nor does it lessen Rockport's rights against you. The success of the payment program which you establish for yourself will depend solely upon you and your willingness to proceed with restitution and monthly payments in satisfactory amounts.

"Very truly yours,

"DE FOREST, PORTER & RUDD

"By

"Alfred White"

Helen Nivens refused to sign the note because she had taken no part in the crime and had received no part of the money which George had embezzled. She looked upon the demand that she sign the note as some sort of confession that she, too, was guilty of criminal conduct or responsible for what had happened. Nivens sensed that their marriage was imperiled, and decided to place no more pressure upon her. He decided that he must have legal advice, and that it would be best to retain a lawyer in Seattle rather than a Bellingham lawyer. Accordingly, he brought his problem to Vernon David of Waterhouse, Porter, Goltra, and David.

David gave consideration to the relief which might be obtained through bankruptcy and the possibility that the debt to Rockport would not be discharged because Section 17(4) of the Bankruptcy Act, 11 U.S.C. 34(4), provides that a bankrupt is not discharged of debts which ". . . were created by his fraud, embezzlement, misappropriation or defalcation while acting as an officer or in any fiduciary capacity." He concluded that Nivens' employment as credit manager neither constituted employment as an "officer" nor in a "fiduciary capacity." But bankruptcy would involve undesirable publicity and probably make current knowledge of the reason for the debt. Moving to a non-community-property state would give Helen Nivens the protection she desired against having any income she might earn subjected to Rockport's claim, but it would not protect any salary Mr. Nivens might earn in that state because of his individual liability. The complaint had been filed more than three years after

Nivens had taken most of the money, but RCW 4.16.080 provided that the statute of limitations did not begin to run until discovery of facts constituting the fraud. Conceivably it could be successfully argued that the statute began to run at such time as Friendly Finance could have discovered the embezzlement if it acted with due diligence upon the facts of which it did have notice. The strongest argument appeared to be that the debt was a separate obligation of Mr. Nivens and not collectible out of community assets.*

David discussed the matter with Mr. White by telephone, and on January 22nd wrote to him making a formal offer concerning a payment program. He prefaced his letter with the observations that in his opinion and on the authority of *McHenry* v. *Short*, 29 Wn.2d 263, 186 P.2d 900 (1947), there was no community liability. He further observed that unless Rockport would renew its surety bond for Nivens, he would be unable to continue in the employment of Bellingham Lumber and Supply. In addition, he reminded White of Helen Nivens' adamant refusal to become individually obligated to pay any portion of the $65,000. Specifically he offered to pay $10,000 at the rate of $75 a month with interest at 6 percent per annum on the declining balance, giving a note which would be accepted as payment of the original obligation. In addition, Rockport would obligate itself to continue bonding Nivens, either under the blanket premium applicable to Bellingham Lumber and Supply, or at a special individual premium, for so long as Nivens made regular payments on the note.

White replied to the letter, stating that he would forward it to Rockport Accident and Indemnity Co. for review and consideration. He further stated that he would advise Rockport that in his opinion the acts of embezzlement did create a community obligation, citing *Local No. 2618* v. *Taylor*, 197 Wash. 515, 85 P.2d 1116 (1938); *La Framboise* v. *Schmidt*, 42 Wn.2d 263, 254 P.2d 485 (1953); and the case of *McHenry* v. *Short*, upon which David had also relied. A month later the answer came, and on February 17, 1965, White wrote to David informing him that the offer had been rejected. Rockport wanted to receive a demand promissory note for the full amount due, signed by Nivens as manager of the community, or the suit would be processed to judgment.

White and David then discussed the possibility of transferring the case from the Superior Court of Whatcom County, in which Bellingham is located, to the Superior Court for King County, in which Seattle is located, so as to minimize the possibilities of adverse publicity. Ultimately they decided that White should take the depositon of Mr. Nivens. It might then be possible to have the controversy over community liability settled on motions for summary judgment, supplemented with affidavits and possibly stipulations of fact. The taking of the deposition occurred in David's office on June 11, 1965.

---

* A detailed description of the community property law of Washington may be found in Cross, *The Community Property Law in Washington*, 49 Wash. L. Rev. 729 (1974).

White tested Nivens on his claim to have lost all the money. Nivens said that some of his largest losses came on five or six days when he had left his home, gone to the Seattle-Tacoma airport, and telephoned his office to report that he was sick. He then flew to Portland, San Francisco, or Los Angeles for an afternoon at the race tracks, returning to Seattle in time for a late dinner. Other losses of $1,000 he explained could take place just as easily as one can pick up a telephone and make a local call. Ultimately he lost everything he had taken, and none of the funds remained.

White inquired primarily, however, into the question of whether or not Nivens had ever used any of the embezzled funds for household purposes. Nivens insisted that he had not, because his wife would have become aware that he had additional income. Indeed, he could recall a few incidents upon which he seriously discussed with his wife their budgeting problems when he had several thousand dollars in his wallet. When asked if he didn't occasionally dip into the money he had taken, he replied, "No. My being an accountant and professional, and that type of person by nature, no, I wouldn't. This had to be separate and distinct."

Ten days later Mr. White filed his motion for summary judgment along with a supporting brief. In the letter transmitting copies to David he reminded David after the deposition had been taken that it would be desirable for Nivens to propose settlement terms, and expressed the hope that a settlement might still be reached. David, who had previously filed an answer denying liability on the part of the community and specifically raising the defense that the statute of limitations had run, also filed a motion for summary judgment in favor of the community.

White's suggestion produced the following offer, which David summarized in a letter written on June 24, 1965: (1) The complaint would be dismissed; (2) Nivens and the community would bind themselves to pay Rockport the sum of $75 per month, beginning September 1, 1965, and every month thereafter until Mr. Nivens reached the age of 65 or sooner died. The claim would not survive his death, nor would he be required to make payments in any month in which he was unable to work for two or more weeks because of accidental injury or sickness or unemployment if reasonable efforts were made to obtain employment. He emphasized that this offer was based upon Nivens' belief that, community property laws entirely aside, he was under an obligation to repay Rockport for the loss he caused the company, provided that the action he took was consistent with his obligations to his wife and children. He also stressed that Helen Nivens objected most strenuously to any attempt to make her personally liable or to apply any portion of the income she might earn to satisfaction of the debt. She would leave her husband if any such agreement were made. He assured Mr. White that $75 per month was the maximum amount Nivens could pay and was perhaps slightly high in terms of his ability to respond.

On August 9, 1965, White replied to David's letter, first by phone and later by confirming letter. Rockport did not agree with some of the proposed terms, but, said White, they were not too far apart regarding the terms of restitution. He proposed that Nivens enter into a written contractual obligation on behalf of himself and the community to pay the $65,000 to Rockport. Restitution payments on this amount would initially be $75 per month. Thereafter, Nivens would furnish copies of his federal income tax return, beginning with the 1965 return. In subsequent years Nivens would pay 15 percent of the amount by which his income was more than $1,000 in excess of his 1965 income. There would be no obligation to increase the payments on account of income earned by Helen Nivens, and a moratorium provision could be inserted to cover periods of unemployment. Rockport was to receive an equitable portion of not less than 25 percent of any substantial windfalls received by Nivens, such as inheritances and gifts. It was also to have the right to file a claim against his estate upon death, although the claim would not be applicable to assets contributed by Mrs. Nivens.

On August 30, 1965, David wrote to inform White that the offer of June 24 was withdrawn and the counteroffer of August 9 was rejected. He added that Mr. Nivens was currently unemployed.

During the summer of 1965, disagreements had arisen between stockholders of Bellingham Lumber and Supply, and a newly formed group appeared ready to challenge management. The general manager of the company felt he could no longer risk the exposure involved in having the office run by a person convicted of embezzlement and accordingly he had terminated Nivens' employment. This situation prevailed for only a few months because the challenging group did succeed in electing a new board of directors, which terminated the employment of the general manager. While conducting their search for a replacement, they called upon Mr. Nivens to serve as acting general manager. He, of course, made certain that the new directors were informed of his prison record.

White and David then undertook to set a date for hearing of their motions for summary judgment. Difficulties encountered in arriving at a date convenient to counsel and the court resulted in a delay until November 22, 1965, when argument on the motions was heard by Judge Bliff of the Superior Court for Whatcom County. On Friday, December 3, 1965, Judge Bliff filed a five-page memorandum decision, granting Rockport's motion for summary judgment. He noted that it was Nivens' employment in a position of trust which gave him access to the funds he had taken. Cases in which the community had been absolved of liability for tortious conduct of the husband were, he thought, to be limited to cases of physical violence where the act complained of could have no benefit to the community. Nivens' presence at the race tracks was, Judge Bliff ruled, legitimate community recreation, and expenditures for his recreation were made for a community purpose. With respect to the defense of the statute of limitations, he believed that it would have been unreasonable to require such measures as would have permitted Friendly Finance to discover the defalcations any earlier than they did.

On December 14, 1965, the *Bellingham Bugle* carried a story reporting upon Judge Bliff's decision in the case, setting forth in detail the facts of the case and the names of the parties as well as the legal theories involved. Because the decision was reported as having precedential value, summaries of the *Bellingham Bugle* story were published by other newspapers throughout the state. Some of the papers were rather thick with advertisements for the coming holidays and the stories were accordingly less prominent.

On January 3, 1966, David wrote to the Nivenses, restating an opinion which he had previously given orally that the chances of defeating the Rockport claim against the community were 50 percent. He strongly urged that an appeal be taken. He also enclosed a statement for services rendered, which then exceeded $750, as well as costs of approximately $100, and requested a substantial payment thereon.

The Nivenses decided to follow his advice, and a notice of appeal was prepared. David and White agreed that the case might be heard on an agreed statement of facts. Other details concerning the appeal were taken care of, and briefs for both sides were prepared, printed, and filed. The litigation between Rockport and the Nivenses subsided as the case lay on the appellate docket awaiting argument.

On October 31, 1966, Mr. Nivens wrote to Mr. David, requesting him to drop all action with respect to the appeal immediately. He reminded David that the story in the *Bellingham Bugle* had come to the attention of the U.S. Internal Revenue Service, and informed him that they had already been assessed for the taxes which should have been paid on the money which he had embezzled. He had now been made general manager of Bellingham Lumber and Supply, but the understanding reached upon making the position permanent was that any further unfavorable publicity would result in termination of that employment. Furthermore, the strain on his wife had made her so ill that she had required hospital treatment, and was still recuperating at home. She would probably leave him if anything further were publicized. He did not mean to suggest that he would not pay for the services performed, but he could not stand additional publicity, and hence was willing to agree to any reasonable payment plan.

David proceeded, however, to reach an agreement with White that the case be argued on March 15 or 16, and appropriate arrangements were made with the clerk of the court. He also approached the Associated Press and United Press news services to see whether they would agree not to use the names of the parties upon publication of a Supreme Court decision, but they refused to do so. On January 4, 1967, David wrote to White, suggesting further consideration of the matter before additional costs and fees were incurred by their clients. He proposed that (1) the appeal be abandoned, leaving Rockport with its judgment against Mr. Nivens and the community; and (2) Rockport refrain from executing on the judgment so long as Nivens made payments of $75 per month, with a provision for renegotiation of the payments should there be a substantial change in Mr. Nivens' (but not Helen Nivens') income. He also advised White of the action taken by the Internal Revenue Service, that Nivens had not yet paid his attorney's fees, and that the assets of the community were exempt from execution. Garnishment would only destroy his employment and any possibility of additional payments.

Telephone conversations and a meeting in White's office produced a restitution agreement which began with a recitation of the events of embezzlements, payment by Rockport, and judgment in a suit by subrogation, and then set forth the following substantive terms of agreement:

"1. NIVENS agrees to pay to ROCKPORT or its order the sum of $65,000.00 payable at the rate of $75.00 per month or more, beginning April 1, 1967, and continuing thereafter on the first of each month until NIVENS either reaches the age of 65 or sooner dies, or repays in full this obligation.

"2. Interest shall accrue on this obligation from date until paid at the rate of 6 percent and payments shall be applied first to interest and then to principal.

"3. NIVENS agrees to pay, in addition to the $75.00 per month, a monthly increase of $10.00 for each $1,000.00 or major part thereof that the adjusted gross income of NIVENS and the marital community exceeds $10,000.00 per year. Any income contributed by the wife of NIVENS as wages or salary shall not be included when determining said income. However, income from all other sources shall be included. NIVENS further agrees that the annual federal income tax returns of both he and his wife, whether filed individually or jointly, beginning with the taxable year 1967, will be supplied, on demand, to ROCKPORT for determination of any said pro rata increase.

"4. During the period that this agreement is in force and effect, or during the period of NIVENS' lifetime, whichever is shorter, the monthly payments due and owing hereunder shall be temporarily suspended during any month in which NIVENS is unemployed for a greater portion of that month.

"5. In the event of the death of NIVENS, the obligation due hereunder shall be cancelled and ROCKPORT will not be entitled to file a creditor's claim against the estate of NIVENS.

"6. NIVENS further agrees that in the event that he defaults under the terms of this agreement, files bankruptcy or otherwise attempts to avoid paying the obligation recited herein, that at the option of ROCKPORT the unpaid balance due shall become immediately payable, without notice given, and ROCKPORT shall be entitled to reduce said debt to judgment, and NIVENS agrees to pay reasonable attorneys' fees in the event that legal action is necessary.

"7. ROCKPORT agrees to satisfy the judgment heretofore rendered against NIVENS in the above referenced case, and to accept installment payments as set forth herein.

"Dated this _____ day of _____, 1967.

> "GEORGE NIVENS, individually, and as man-
> ager of the community of
> GEORGE AND HELEN NIVENS
>
> "ROCKPORT ACCIDENT & INDEMNITY COMPANY
> "By _____
>   "Its _____

"STATE OF WASHINGTON)
)ss.
"COUNTY OF   )

"On this day personally appeared before me GEORGE NIVENS, to me known to be the individual described in and who executed the within and foregoing instrument, and acknowledged that he signed the same as his free and voluntary act and deed, for uses and purposes therein mentioned.

"Given under my hand and official seal this _____ day of _____, 1967.

> "NOTARY PUBLIC in and for the State
> of Washington"

On March 8, 1967, David mailed the agreement to Nivens, advising him to sign it, and informing him that it was not necessary for the notary to read the document in order to notarize it. He warned him that the appeal would have to be dismissed by a formal order, but suggested that it was extremely unlikely that any publicity would result. Finally, he requested some payment on his bill for fees and costs.

Nivens executed the agreement, and returned it to David, who, with White, agreed to a dismissal of the appeal. The dismissal received no publicity.

There remained the matter of Nivens' liability for income taxes due on the money which he had embezzled. David decided to let Nivens handle that aspect of his problem with only general guidance. Nivens opened with an offer of paying $50 per month for 12 months, and the Service responded by asking for an additional 20 percent of his income in excess of $7,000 for the next 10 years. Ultimately agreement was reached on the basis of Nivens paying $50 per month for 12 months, 10 percent of his income in excess of $7,000 for the next five years, and waiving his right to deduct for income tax purposes the amount credited to interest under his restitution agreement with Rockport.

QUESTIONS

1. Are you satisfied with the precautions taken by counsel for both parties to prevent publication of George Niven's criminal record? What were they?

2. Why did David explore relief possible through bankruptcy if he knew it was unsatisfactory because of the publicity it would involve?

3. What do you think of the argument David constructed around the statute of limitations? Did it serve any purpose in the long run?

4. What do you think of David's argument that the debt was not an obligation of the community? Do you think it was a factor in bringing about the final restitution agreement?

5. Should White have assumed that Nivens could pay more than $75 per month because that was the amount David first suggested? Would the interest at 6 percent per annum of $65,000 exceed $75 per month? If the payment of interest is deductible for tax purposes, how much was Nivens going to be out of pocket by paying $75 per month?

6. Why was White so cooperative in avoiding publicity concerning the suit? Could he have obtained more for his client by adopting a less cooperative attitude? Did the publicity which in fact occurred injure his client?

7. Do you believe Nivens really lost all the money he embezzled? Does the restitution agreement protect Rockport if he still has all or part of the funds? Would you have insisted upon some clause dealing specifically with that contingency?

8. Note that it was White who invited a settlement offer after the taking of the deposition. Would you have done so? What should David have done if the invitation had not been made?

9. Do you believe David believed that $75 per month was the most Nivens could pay? If not, was it ethical for him to make such a statement to White?

10. What aspect of Rockport's counterproposal of August 9, 1965, presented the greatest obstacle to agreement? Was it worth insisting upon?

11. Why didn't David tell White what were the most objectionable features of the counterproposal?

12. Would you have recommended that an appeal be taken? If so, would you have expected to carry it through?

13. Why did David proceed to agree with White on a date for argument after receiving Nivens' letter of October 31, 1966, directing him to withdraw the appeal? Was it ethical for him to do so, knowing he lacked authorization to continue with the appeal?

14. Would you have insisted upon 1967 income rather than $10,000 as the base from which increased payments were to be computed? When did White and Rockport learn what Nivens' income currently was? Would

you have assumed he could not have bettered his financial situation after 15 months in the state penitentiary?

15. To whose advantage was the provision that payments would be applied first to interest and then to principal?

16. Why was it important to have the judgment satisfied? If you had been White, would you have agreed to do so?

17. What happens if Helen Nivens dies or divorces George and he remarries, establishing a new community? Could White have given Rockport protection against this contingency?

18. Why did David allow Nivens to handle the negotiations with the Internal Revenue Service? Would you have done so? How does Nivens' result compare with the result David's negotiations produced?

E. Negotiation and Publicity

Avoidance of publicity was an important objective for both parties in the case of George Nivens. For Mr. Nivens, however, the threat that publicity would destroy his earning capacity and thus eliminate any possibility of recovery was also a strong bargaining tool. The dangers attending any further publicity effectively ended the opportunity to test his legal defense, which absent those dangers would have been worth pursuing. Cf. *Smith v. Retallick*, 48 Wn.2d 360, 293 P.2d 745 (1956), holding that the community was not liable for an assault and battery committed by the husband, with the consequence that the plaintiff was unable to obtain satisfaction of his judgment from income earned by the husband while married.

Publicity, or the threat of publicity, had important effects in other cases presented earlier. Thus, it seems to be agreed that the effect of publicizing General Electric's first and final offer (p. 122) was to freeze its position and make even minor adjustments less likely. The threat of publicity undoubtedly was a factor in the decision of the heirs to withdraw their contest of the will of Abigail Schnure (p. 25). Counsel for the defendants in the case of Charles Hoague (p. 47) obviously became concerned that publicity concerning the assault might make it impossible to arrange a favorable plea. In the case of Eleanor Bean's Whiplash (p. 17), the insurance company's decision not to appeal the unfavorable decision in the declaratory judgment proceeding, obviously was directed by its concern that the fact finding that it had wilfully mislead an insured, might be given circulation by being printed in the official reports of the decisions of the state supreme court. As indicated in the note at p. 74, EEOC effectively used the threat of publicity concerning AT&T's employment practices as a bargaining tool to obtain a settlement agreement costing the company over $50 million.

Publicity or the threat of publicity had an important effect in each of these cases, but not the same effect and not for the same reason. As with other aspects of the negotiation process, it is possible to say that publicity may be an important factor in producing or preventing agreement. One cannot say that publicity is "good" or "bad" for negotiation, but only that it is a factor of varying significance in the totality of the process and that its effect must be considered in assessing the bargaining positions of the parties.

F. Agreements in On-Going Relationships

Considering the vagueness and uncertainty which may remain even after the most careful use of language in a relatively simple contract, it is at least questionable whether parties ever have reached a full agreement upon any matter. That they had no dispute, may be attributable to the fact that problems did not arise rather than to the completeness of their agreement. In fact, courts do not look to the completeness of an agreement to determine whether it is an enforceable contract, but rather to whether the parties intended to enter into a binding contract. As Professor Corbin puts it, "If the parties have concluded a transaction in which it appears that they intend to make a contract, the court should not frustrate their intention if it is possible to reach a fair and just result, even though this requires a choice among conflicting meanings and the filling of some gaps that the parties have left." 1 CORBIN ON CONTRACTS 400 (1963). Section 2-204(3) of the Uniform Commercial Code adopts the same attitude with its provision, "[e]ven though one or more terms are left open, a contract for sale does not fail for indefiniteness if the parties have intended to make a contract and there is a reasonably certain basis for giving an appropriate remedy." See also Sections 2-305 to 2-311.

It is thus possible to view contracts as agreements to be bound by a court's determination on those matters upon which the parties have not reached agreement. And, where litigation is possible, so is negotiation. In this respect, even agreements made in what could be considered single phase transactions involve a commitment to possible future negotiation.

The commitment to possible future negotiations is much greater and more obvious in on-going relationships, such as the labor-management relation established by a collective bargaining agreement or the landlord-tenant relationship established by a long-term lease. Thus, at least 94 percent of the collective bargaining agreements in effect in the United States contain grievance and arbitration procedures that provide for final and binding arbitration of disputes which arise between the parties (BLS Bulletin 1425-1 (1969)). Even if the procedures thus established are limited to grievances concerning the meaning and application of the collective bargaining agreement, the parties have thus shown their commitment to future negotiation by establishing the procedures for determining what rights were created by that agreement.

It is wrong, however, to view a collective bargaining agreement as the sole source of the rights and obligations of the parties in a way comparable to that of the typical commercial contract for a single phase transaction. The point is well illustrated by the following excerpt from the opinion of justice Douglas in *United Steelworkers* v. *Warrior and Gulf Navigation Co.*, 363 U.S. 574, 46 LRRM 2416 (1960), at 578-581:

"The collective bargaining agreement states the rights and duties of the parties. It is more than a contract; it is a generalized code to govern a myriad of cases which the draftsmen cannot wholly anticipate. See Shulman, *Reason, Contract, and Law in Labor Relations,* 68 Harv. L. Rev. 999, 1004-1005. The collective agreement covers the whole employment relationship. It calls into being a new common law—the common law of a particular industry or of a particular plant. As one observer has put it:[6]

" '. . . [I]t is not unqualifiedly true that a collective-bargaining agreement is simply a document by which the union and employees have imposed upon management limited, express restrictions of its otherwise absolute right to manage the enterprise, so that an employee's claim must fail unless he can point to a specific contract provision upon which the claim is founded. There are too many people, too many problems, too many unforeseeable contingencies to make the words of the contract the exclusive source of rights and duties. One cannot reduce all the rules governing a community like an industrial plant to fifteen or even fifty pages. Within the sphere of collective bargaining, the institutional characteristics and the governmental nature of the collective-bargaining process demand a common law of the shop which implements and furnishes the context of the agreement. We must assume that intelligent negotiators acknowledged so plain a need unless they stated a contrary rule in plain words.'

"A collective bargaining agreement is an effort to erect a system of industrial self-government. When most parties enter into contractual relationship they do so voluntarily, in the sense that there is no real compulsion to deal with one another, as opposed to dealing with other parties. This is not true of the labor agreement. The choice is generally not between entering or refusing to enter into a relationship, for that in all probability preexists the negotiations. Rather it is between having that relationship governed by an agreed-upon rule of law or leaving each and every matter subject to a temporary resolution dependent solely upon the relative strength, at any given moment, of the contending forces. The mature labor agreement may attempt to regulate all aspects of the complicated relationship, from the most crucial to the most minute over an extended period of time. Because of the compulsion to reach agreement and the breadth of the matters covered, as well as the need for a fairly concise and readable instrument, the product of negotiations (the writ-

---

[6] [Footnote numbered as in original—Ed.] Cox, *Reflections Upon Labor Arbitration,* 72 Harv. L. Rev. 1482, 1498-1499 (1950).

ten document) is, in the words of the late Dean Shulman, "a compilation of diverse provisions: some provide objective criteria almost automatically applicable; some provide more or less specific standards which require reason and judgment in their application; and some do little more than leave problems to future consideration with an expression of hope and good faith." Shulman, *supra*, at 1005. Gaps may be left to be filled in by reference to the practices of the particular industry and of the various shops covered by the agreement. Many of the specific practices which underlie the agreement may be unknown, except in hazy form, even to the negotiators. Courts and arbitration in the context of most commercial contracts are resorted to because there has been a breakdown in the working relationship of the parties; such resort is the unwanted exception. But the grievance machinery under a collective bargaining agreement is at the very heart of the system of industrial self-goverment. Arbitration is the means of solving the unforeseeable by molding a system of private law for all the problems which may arise and to provide for their solution in a way which will generally accord with the variant needs and desires of the parties. The processing of disputes through the grievance machinery is actually a vehicle by which meaning and content are given to the collective bargaining agreement.

"Apart from matters that the parties specifically exclude, all of the questions on which the parties disagree must therefore come within the scope of the grievance and arbitration provisions of the collective agreement. The grievance procedure is, in other words, a part of the continuous collective bargaining process. It, rather than a strike, is the terminal point of a disagreement."

G. Failure of Negotiation

Negotiations sometimes fail to produce agreement because the parties have been unable to arrive at an arrangement which is more attractive to both than the lack of agreement. If both ultimately make a sufficiently attractive agreement with others, or find some way to accomplish their objectives, the earlier failure to reach agreement probably was desirable in the sense that the substitute arrangements better serve the interests of the parties. However, parties may fail to reach agreement in circumstances which result in deterioration of the situation of both parties.

Such a failure may occur because of unreasonable expectations held by one or the other of the parties—expectations which the other bargaining party could not alter. For example, when a husband and wife set unrealistic standards for one another, and are unable to compromise their differences, a fiercely litigated divorce may leave both in a worse condition, emotionally and economically. The hard bargaining which took place between New York city newspapers and the unions of their employees presents a comparable failure in the labor relations area. In the attempt to live with the labor conditions established by collective bargaining after a 140-day strike, the *World-Telegram and Sun,* the *Journal-American,* and the *Herald Tribune* merged to form a single newspaper which began publication on September 18, 1966. However, after less than eight months of publication that newspaper, the *New York World Journal Tribune* on May 5, 1967, ceased publication, blaming its demise chiefly upon labor costs. It seems probable that the unions had held unrealistic expectations as to the ability of the employers to pay. The city of New York was left with but two daily newspapers, and the former newspaper employees with greatly restricted employment opportunities.

Negotiations may fail because the ineptness of one or the other of the negotiating parties produces irrational and self-defeating reactions from the other, who becomes willing to forego the known advantages of agreement over lack of agreement because of unrelated matters with great motivational power. Or negotiations may fail because the matter simply is not negotiable.

One of the most conspicuous failures of negotiation in American labor relations is the failure of American railroads and the unions of railroad employees to reach agreement on the subjects of firemen on diesel locomotives engaged in freight and yard-switching operations and the "crew consist" problem. Among the many excellent discussions of the problems are Kaufman, *The Railroad Labor Dispute: A Marathon of Maneuver and Improvisation,* 18 Ind. & Lab. Rel. Rev. 196 (1965), and Levine, *The Railroad Crew Size Controversy Revisted,* 20 Lab. L.J. 373 (1969). According to management, technological changes have rendered unnecessary the services of firemen on freight and diesel locomotives and services of a brakeman in addition to the conductor and switchman who make up the remainder of the nonlocomotive workmen on a freight train. While it is hazardous to present a brief analysis of such a complicated problem, it seems likely that two factors have been of prime importance in producing that failure of collective bargaining. The first factor is that the railroad employers would prefer arbitration to negotiation and bargaining, and feel quite secure in resisting bargaining demands because they believe that the nation could not and would not tolerate a prolonged railroad strike. The second factor is that, because the institutional organization of railroad unions limits their membership to employees performing tasks peculiar to railroading, the objective sought by management would drastically reduce the size and importance of the unions with which negotiations are conducted. Thus, following a 1963 arbitration award made pursuant to emergency legislation, the railroads eliminated 18,000 of their 35,000 firemen. Levine, *op. cit. supra,* at 377. It is self-evident that parties are unlikely to succeed in negotiating the elimination of one of them.

That negotiation is not likely to succeed where the object of one party is the elimination of the other was demonstrated by the "peace talks" which took place in Paris at various times from January of 1969 to January of 1973. The original objective of the representatives of the

United States and the government of South Vietnam was the preservation of the government of South Vietnam, with only such changes taking place as were permitted by the political processes of that government. That objective necessarily required liquidation of the National Liberation Front and abandonment by the government of North Vietnam of the objective of a unified Vietnam. The North Vietnamese denied the legitimacy of the government of South Vietnam and sought to exclude from any government formed to replace it those persons associated with the government of South Vietnam. So long as those remained the objectives of the parties agreement was impossible, and the talks remained "stalled."

On January 23, 1973, President Nixon announced the terms of an agreement to bring an end to the war. Terms of the agreement included recognition by the North Vietnamese that the people of South Vietnam had a right to self-determination, recognition by the United States of the government of North Vietnam, and the establishment of a National Council of National Reconciliation and Concord to organize elections as agreed upon by the parties, looking forward to reunification of the country only by peaceful means. The agreement also provided for removal of all United States troops from Vietnam within 60 days and a ban on infiltration of troops or war supplies into South Vietnam. But by April 16, 1974, the government of South Vietnam announced suspension of talks with the National Liberation Front because of truce violations.

Cool and detached appraisal of the events remains difficult if not impossible. It may, nevertheless, be asked whether agreement was reached in 1973 because the United State's objective had changed to that of arranging for withdrawal from the war with some appearances of dignity, to which the government of North Vietnam and the National Liberation Front acceded, over the protests earlier made by the government of South Vietnam that the draft of the peace treaty amounted to "a surrender of the South Vietnamese people to the Communists."

4. Roles in the Negotiation Process

A. Distinguishing the Advisor Role From the Negotiator Role

Not everyone present in a room in which negotiation takes place is a negotiator, even though his presence may be necessary and may go far to shape the developments in the negotiation process. A lawyer may participate in negotiations as an advisor to the client. The client may conduct the negotiation accepting such suggestions as the lawyer may make and relying upon his advice as to the legal consequences of various undertakings. The advice given by the lawyer may be limited to technical legal matters, or it may be related to matters of strategy and psychology as well as business or personal policy.

Which role is preferable for the lawyer depends in large part upon the negotiating competence of the lawyer as compared with the negotiating competence of those whom he might advise. That competence will vary with the subject matter of the negotiation, as well as the experience of the lawyer and client. In dispute settlements, ordinarily the lawyer's greater familiarity with judicial procedures and the possible outcome of litigation make it desirable for him to conduct the negotiations even though the ultimate right to accept or reject a proposed settlement must remain with the client. Of course, in disputes involving parties who know each other well—divorce proceedings or contested probate proceedings—where correct appraisal of the expectations and determination of the other party is important, the lawyer must be attentive to the advice which he receives from his client.

In commercial transactions or labor negotiations in which familiarity with the methods of doing business or the manufacturing processes involved is of great importance, it may be better for the lawyer to restrict his role to that of advisor because of his client's greater competence. In some situations, such as negotiation of a lease, it may be possible to identify those subjects which involve primarily business or economic judgments and those subjects which involve a judgment about law, assigning some for negotiation to the client and others to the lawyer. It is not unknown, however, for a matter which produces a great legal controversy between lawyers to have so little practical significance to the parties to the negotiation that its resolution is neither necessary for agreement nor rewarding as an activity.

Generally speaking, in addition to his ability to predict the outcome of litigation, a lawyer will have a greater competence than his client in marshalling data or evidence and presenting it in a manner which most effectively supports a particular argument. A lawyer will probably also be more competent than his client at detecting and exploiting weaknesses in the arguments presented by others. He will also probably excel his client in the ability to formulate an understanding in general principles with exact language, and thus be better at stating that understanding in a form which is acceptable to the other party. Generally speaking, a lawyer must be on guard against an excessive legalism which leads him to insist that every contingency be covered even though that matter may have no significance except that the difficulty of resolving it prevents the attaining of agreement. He should also be on guard against using legal arguments stated in highly generalized language as a substitute or cover for the economic realities of a particular business transaction.

B. Separating and Distinguishing Between Client Goals and Lawyer or Negotiator Goals

The stresses imposed upon members of the legal profession by the conflicting objectives which they are expected to pursue are extraordinary. A lawyer is, of course, an officer of the court and expected to behave in a manner befitting that office, always serving and never acting contrary to the public interest. Indeed, he is ethically obligated to divulge to a court those legal authorities which are contrary to the argument he makes or the position he seeks to establish. At the same time, he is expected to give unswerving devotion to the service of his client's interests, relentlessly utilizing every means legally and ethically available for that purpose. He is also expected, at least by his family, to derive sufficient income to earn a living from his activities, and the opportunities for economic gain frequently are great. That more lawyers do not develop a three-way personality split is perhaps amazing. As is true with so many intrapersonal conflicts, the best means for resolving them is to bring them into the open for analysis and conscious appraisal.

For example, the lawyer representing Charles Hoague in the case history beginning at p. 47 recognized a minor conflict between the understandable desire of the parents and Hoague to be released from jail as soon as possible and his professional judgment that the court would be more favorably inclined to lenient treatment if it knew that Hoague had experienced some of the unpleasantness of jail life. That conflict was one which he could easily resolve because it was his professional judgment that in the long run his failure to satisfy his client's immediate desires would be beneficial to the client. However, other aspects of the case involved the lawyer personally because his reputation and record for accurate appraisal with persons with whom he regularly dealt were at stake. A program of rehabilitation imposing conditions restricting the client's activities as the bargained-away terms for a reduced or deferred charge may enhance a lawyer's reputation and record for accurate and dependable appraisal of his clients generally, but may do less than might have been obtained in the way of liberty or freedom if the bargaining turned only on the problems of proof and the possibilities of conviction. On the other hand, the lawyer must not allow any individual client the benefit of a bargained-for plea which comes, not from a careful appraisal of the client's ability to avoid further clashes with the law, but instead from the lawyer's reputation for making such careful appraisals.

As mentioned in the introduction, a lawyer considering a settlement offer in a personal injury case must take care to ensure that his appraisal of the worth of the claim is not affected by a consideration of the amount of flattering publicity which would come from litigation resulting in the recovery of a sum of money as large as the amount offered or possibly larger. On the other hand, he also must guard against the possibility that he will use up an established reputation as an adversary and appraiser of claims for the benefit of a single client if he attempts to obtain more for that client than what in his best judgment is the value of the claim discounted by the hazards of litigation. In short, how he performs as a negotiator or litigator in each particular case will have an effect upon how well he can serve his clients in other cases. As he builds a reputation which will benefit other clients he necessarily builds a reputation from which he benefits personally.

The conflict between the interests of negotiator and client appear in contexts other than those of litigation. Professor Mathews has described an instance in the negotiation of the first collective bargaining agreement after a successful union organizing campaign. The parties had reached agreement on practically every matter which had been brought up for discussion. Management representatives, concerned lest they be charged with bad faith, then informed the union representatives that a shortage of business would soon require layoffs in one of the manufacturing departments. The union representatives, agreeing with management that some employees might interpret the layoffs as having been caused by the agreed-upon wage increases, suggested that the easy way to handle the matter was to lay off the employees immediately rather than after the agreement had been executed. Such a course of action would, of course, have protected the union's reputation from the tarnishing effect of an event which both management and the union recognized as inevitable, but it hardly would have served the interests of the employees who would have been laid off. Indeed, it most likely would have been a breach of the duty of fair representation owed by the union to employees in the bargaining unit, and hence subject to redress under the standards established by *Steele* v. *Louisville & Nashville Road Co.,* 323 U.S. 192, 15 LRRM 708 (1944); *Humphrey* v. *Moore,* 375 U.S. 335, 55 LRRM 2031 (1964), and *Miranda Fuel Company,* 140 NLRB 181, 51 LRRM 1584 (1962). Acceptance of the proposal by the company probably also would have violated Section 8(a)(1) of the NLRA.

The sale of a small company to a larger, unionized company, followed by a consolidation of operations at the plant of the larger company, may produce a conflict of interest between the union and/or its officers and former employees of the smaller company. The seniority list for the consolidated operation might be established by "dovetailing" the two seniority lists previously used when the operations were separate—that is, fixing an employee's seniority on the basis of the total length of time worked for both employers. Alternatively, the seniority list for the con-solidated operation might be established by "endtailing" the seniority of the employees transferring from the former smaller operation—that is, giving them seniority only on the basis of the length of time worked at the plant of the larger employer. "Dovetailing" has an apparent fair-ness and would obviously be preferable from the viewpoint of an em-ployee of the former smaller operation, but "endtailing" can be rational-ized on the basis that in many situations seniority is determined on the basis of the length of time an employee works at a particular plant, even for an employer who has a multiplant operation. "Endtailing," which favors the more numerous employees of the larger company, has an obviously political appeal which may be used by persons seeking elec-tion or reelection to union offices. In *Barton Brands, Ltd.*, 213 NLRB 640, 87 LRRM 1231 (1974), the NLRB concluded that a union violated its duty of fair representation when it "endtailed" the seniority of em-ployees transferred from a smaller operation purchased by the employer largely, if not solely, for the advancement of a political cause of a union official. The reviewing court of appeals disagreed and found that the "endtailing" proposal arose from the rank and file employees and not to serve the political cause of the official. However, it concluded that the Board's order against the union could be enforced because the "end-tailing" had taken place for no other apparent reason than political expediency and that to be absolved of liability the union would have to show some objective justification for its conduct beyond that of pla-cating the desires of the majority of the employees in the unit at the expense of a minority. *Barton Brands, Ltd.* v. *NLRB,* 529 F.2d 793, 91 LRRM 2241 (7th Cir. 1976).

The case illustrates the difficulty of applying the standard of fair repre-sentation to collective bargaining or the processing of grievances. A breach of that duty occurs whenever the union's conduct toward a member of the bargaining unit is arbitrary, discriminatory, or in bad faith. *Vaca* v. *Sipes,* 386 U.S. 171 at 190, 64 LRRM 2369 (1967). In this sense, dis-crimination consists of treating persons or things which should be dealt with similarly in variant ways because of an irrelevant factor. Variant treatment is not discriminatory if it is based upon criteria which are relevant to achieving a legitimate objective. Conduct is not arbitrary if it is controlled by principle even if the controlling principle is not the best which could be formulated. The conclusion that criteria such as race, religion, sex, or age may not be considered relevant factors for producing variant treatment is one easily reached in light of constitutional and statutory provisions condemning their use. But, given the multitude of objectives which legitimately appeal to both management and unions and the variety of ways in which those objectives may be pursued, it becomes extremely difficult to condemn the use of any other particular criterion or principle unless its use can be said to have been solely for the benefit of the negotiator rather than for the employees represented.

An adverse effect upon one group of employees, or even a particular employee, does not establish a case of arbitrary, discriminatory, or bad-faith conduct. In negotiations to establish conditions of employment for the future, unions frequently must choose between objectives which will provide greater benefits for some employees and lesser benefits for other employees. An across-the-board wage increase is more favorable to employees in lower wage classifications than a wage increase costing the employer exactly the same amount but made as a percentage of the existing wage rates. Allocation of a large portion of the economic package to retirement benefits is more favorable to older employees than its allocation to wage increases or a medical plan which provides benefits to dependents. The decision as to which course to follow frequently has political implications within the union, and hence the decision may represent a political judgment rather than an appraisal of what is better for the entire group of employees represented. But can such a decision made by representatives selected on a political basis be said to be a bad-faith action? Any decision on a matter which divides the constituency will have a political effect. It is neither unprincipled nor wrong to make that decision which it is believed will win approval from the greatest number of those represented.

With respect to claims which arise under an existing contract, there is a widely held belief that each claim deserves to be judged on its merits. That belief probably has its roots in the judicial analogy, pursuant to which each man is entitled to justice in his case. If management and a union engage in trading favorable settlements of grievances without regard to their individual merits, they are making unprincipled and, hence, arbitrary decisions. Moreover, the union negotiators have been spared the burden of careful appraisal and presentation of the particular grievances, and the union's reputation has been enhanced by the favorable settlements which it received in the trades. Such an appropriation of the value of the employee's claim for the benefits of the negotiator cannot be justified by the benefit improperly conferred upon other employees, and hence stands as bad-faith conduct.

It is not so easy to apply the fair-representation test to other dispositions of individual grievances under existing collective bargaining agreements. The difficulty arises in large part because so many grievances stem from ambiguities or lack of full and complete agreement by parties who failed to anticipate all the possible situations to which the language they used might apply. In such a case, the disposition of a particular grievance constitutes the completion of the bargaining process. The same lack of standards for determining whether a union violated its duty in pursuing one of a number of alternative objectives in negotiating a new collective bargaining agreement precludes judgment on how well the union performed its representational duties in processing the grievance.

The subject is a difficult and complicated one, and has been the subject of a number of thoughtful articles. See Cox, *Rights Under a Labor Agreement*, 69 Harv. L. Rev. 601 (1956); Blumrosen, *Legal Protection for Critical Job Interests: Union-Management Authority Versus Employee Autonomy*, 13 Rutgers L. Rev. 631 (1959); Aaron, *The Individual's Legal Rights as an Employee*, 86 Mo. L. Rev. 666 (1963).

Personal injury specialists who have a number of claims against persons insured by the same company have occasions upon which they might also engage in a mass settlement of claims. The final result might be financially as acceptable to an attorney who had all of the cases on a contingent fee, and it would not involve the work of preparing the cases or a loss of costs advanced on those cases in which a plaintiff did not prevail. Settlement of a large number of cases might be attractive to an insurance adjuster, whose outstanding case load would be reduced, with a beneficial effect on the reserves he must maintain for the cases assigned to him. It would, of course, be unethical for an attorney to behave in such a manner and should result in malpractice liability to those clients whose cases were settled for less than fair value.

Negotiators must be on guard against other influences adverse to their clients' interests which can be defined with no greater precision than the duty of fair representation. Few persons enjoy having a reputation of being unreasonable or difficult to work with; most persons probably prefer to be considered open, outgoing, and generous. But the open, outgoing negotiator may inform his opposite of all his objectives, priorities, and limitations and yet obtain no equal return of information from the opposite, and thereby greatly weaken his client's position vis à vis the opposite. It is difficult for many people to be uncommunicative or enigmatic, but just such conduct may be necessary to elicit information from the bargaining opposite. Where negotiations take place within a peer group, such as the legal profession, that group may contain a number of friends and close acquaintances. A lawyer representing a client on a single claim or a one-phase transaction may be more concerned about the esteem in which he is held by his bargaining opposite than that of his client. He must not let that concern affect his performance. Union negotiators who have dealt with the management of a company for a number of years may feel it necessary to show that they understand the problems of the industry as well as those on the other side of the table, and in doing so they may fail to obtain for their membership all that is available.

Uncertainty is an uncomfortable state for most persons. Unsettled negotiations, of course, involve a state of uncertainty. The negotiator must guard against the possibility that his desire to eliminate uncertainty which makes him uncomfortable leads to acceptance of proposed terms which are less advantageous than those which could be obtained if he persisted. Indeed, if negotiations are prolonged over a number of days and late into the night, as frequently occurs in labor-management negotiations, matters of physical comfort might, if not guarded against, adversely affect a negotiator's performance. Considerations such as this make it appropriate to give consideration to the psychodynamics of the negotiation process.

5. Psychodynamics of the Negotiation Process

A. PERSONALITY TYPES AND TRAITS

OF NEGOTIATING

From the Essayes or Councels,
Civill and Morall by
Francis Bacon, Lo. Vervlam,
Viscount St. Alban (1625)

It is generally better to *deale* by Speech, then by Letter; And by the Mediation of a Third, then by a Mans Selfe. Letters are good, when a Man would draw an Answer by Letter backe againe; Or when it may scrue, for a Mans Justification, afterwards to produce his owne Letter; Or where it may be Danger to be interrupted, or heard by Peeces. To *deale in Person* is good, when a Mans Face breedeth Regard, as Commonly with Inferiours; Or in Tender Cases, where a Mans Eye, upon the Countenance of him with whom he speaketh, may give him a Direction, how farre to goe: And generally, where a Man will reserve to himselfe Libertie, either to Disavow, or to Expound. In Choice of *Instruments*, it is better, to choose Men of a Plainer Sort, that are like to doe that, that is committed to them, and to report back again faithfully the Successe; Then those, that are Cunning to Contrive out of other Mens Businesse, somewhat to grace themselves; And will helpe the Matter, in Report, for Satisfaction sake. Use also, such Persons, as affect the Businesse, wherein they are Employed; For that quickneth much; And such, as are Fit for the Matter; As Bold Men for Expostulation, Faire spoken Men for Perswasion, Craftie Men for Enquiry and Observation, Froward and Absurd Men for Businesse that doth not well beare out it selfe. Use also such, as have beene Luckie, and Prevailed before in Things wherein you have Emploied them; For that breeds Conficence, and they will strive to maintain their Prescription. It is better, to sound a Person, with whom one *Deales,* a farre off, then to fall upon the Point at first; Except you meane to surprize him by some Short Question. It is better *Dealing* with Men in Appetite, then with those that are where they would be. If a Man *Deale* with another upon Conditions, the Start or First Performance is all; Which a Man cannot reasonably Demaund, except either the Nature of the Thing be such, which must goe before; Or Else a Man can perswade the other Partie, that hee shall still need him, in some other Thing; Or else that he be counted a Honester Man. All Practise, is to *Discover,* or to *Worke.* Men *Discover* themselves, in Trust; In Passion; At unawares; And of Necessitie, when they would have somewhat done, and cannot finde an apt Pretext. If you would *Worke* any man, you must either know his Nature and Fashions, and so Lead him; Or his Ends, and so Perswade him; Or his Weaknesse, and Disadvantages, and so Awe him; or those that have Interest in him, and so Governe him. In *Dealing* with Cunning Persons, we must ever Consider their Ends, to interpret their Speeches; And it is good, to say little to them, and that which they least looke for. In all *Negociations* of Difficultie, a Man may not looke, to Sowe and Reape at once; But must Prepare Businesse, and so Ripen it by Degrees.

As Bacon's essay on negotiating illustrates, one need not be a psychiatrist to have a keen appreciation of the psychodynamics of the negotiation process and the significance of the personality types involved in a particular negotiation. Indeed, the intuitive understanding of the process is probably one of the most valuable traits of the successful negotiator. Conscious attempts to be other than "one's real self" in negotiation situations are unlikely to succeed. They are unlikely to succeed because one is apt to make "mistakes" in living out his adopted personality. They are also unlikely to succeed because the other bargaining parties will probably sense the falseness of the adopted personality, and react negatively to proposals made for lack of confidence in the actor. But this is not to say that one interested in negotiation should not become familiar with personality types and traits in order to enhance his understanding of his own actions and those of persons with whom he deals.

Much of what has been written about psychiatry and the law concerns persons who are psychopathic—persons who might loosely be described as in trouble mentally and out of control. Conceivably one may have to negotiate with such persons, but that presents problems not germane to the negotiation process in general. There are, however, typical personality traits which should be recognized and appreciated in those persons generally considered normal, which includes those with recognizable mental problems who are still in control to the extent of conforming to generally accepted social standards.

(1) Transference Problems

One of the irrationalities affecting the exchange of information between persons attempting to understand a problem is the phenomena which psychiatrists have labeled "transference." Strictly speaking, problems of transference are those which the patient or client encounters in his attempt to understand or relate to the professional whom he has consulted, and problems of counter-transference are those which the professional encounters in attempting to understand or relate to the patient or client who has come to him. See, *e.g.,* Watson, PSYCHIATRY

FOR LAWYERS 4-9, 16-17 (1968); Menninger, THE THEORY OF PSYCHO-
ANALYTIC TECHNIQUE 76-98 (1958). The irrationalities of transference and
counter-transference may affect the effectiveness of communications not
only between lawyer and client but between lawyer and opposing lawyer,
between opposing clients, or between lawyer and opposing client.

The transference phenomenon occurs when the observer attributes
to the person with whom communication is being attempted meanings,
value judgments, and motivations based not upon what he has in fact
observed or heard but instead upon what he is reminded of from a
former experience with another person, whose characteristics are attributed to the person attempting to communicate. Thus, a client impressed
by the social status of his lawyer may, if the lawyer bears a resemblance
to the client's father, attribute to the lawyer characteristics of his father
without regard to whether they are in fact characteristics of the lawyer.
Fear of disapproval may then lead to less than full disclosure of the
relevant facts. Or a lawyer, dealing with opposing counsel and opposing
client, may attribute to one or the other of them the traits of a former
school teacher who hid his deficiencies in stubborn and dogmatic behavior and thus fail to recognize the quick, perceptive, but understanding
approach of a person of intelligence who is open to persuasion.

If time and expense were of no significance, preparation of a person
for the practice of law would probably include a period of psycho-
analysis to enable him to understand his reactions to the people whom
he will counsel or with whom he will negotiate. Unfortunately, lawyers
do not receive such a preparation for dealing with the intense interpersonal relationships in which they will be involved. It is desirable,
however, for a lawyer to engage in a deliberate and explicit analysis of
his social and economic background and attempt to recognize the manner
in which it will affect his relationships with other persons. Review of
one's emotional responses to characters in novels, plays, movies, and television programs may give insight concerning the value system with which
one judges others and their conduct.

Some of the tests suggested for detection of counter-transferences in the
relationship between a psychiatrist and his patient seem useful in detecting the presence of a transference or counter-transference in negotiation situations. Thus a feeling that the other person is incomplete,
unreal, or mechanical may result from a transference. Persistent tardiness or carelessness in regard to arrangements for conferences, or persistent
drowsiness during negotiations despite adequate rest, should serve as a
warning. Obvious attempts to obtain approval from or engage in arguments with a client, a compulsive tendency to repeat certain points, and
a strong personal and emotional response to arguments or statements are
also indicative of the phenomenon. The same is true if the negotiator
finds himself reliving the counseling or negotiation session in an em-
bellished reverie. The list could be made longer without becoming complete. See, *e.g.*, Menninger, THE THEORY OF PSYCHOANALYTIC TECHNIQUE
88-93 (1958). The short of it is that one engaged in negotiations should

be willing to engage in introspective evaluation of his reactions and conduct and an analysis of the conduct of others for the purpose of determining whether the communication process has been affected by the irrationality of a transference. A brief consultation with a partner or associate who is familiar with the lawyer but not involved in the relationship may provide insights to the cause of the transference which are not apparent to the lawyer.

In making such an analysis, one should be aware that he is not concerned merely with one person's reaction to another as a fixed relationship. He is instead concerned with how one person reacts to another person's reactions, or with how the persons interact with each other.

(2) Nonverbal Communications

An accomplished negotiator is aware that many communications are nonverbal, and he is attentive and observant so that he may learn as much as possible about the persons with whom he is dealing from those communications. Indeed, they may be among the most valuable communications he receives, since it is quite possible that the party making the communication is totally unaware of the fact that he is doing so. He may thereby disclose an appraisal of the status of the negotiations which he has attempted to hide in the statements he makes orally or in writing.

The homely advice that a handshake should be firm but friendly is so prevalent that such a greeting may have no significance, but one which is excessively forceful may be a better indication of the greeter's desire to make a good impression than it is of the strength of his forearm. The palm which is warm and moist strongly indicates that the greeter has reached that state of tension at which the sympathetic division of his autonomic nervous system has produced these involuntary signs of the "fight or flight" reaction. That phenomenon may also be manifested in the dilation of the pupils of his eyes or visible perspiration produced by the stimulation of sweat glands. The same direction from the autonomic nervous system probably caused a sinking feeling in his stomach as the flow of blood to the viscera was cut off and redirected to his brain and skeletal muscles. The excess of adrenaline in the blood supplied those muscles may produce foot or hand tapping or even involuntary muscular twitching. These reactions may occur, of course, at any time during negotiations. If they do, the observant negotiator will attempt to determine not only what was the cause, but whether to discontinue the negotiations until tensions have dropped or to attempt to pursue the matter to an immediate conclusion.

Internal tensions may be manifested in other ways. Thus, as emotions and tension increase, the voice level generally rises. Nervous laughter or giggles likewise reveal internal tensions. It is not only Frenchmen who talk with their hands. The relaxed and confident person is likely to gesticulate with opened hands and wide circular movements. The person who feels tense and threatened is more likely to use clenched fists and jabbing motions. The person who is confident of his position in the negotiations will be willing to sit at the table or desk, whereas the person who is dissatisfied with the current posture of negotiations will be inclined to manifest his desire for a change by movement in his chair or even by moving about in the room.

Persons who are interested, confident, and assured will generally maintain eye contact with someone with whom they are conversing. One who looks sidewise while speaking perhaps does so because of his lack of confidence in the accuracy of his statement or the power of his position. A person may similarly indicate such lack of confidence by partially covering his mouth with his hand while speaking. Even the way in which arms or legs are positioned may reflect a person's inner feelings, as when a man brings his arms together before him in the protective position assumed by boxers. A surprising number of people unconsciously indicate their agreement or disagreement with statements by nodding or shaking their heads. A yawn or obvious drowsiness may indicate more than a lack of sufficient rest the night before.

Physical movements may also indicate interest or approval. Acceptance of drafts, exhibits, or samples, the taking of notes, and physical examination of a site involved give such indication. A person who stops taking notes or making calculations manifests a change in attitude, perhaps a loss of interest or a conviction that agreement will not be reached in that session. A glance at a wrist watch or wall clock conveys a message that the actor is becoming bored or that there are other engagements which he wishes to make. Usually, one engages in such conduct unconsciously and is therefore unaware of the message being communicated, but such movements may be put to use for the purpose of conveying a message one does not wish to state. Indeed, there is the story, perhaps apocryphal, of the students of the psychologist Skinner who managed to confine an otherwise peripatetic instructor to one corner of the lecture room through an agreement that it would be his "reward corner," from which his comments provoked active note-taking, inquiries, and animated discussion not given comments spoken elsewhere.

People communicate much to one another in the distance which they place between themselves. One does not approach closely an authority figure or one of whom he is in awe, at least not if that person is standing or seated at the same level. Friendliness, trust, and agreement brings persons physically closer together, whereas distrust or growing antagonism tend to make persons move apart from one another so long as they consider themselves equals in power. On the other hand, one who believes he has the advantage in power may draw closer to the bargaining opposite as his distrust or antagonism grow. Not only has the negotiator who moves out from behind his desk to sit in the same style of chair as he has offered to his bargaining opposite given a friendly suggestion of equality of position; he has removed what may be a barrier in more than a physical sense. A return to the desk or an increase in the distance between the parties may signal his unstated conclusion that negotiations are not going well and that agreement seems further away than the person moving originally thought. An accomplished negotiator will therefore watch the physical movements of his bargaining opposite for the indications they may give of his appraisal of the bargaining situation and his willingness to reach agreement. Obviously, one should not rely upon such movements as infallible indicators, but likewise one should not ignore them.

Clothing also can tell much not only about the wearer but about his appraisal of the person with whom he has met. The man who appears in his "Sunday best" for a meeting gives good evidence of his standards of taste and level of sophistication. He also reveals that he holds the other in esteem. The president of a company or a senior partner in a law firm, enjoying the confidence that comes from the power of position, much more easily discusses a problem with a subordinate while wearing sports clothing than would the subordinate if the situation were reversed. Indeed, a moment's reflection about the many times when one has decided what clothing he will wear for a particular day or occasion should be convincing proof that the clothing worn says much about what the wearer thinks about a situation and the messages he desires to communicate.

Ordinarily one is not late for an appointment which he views as important and of potential benefit. An early arrival may thus signal much about how the person feels about the matter to be discussed. If he is late, the length of time which provokes an apology and the elaborateness of the apology tells much about the esteem he holds for the party with whom he is meeting. The negotiator who attends to the physical needs and comfort of a bargaining opposite not only has done favors which create a sense of obligation but has manifested that he is sufficiently relaxed and confident that he can give attention to needs other than his own. The negotiator whose file is so well organized and familiar to him that he can promptly produce the document or information required has thereby given an indication of his desire to reach agreement and his understanding of the bargaining situation. The negotiator who is unfamiliar with his file or whose file is disorganized is less likely to be ready to reach agreement.

Of course, one of the difficulties encountered in assessing nonverbal communications is that, just as they have been described here, many of them can be learned and put to use by negotiators who desire to send out false messages. But the same is true of the verbal communications. The accomplished negotiator must learn which of the nonverbal communications he will trust just as he must learn which of the verbal communications he will credit.

(3) *Uncertainty, Ambiguity, Silence, and Delay*

As indicated in the excerpt from Hermann's book, BETTER SETTLEMENTS THROUGH LEVERAGE, *supra* p. 13, and the note on the *General Electric* case *supra* p. 146, uncertainty is a very important device for producing agreement. Uncertainty is also an unpleasant state which most people do not enjoy. We do not worry about *whether* we will grow old or die; we worry about *how* we will grow old or die. We do not worry about whether there will be another day tomorrow; we worry about whether it will rain and spoil an outing we have planned. And we naturally seek to eliminate as many of our worries as we can.

The professional negotiator must learn, however, to live with uncertainty and even to create it so that his bargaining opposite will seek the certainty available in accepting the negotiator's proposal. The lawyer engaged in dispute settlement not only must learn to tolerate uncertainty himself. He must, through advice and counseling, eliminate as many as possible of his client's uncertainties and give him support to tolerate those uncertainties which cannot be eliminated.

One method for creating uncertainty is by making ambiguous statements which have a plausibility to one who considers them. As Hermann points out, the statement or demand which is ridiculous or implausible will not create uncertainty. Another method of creating uncertainty is to remain silent about a matter of common interest. The social nature of most people makes it difficult for them to tolerate long periods of silence while in the company of others. The negotiator who has the strength to say nothing may be able to force his bargaining opposite to speak. If the bargaining opposite does speak, the negotiator probably has gained some information about the opposite's view of the matter and the range of possible settlement, while having disclosed none of his own views. The negotiator who remains an enigma to his bargaining opposite may likewise provoke comments or inquiries which will give him valuable information about the opposing side. The negotiator who is transparent will do no better than the poker player who holds his cards so that the other players may see them.

(4) *Territory or Situs*

Robert Ardrey's book, THE TERRITORIAL IMPERATIVE (1966), has been the subject of considerable debate. Some consider it to be an important contribution to our understanding of life processes, while others have criticized it as an unscientific, popularized presentation of serious but unconnected studies. One of Ardrey's propositions is that animals or birds, having established domination of a particular territory, are more likely to win combat with other members of their species which takes place on that territory than combat which occurs elsewhere. This he suggests is so without regard to the relative strength of the combatants. See pp. 59-62, 90-91, 214, 248-253. Ardrey's basic proposition is that what we observe in the animal world has an applicability to affairs of men.

It is, of course, quite a leap to apply the principle of territoriality, if established, to the affairs of men. But any lawyer who has handled a property line dispute between neighbors will probably agree that such a dispute generates greater emotional content and involves more irrational and uneconomic behavior than most other disputes. The reduction in the value of either piece of property resulting from the loss of the disputed six inches or one foot of ground cannot be what is really at issue. And it is common lore in labor negotiations and the arbitration of labor grievances that some neutral territory should be found even though the offices of either the employer or the union may contain a more than adequate conference room.

The person who negotiates on his own territory has a number of potential advantages over his visiting opposite. He may have his desk so located that it identifies the person behind it as the authority figure in the room. He may, if he so desires, perform the friendly and obligation-inducing act of coming out from behind it, or he may remain behind it and utilize the psychological defense its physical presence creates. He is the host, and by attending to the physical needs and comforts of his visitors he may, as mentioned above, display his relaxed confidence and at the same time create a sense of obligation. By being the one who calls for the files, supplies the books, or provides the services, he may reemphasize his authority status. Being familiar with all aspects of his surroundings, he can concentrate on the matter at hand undisturbed by any novelties of the situation. Of course, whether these possibilities are real advantages depends upon the details of the particular matter being negotiated, and in some bargaining relationships they may instead be disadvantages. The negotiator must also consider the possibility that the physical characteristics of his office will be considered so obviously inferior to those of his bargaining opposite that the comparison will instead only create confidence in the opposite. The evaluation is subjective, but nonetheless important. The most important thing is that a negotiator be aware that the situs of negotiations may affect his and his bargaining opposite's behavior.

(5) Cultural Aspects of Negotiation

Most of what has been set out above concerning the psychodynamics of the negotiation process has been directed to that process as practiced by an American lawyer dealing with the various white American clients met in a traditional law practice. Conduct which carries one message in that context may project a different message or no message when persons with other cultural backgrounds are involved. Americans consider punctuality to be of great importance, even though there are minor regional variations concerning when tardiness is great enough to require apology or explanation. Latin Americans generally do not consider time to have such a great significance and indeed insistence upon punctuality conflicts with other more important values in life. Americans make extensive use of what are otherwise social occasions to discuss important aspects of a transaction being negotiated, hoping that somehow the relaxed or informal atmosphere will make possible progress not attainable in a formal negotiating setting. Japanese, on the other hand, do not believe it is proper to do business on a social occasion and an American who does so may offend his Japanese counterparts by what appears to be uncultivated overreaching. Mediterranean people stand much closer to persons with whom they converse than do Americans, and close presence which would suggest aggressiveness in an American has no such significance for an Italian or Greek.

America contains a number of subcultures, and members of different subcultures may experience similar distortions of things said or done during negotiations. Many whites, blacks, Chicanos, and Asians hold stereotyped views of persons in other racial groups. Stereotypes provide a great source of difficulties in communication similar to those of the transference phenomenon. Given the history of relations between the two races, sincere white negotiators may experience greater difficulty in achieving credibility with black negotiators than they experience with members of their own race. Given white stereotypes of blacks as argumentative, emotional, or ostentatious, a thoroughly prepared black negotiator may experience greater difficulty in obtaining appraisal of the merits of his proposal from a white negotiator than he would experience with a member of his own race. Appraisal of one's attitudes toward members of another race is essential to effective negotiation between members of different racial subcultures. In some instances explicit discussion of or at least allusion to the problem may be appropriate.

An interesting set of readings on the cultural aspect of negotiation may be found in Chapter 7 of H. Edwards and J. White, THE LAWYER AS A NEGOTIATOR (1977).

(6) Sex and Negotiation

Only in recent years has a substantial proportion of the persons admitted to the practice of law been female. These women enter a profession which is still predominately male, consisting largely of men who graduated from law schools when a woman lawyer was a rarity. They practice law before a judiciary which consists primarily of older men. Attitudes toward sex roles and sex stereotypes are certain to be a factor in the negotiations which take place between lawyers when they are members of the opposite sex, particularly if there is a difference in age.

This editor's experience in teaching a course in negotiation to women and men who were approximately the same age has led him to conclude that many persons still prefer to negotiate with members of their own sex. Both men and women sense something in the nature of a subcultural clash and its concomitant problems of communication and interpretation. Some men may prefer to negotiate with women because of a conviction that women do not try as hard as men to win, but an aggressive woman negotiator poses a problem for a man reared with traditional standards. Childhood training teaches men how to deal with aggressive men: never start the fight, but if another boy does, be sure you are the one to finish it. That same training teaches that a boy must not strike a girl and that, while they may be teased, girls are to be protected. An aggressive woman, aware of this ability to incapacitate, may make inroads upon a male's position that would not be possible for a man. On the other hand, discussions with students indicate that women believe men are more likely to lie in negotiating than women—a belief that may have its origins in traditional romantic male pursuit of women. Negotiation between members of different sexes can also involve a variant of the threat that a client's interests will not be fully served because of the lawyer's concern for obtaining the approval of his opposing negotiator.

As men and women accumulate more experience in negotiation and the presence of a woman lawyer becomes familiar, the problems associated with sex differences will almost certainly change and may even disappear. In the meantime, however, it would be well for both women and men consciously to evaluate how a difference in the sex of a negotiating opposite affects their approach to negotiation.

(7) *Stages of Negotiation*

Another important subjective feeling which the negotiator must develop is that of knowing to what stage negotiations have progressed, and whether the time is ripe for pressing for agreement. An important book dealing with collective bargaining negotiations suggests that there are three identifiable stages in that process. Douglas, INDUSTRIAL PEACE-MAKING 13-99 (1962). The first stage is that of establishing the negotiating range. It is marked by elaborate declarations of purpose, dogmatic pronouncements, and vehement assertions of what must be accepted as uncompromisable principles, all of which are heard by the other side largely without interruption. The second stage is that of reconnoitering the ranges previously stated for discovery of the areas of possible agreement even though there is no admission of willingness to make concessions. The third and final stage is that of precipitating the decision-reaching crisis, in which the pace quickens and the tensions grow greater as the parties establish what are in fact their last positions with respect to various issues. Other types of negotiation may develop different but identifiable phases. The important thing for the negotiator is to recognize that he is involved in a developing process and that it is of utmost importance to him to have in mind exactly where it is that the parties have arrived in the pursuit of that process.

B. GROUP DYNAMICS IN NEGOTIATION

What has been said thus far finds primary application in person-to-person relationships. Many negotiations, however, involve teams of negotiators representing each party, and they may involve three or more parties. The dynamics of group behavior are even more complicated than the dynamics of a two-person bargaining relationship. But one has made a significant advance as a negotiator if he is aware of and alert to the differences between interpersonal dynamics and group dynamics.

Ordinarily a negotiating team has one, or possibly two, spokesmen. Other members of the team play subsidiary and supportive roles, though on some teams individual members may be assigned primary responsibility for particular subjects or areas. Negotiating teams make frequent use of the system of caucusing separately for an exchange of views among team members. At this time not only may notes be compared on the comments and attitude of the opposing spokesman, but attention may be given to statements made by supporting members of the opposing team. Overall strategy may be reviewed, and specific tactics for the next session agreed upon. A person participating as a member of such a bargaining team should be attentive to the dynamics of the group, its developing deference patterns, and the possibility that a member who would otherwise have an effective role to play has been prevented from doing so. And, recognizing that the other team will attempt to evaluate the significance of a chance remark of a subordinate member of the team, the caucus serves as a refresher for review by the team membership of the positions to be asserted and the subjects to be avoided in discussion with the opposing side.

The previously mentioned book by Douglas, INDUSTRIAL PEACEMAKING, may be of interest to one who wishes to study the group dynamics of a bargaining team. It contains the case histories of four different collective bargaining negotiations, with verbatim transcripts of the discussions in the party caucuses as well as in the formal negotiating sessions. See also Bales, *How People Interact in Conferences,* Scientific American 3-7 (March 1955).

Where bargaining involves more than two parties, whether represented by individuals or by negotiating teams, additional complications of group dynamics result. In addition to the possibilities of alliance and cooperation, interpersonal relations may lead to one of the negotiators performing a dominant role. Or one of the negotiators may, by suggesting more moderate stands, take on the function of mediator or problem solver. The number of possible variations is immense, and generalization is difficult. It is safe to say, however, that a person engaged in multiparty negotiation should be aware of the differences between such negotiation and two-party negotiation.

6. Negotiation Tactics

A. Establishing a Commitment

SCHELLING, AN ESSAY ON BARGAINING*

This chapter presents a tactical approach to the analysis of bargaining. The subject includes both explicit bargaining and the tacit kind in which adversaries watch and interpret each other's behavior, each aware that his own actions are being interpreted and anticipated, each acting with a view to the expectations that he creates. In economics the subject covers wage negotiations, tariff negotiations, competition where competitors are few, settlements out of court, and the real estate agent and his customer. Outside economics it ranges from the threat of massive retaliation to taking the right of way from a taxi.

Our concern will *not* be with the part of bargaining that consists of exploring for mutually profitable adjustments, and that might be called the "efficiency" aspect of bargaining. For example, can an insurance firm save money, and make a client happier, by offering a cash settlement rather than repairing the client's car; can an employer save money by granting a voluntary wage increase to employees who agree to take a substantial part of their wages in merchandise? Instead, we shall be concerned with what might be called the "distributional" aspect of bargaining: the situations in which a better bargain for one means less for the other. When the business is finally sold to the one interested buyer, what price does it go for? When two dynamite trucks meet on a road wide enough for one, who backs up?

These are situations that ultimately involve an element of pure bargaining—bargaining in which each party is guided mainly by his expectations of what the other will accept. But with each guided by expectations and knowing that the other is too, expectations become compounded. A bargain is struck when somebody makes a final, sufficient concession. Why does he concede? Because he thinks the other will not. "I must concede because he won't. He won't because he thinks I will. He thinks I will because he thinks I think he thinks so. . . ." There is some range of alternative outcomes in which any point is better for both sides

* From THE STRATEGY OF CONFLICT by Thomas C. Schelling. Harvard University Press (1960). The essay first appeared in Volume 46 of the American Economic Review (June, 1956), which holds the original copyright. It is used here with the permission of the author, The American Economic Association, and the Harvard University Press. Footnotes omitted.

than no agreement at all. To insist on any such point is pure bargaining, since one always *would* take less rather than reach no agreement at all, and since one always *can* recede if retreat proves necessary to agreement. Yet if both parties are aware of the limits to this range, *any* outcome is a point from which at least one party would have been willing to retreat and the other knows it! There is no resting place.

There is, however, an outcome; and if we cannot find it in the logic of the situation we may find it in the tactics employed. The purpose . . . is to call attention to an important class of tactics, of a kind that is peculiarly appropriate to the logic of indeterminate situations. The essence of these tactics is some voluntary but irreversible sacrifice of freedom of choice. They rest on the paradox that the power to constrain an adversary may depend on the power to bind oneself; that, in bargaining, weakness is often strength, freedom may be freedom to capitulate, and to burn bridges behind one may suffice to undo an opponent.

BARGAINING POWER: THE POWER TO BIND ONESELF

"Bargaining power," "bargaining strength," "bargaining skill" suggest that the advantage goes to the powerful, the strong, or the skillful. It does, of course, if those qualities are defined to mean only that nego-tiations are won by those who win. But, if the terms imply that it is an advantage to be more intelligent or more skilled in debate, or to have more financial resources, more physical strength, more military potency, or more ability to withstand losses, then the term does a disservice. These qualities are by no means universal advantages in bargaining situations; they often have a contrary value.

The sophisticated negotiator may find it difficult to seem as obstinate as a truly obstinate man. If a man knocks at a door and says that he will stab himself on the porch unless given $10, he is more likely to get the $10 if his eyes are bloodshot. The threat of mutual destruction cannot be used to deter an adversary who is too unintelligent to comprehend it or too weak to enforce his will on those he represents. The government that cannot control its balance of payments, or collect taxes, or muster the political unity to defend itself, may enjoy assistance that would be denied it if it could control its own resources. And, to cite an example familiar from economic theory, "price leadership" in oligopoly may be an unprofitable distinction evaded by the small firms and assumed per-force by the large one.

Bargaining power has also been described as the power to fool and bluff, "the ability to set the best price for yourself and fool the other man into thinking this was your maximum offer." Fooling and bluffing are certainly involved; but there are two kinds of fooling. One is de-ceiving about the facts; a buyer may lie about his income or misrepre-sent the size of his family. The other is purely tactical. Suppose each knows everything about the other, and each knows what the other knows.

What is there to fool about? The buyer may say that, though he'd really pay up to twenty and the seller knows it, he is firmly resolved as a tactical matter not to budge above sixteen. If the seller capitulates, was he fooled? Or was he convinced of the truth? Or did the buyer really not know what he would do next if the tactic failed? If the buyer really "feels" himself firmly resolved, and bases his resolve on the conviction that the seller will capitulate, and the seller does, the buyer may say afterwards that he was "not fooling." Whatever has occurred, it is not adequately conveyed by the notions of bluffing and fooling.

How does one person make another believe something? The answer depends importantly on the factual question, "Is it true?" It is easier to prove the truth of something that is true than of something false. To prove the truth about our health we can call on a reputable doctor; to prove the truth about our costs or income we may let the person look at books that have been audited by a reputable firm or the Bureau of Internal Revenue. But to persuade him of something false we may have no such convincing evidence.

When one wishes to persuade someone that he would not pay more than $16,000 for a house that is really worth $20,000 to him, what can he do to take advantage of the usually superior credibility of the truth over a false assertion? Answer: make it true. How can a buyer make it true? If he likes the house because it is near his business, he might move his business, persuading the seller that the house is really now worth only $16,000 to him. This would be unprofitable; he is no better off than if he paid the higher price.

But suppose the buyer could make an irrevocable and enforceable bet with some third party, duly recorded and certified, according to which he would pay for the house no more than $16,000, or forfeit $5,000. The seller has lost; the buyer need simply present the truth. Unless the seller is enraged and withholds the house in sheer spite, the situation has been rigged against him; the "objective" situation—the buyer's true incentive—has been voluntarily, conspicuously, and irreversibly changed. The seller can take it or leave it. This example demonstrates that if the buyer can accept an irrevocable *commitment*, in a way that is unambiguously visible to the seller, he can squeeze the range of indeterminacy down to the point most favorable to him. It also suggests, by its artificiality, that the tactic is one that may or may not be available; whether the buyer can find an effective device for commiting himself may depend on who he is, who the seller is, where they live, and a number of legal and institutional arrangements (including, in our artificial example, whether bets are legally enforceable).

If both men live in a culture where "cross my heart" is universally accepted as potent, all the buyer has to do is allege that he will pay no more than $16,000, using this invocation of penalty, and he wins—or at least he wins if the seller does not beat him to it by shouting "$19,000, cross my heart." If the buyer is an agent authorized by a board of directors to buy at $16,000 but not a cent more, and the directors cannot constitutionally meet again for several months and the buyer cannot exceed his authority, and if all this can be made known to the seller, then the buyer "wins"—if, again, the seller has not tied himself up with a commitment to $19,000. Or, if the buyer can assert that he will pay no more than $16,000 so firmly that he would suffer intolerable loss of personal prestige or bargaining reputation by paying more, and if the fact of his paying more would necessarily be known, and if the seller appreciates all this, then a loud declaration by itself may provide the commitment. The device, of course, is a needless surrender of flexibility unless it can be made fully evident and understandable to the seller.

Incidentally, some of the more contractual kinds of commitments are not as effective as they at first seem. In the example of the self-inflicted penalty through the bet, it remains possible for the seller to seek out the third party and offer a modest sum in consideration of the latter's releasing the buyer from the bet, threatening to sell the house for $16,000 if the release is not forthcoming. The effect of the bet—as of most such contractual commitments—is to shift the locus and personnel of the negotiation, in the hope that the third party will be less available for negotiation or less subject to an incentive to concede. To put it differently, a *contractual* commitment is usually the assumption of a contingent "transfer cost," not a "real cost"; and if all interested parties can be brought into the negotiation the range of indeterminacy remains as it was. But if the third party were available only at substantial transportation cost, to that extent a truly irrevocable commitment would have been assumed. (If bets were made with a number of people, the "real costs" of bringing them into the negotiation might be made prohibitive.)

The most interesting parts of our topic concern whether and how commitments can be taken; but it is worth while to consider briefly a model in which practical problems are absent—a world in which absolute commitments are freely available. Consider a culture in which "cross my heart" is universally recognized as absolutely binding. Any offer accompanied by this invocation is a final offer, and is so recognized. If each party knows the other's true reservation price, the object is to be first with a firm offer. Complete responsibility for the outcome then rests with the other, who can take it or leave it as he chooses (and who chooses to take it). Bargaining is all over; the commitment (that is, the first offer) wins.

Interpose some communication difficulty. They must bargain by letter; the invocation becomes effective when signed but cannot be known to the other until its arrival. Now when one party writes such a letter the other may already have signed his own, or may yet do so before the letter of the first arrives. There is then no sale; both are bound to incompatible positions. Each must now recognize this possibility of stalemate and take into account the likelihood that the other already has, or will have, signed his own commitment.

An asymmetry in communication may well favor the one who is (and is known to be) unavailable for the receipt of messages, for he is the one who cannot be deterred from his own commitment by receipt of the other's.

(On the other hand, if the one who cannot communicate can feign ignorance of his own inability, the other too may be deterred from his own commitment by fear of the first's unwitting commitment.) If the commitments depend not just on words but on special forms or ceremonies, ignorance of the other party's commitment ceremonies may be an advantage if the ignorance is fully appreciated, since it makes the other aware that only his own restraint can avert stalemate.

Suppose only part of the population belongs to the cult in which "cross my heart" is (or is believed to be) absolutely binding. If everyone knows (and is known to know) everyone else's affiliation, those belonging to this particular cult have the advantage. They can commit themselves, the others cannot. If the buyer say "$16,000, cross my heart" his offer is final; if the seller says $19,000" he is (and is known to be) only "bargaining."

If each does not know the other's true reservation price there is an initial stage in which each tries to discover the other's and misrepresent his own, as in ordinary bargaining. But the process of discovery and revelation becomes quickly merged with the process of creating and discovering commitments; the commitments permanently change, for all practical purposes, the "true" reservation prices. If one party has, and the other has not, the belief in a binding ceremony, the latter pursues the "ordinary" bargaining technique of *asserting* his reservation price, while the former proceeds to *make* his.

The foregoing discussion has tried to suggest both the plausibility and the logic of self-commitment. Some examples may suggest the relevance of the tactic, although an observer can seldom distinguish with confidence the consciously logical, the intuitive, or the inadvertent use of a visible tactic. First, it has not been uncommon for union officials to stir up excitement and determination on the part of the membership during or prior to a wage negotiation. If the union is going to insist on $2 and expects the management to counter with $1.60, an effort is made to persuade the membership not only that the management could pay $2 but even perhaps that the negotiators themselves are incompetent if they fail to obtain close to $2. The purpose—or, rather, a plausible purpose suggested by our analysis—is to make clear to the management that the negotiators could not accept less than $2 *even if they wished to* because they no longer control the members or because they would lose their own positions if they tried. In other words, the negotiators reduce the scope of their own authority and confront the management with the threat of a strike that the union itself cannot avert, even though it was the union's own action that eliminated its power to prevent the strike.

Something similar occurs when the United States Government negotiates with other governments on, say, the uses to which foreign assistance will be put, or tariff reduction. If the executive branch is free to negotiate the best arrangement it can, it may be unable to make any position stick and may end by conceding controversial points because its partners know, or believe obstinately, that the United States would rather concede than terminate the negotiations. But, if the executive branch negotiates under legislative authority, with its position constrained by law, and it is evident that Congress will not be reconvened to change the law within the necessary time period, then the executive branch has a firm position that is visible to its negotiating partners.

When national representatives go to international negotiations knowing that there is a wide range of potential agreement within which the outcome will depend on bargaining, they seem often to create a bargaining position by public statements, statements calculated to arouse a public opinion that permits no concessions to be made. If a binding public opinion can be cultivated and made evident to the other side, the initial position can thereby be made visibly "final."

These examples have certain characteristics in common. First, they clearly depend not only on incurring a commitment but on communicating it persuasively to the other party. Second, it is by no means easy to establish the commitment, nor is it entirely clear to either of the parties concerned just how strong the commitment is. Third, similar activity may be available to the parties on both sides. Fourth, the possibility of commitment, though perhaps available to both sides, is by no means equally available; the ability of a democratic government to get itself tied by public opinion may be different from the ability of a totalitarian government to incur such a commitment. Fifth, they all run the risk of establishing an immovable position that goes beyond the ability of the other to concede, and thereby provoke the likelihood of stalemate or breakdown.

INSTITUTIONAL AND STRUCTURAL CHARACTERISTICS
OF THE NEGOTIATION

Some institutional and structural characteristics of bargaining situations may make the commitment tactic easy or difficult to use, or make it more available to one party than the other, or affect the likelihood of simultaneous commitment or stalemate.

Use of a Bargaining Agent. The use of a bargaining agent affects the power of commitment in at least two ways. First, the agent may be given instructions that are difficult or impossible to change, such instructions (and their inflexibility) being visible to the opposite party. The principle applies in distinguishing the legislative from the executive branch, or the management from the board of directors, as well as to a messenger-carried offer when the bargaining process has a time limit and the principal has interposed sufficient distance between himself and his messenger to make further communication evidently impossible before the time runs out.

Second, an "agent" may be brought in as a principal in his own right, with an incentive structure of his own that differs from his principal's. This device is involved in automobile insurance; the private citizen, in settling out of court, cannot threaten suit as effectively as the insurance company since the latter is more conspicuously obliged to carry out such threats to maintain its own reputation for subsequent accidents.

Secrecy vs. Publicity. A potent means of commitment, and sometimes the only means, is the pledge of one's reputation. If national representatives can arrange to be charged with appeasement for every small concession, they place concession visibly beyond their own reach. If a union with other plants to deal with can arrange to make any retreat dramatically visible, it places its bargaining reputation in jeopardy and thereby becomes visibly incapable of serious compromise. (The same convenient jeopardy is the basis for the universally exploited defense, "If I did it for you I'd have to do it for everyone else.") But to commit in this fashion publicity is required. Both the initial offer and the final outcome would have to be known; and if secrecy surrounds either point, or if the outcome is inherently not observable, the device is unavailable. If one party has a "public" and the other has not, the latter may try to neutralize his disadvantage by excluding the relevant public; or if both parties fear the potentialities for stalemate in the simultaneous use of this tactic, they may try to enforce an agreement on secrecy.

Intersecting Negotiations. If a union is simultaneously engaged, or will shortly be engaged, in many negotiations while the management has no other plants and deals with no other unions, the management cannot convincingly stake its bargaining reputation while the union can. The advantage goes to the party that can persuasively point to an array of other negotiations in which its own position would be prejudiced if it made a concession in this one. (The "reputation value" of the bargain may be less related to the outcome than to the firmness with which some initial bargaining position is adhered to.) Defense against this tactic may involve, among other things, both misinterpretation of the other party's position and an effort to make the eventual outcome incommensurable with the initial positions. If the subjects under negotiation can be enlarged in the process of negotiation, or the wage figure replaced by fringe benefits that cannot be reduced to a wage equivalent, an "out" is provided to the party that has committed itself; and the availability of this "out" weakens the commitment itself, to the disadvantage of the committed party.

Continuous Negotiations. A special case of interrelated negotiations occurs when the same two parties are to negotiate other topics, simultaneously or in the future. The logic of this case is more subtle; to persuade the other that one cannot afford to recede, one says in effect, "If I conceded to you here, you would revise your estimate of me in our other negotiations; to protect my reputation with you I must stand firm." The second party is simultaneously the "third party" to whom one's bargaining reputation can be pledged. This situation occurs in the threat of local resistance to local aggression. The party threatening achieves its commitment, and hence the credibility of its threat, not by referring to what it would gain from carrying out the threat in this particular instance but by pointing to the long-run value of a fulfilled threat in enhancing the credibility of future threats.

The Restrictive Agenda. When there are two objects to negotiate, the decision to negotiate them simultaneously or in separate forums or at separate times is by no means neutral to the outcome, particularly when there is a latent extortionate threat that can be exploited only if it can be attached to some more ordinary, legitimate, bargaining situation. The protection against extortion depends on refusal, unavailability, or inability, to negotiate. But if the object of the extortionate threat can be brought onto the agenda with the other topic, the latent threat becomes effective.

Tariff bargaining is an example. If reciprocal tariffs on cheese and automobiles are to be negotiated, one party may alter the outcome by threatening a purely punitive change in some other tariff. But if the bargaining representatives of the threatened party are confined to the cheese-automobile agenda, and have no instructions that permit them even to take cognizance of other commodities, or if there are ground rules that forbid mention of other tariffs while cheese and automobiles remain unsettled, this extortionate weapon must await another opportunity. If the threat that would be brought to the conference table is one that cannot stand publicity, publicity itself may prevent its effective communication.

The Possibility of Compensation. As Fellner has pointed out, agreement may be dependent on some means of redistributing costs or gains. If duopolists, for example, divide markets in a way that maximizes their combined profits, some initial accrual of profits is thereby determined; any other division of the profits requires that one firm be able to compensate the other. If the fact of compensation would be evidence of illegal collusion, or if the motive for compensation would be misunderstood by the stockholders, or if the two do not sufficiently trust each other, some less optimum level of *joint* profits may be required in order that the initial accrual of profits to the two firms be in closer accordance with an agreed division of gains between them.

When agreement must be reached on something that is inherently a one-man act, any division of the cost depends on compensation. The "agenda" assumes particular importance in these cases, since a principal means of compensation is a concession on some other object. If two simultaneous negotiations can be brought into a contingent relationship with each other, a means of compensation is available. If they are kept separate, each remains an indivisible object.

It may be to the advantage of one party to keep a bargain isolated, and to the other to join it to some second bargain. If there are two projects, each with a cost of three, and each with a value of two to A and a value of four to B, and each is inherently a "one-man" project in its execution, and if compensation is institutionally impossible, B will be forced to pay the entire cost of each as long as the two projects are kept separate. He cannot usefully threaten nonperformance, since A has no incentive to carry out either project by himself. But if B can link the projects together, offering to carry out one while A carries out the other, and can effectively threaten to abandon both unless A carries out one of them, A is left an option with a gain of four and a cost of three, which he takes, and B cuts his cost in half.

An important limitation of economic problems, as prototypes of bargaining situations, is that they tend disproportionately to involve divisible objects and compensable activities. If a drainage ditch in the back of one house will protect both houses; and if it costs $1,000 and is worth $800 to each home-owner; neither would undertake it separately, but we nevertheless usually assume that they will get together and see that this project worth $1,600 to the two of them gets carried out. But if it costs 10 hours a week to be scoutmaster, and each considers it worth 8 hours of his time to have a scout troop but one man must do the whole job, it is far from certain that the neighbors will reach a deal according to which one puts 10 hours on the job and the other pays him cash or does 5 hours' gardening for him. When two cars meet on a narrow road, the ensuing deadlock is aggravated by the absence of a custom of bidding to pay for the right of way. Parliamentary deadlocks occur when logrolling is impracticable. Measures that require unanimous agreement can often be initiated only if several are bundled together.

The Mechanics of Negotiation. A number of other characteristics deserve mention, although we shall not work out their implications. Is there a penalty on the conveyance of false information? Is there a penalty on called bluffs, that is, can one put forth an offer and withdraw it after it has been accepted? Is there a penalty on hiring an agent who pretends to be an interested party and makes insincere offers, simply to test the position of the other party? Can all interested parties be recognized? Is there a time limit on the bargaining? Does the bargaining take the particular structure of an auction, a Dutch auction, a sealed bid system, or some other formal arrangement? Is there *a status quo,* so that unavailability for negotiation can win the *status quo* for the party that prefers it? Is renegotiation possible in case of stalemate? What are the costs of stalemate? Can compliance with the agreement be observed? What, in general, are the means of communication, and are any of them susceptible of being put out of order by one party or the other? If there are several items to negotiate, are they negotiated in one comprehensive negotiation, separately in a particular order so that each piece is finished before the next is taken up, or simultaneously through different agents or under different rules.

The importance of many of these structural questions becomes evident when one reflects on parliamentary technique. Rules that permit a president to veto an appropriation bill only in its entirety, or that require each amendment to be voted before the original act is voted on, or a priority system accorded to different kinds of motions, substantially alter the incentives that are brought to bear on each action. One who might be pressured into choosing second best is relieved of his vulnerability if he can vote earlier to eliminate that possibility, thereby leaving only first and third choices about which his preference is known to be so strong that no threat will be made.

Principles and Precedents. To be convincing, commitments usually have to be qualitative rather than quantitative, and to rest on some rationale. It may be difficult to conceive of a really firm commitment to $2.07½; why not $2.02¼? The numerical scale is too continuous to provide good resting places, except at nice round numbers like $2.00. But a commitment to the *principle* of "profit sharing," "cost-of-living increases," or any other basis for a numerical calculation that comes out at $2.07½, may provide a foothold for a commitment. Furthermore, one may create something of a commitment by putting the principles and precedents themselves in jeopardy. If in the past one has successfully maintained the principle of, say, nonrecognition of governments imposed by force, and elects to nail his demands to that principle in the present negotiation, he not only adduces precedent behind his claim but risks the principle itself. Having pledged it, he may persuade his adversary that he would accept stalemate rather than capitulate and discredit the principle.

Casuistry. If one reaches the point where concession is advisable, he has to recognize two effects: it puts him closer to his opponent's position, and it affects his opponent's estimate of his firmness. Concession not only may be construed as capitulation, it may mark a prior commitment as a fraud, and make the adversary skeptical of any new pretense at commitment. One, therefore, needs an "excuse" for accommodating his opponent, preferably a rationalized reinterpretation of the original commitment, one that is persuasive to the adversary himself.

More interesting is the use of casuistry to release an opponent from a commitment. If one can demonstrate to an opponent that the latter is not committed, or that he has miscalculated his commitment, one may in fact undo or revise the opponent's commitment. Or if one can confuse the opponent's commitment, so that his constituents or principals or audience cannot exactly identify compliance with the commitment— show that "productivity" is ambiguous, or that "proportionate contributions" has several meanings—one may undo it or lower its value. In these cases it is to the opponent's disadvantage that this commitment be successfully refuted by argument. But when the opponent has resolved to make a moderate concession one may help him by proving that he *can* make a moderate concession consistent with his former position, and that if he does there are no grounds for believing it to reflect on his original principles. One must seek, in other words, a rationalization by which to deny oneself too great a reward from the opponent's concession, otherwise the concession will not be made.

THE THREAT

When one threatens to fight if attacked or to cut his price if his competitor does, the threat is no more than a communication of one's own incentives, designed to impress on the other the automatic consequences of his act. And, incidentally, if it succeeds in deterring, it benefits both parties.

But more than communication is involved when one threatens an act that he would have no incentive to perform but that is designed to deter through its promise of mutual harm. To threaten massive retaliation against small encroachments is of this nature, as is the threat to bump a car that does not yield the right of way or to call a costly strike if the wage is not raised a few cents. The distinctive feature of this threat is that the threatener has no incentive to carry it out either before the event or after. He does have an incentive to bind himself to fulfill the threat, if he thinks the threat may be successful, because the threat and not its fulfillment gains the end; and fulfillment is not required if the threat succeeds. The more certain the contingent fulfillment is, the less likely is actual fulfillment. But the threat's efficacy depends on the credulity of the other party, and the threat is ineffectual unless the threatener can rearrange or display his own incentives so as to demonstrate that he would, *ex post,* have an incentive to carry it out.

We are back again at the commitment. How can one commit himself in advance to an act that he would in fact prefer not to carry out in the event, in order that his commitment may deter the other party? One can of course bluff, to persuade the other falsely that the costs or damages to the threatener would be minor or negative. More interesting, the one making the threat may pretend that he himself erroneously believes his own costs to be small, and therefore would mistakenly go ahead and fulfill the threat. Or perhaps he can pretend a revenge motivation so strong as to overcome the prospect of self-damage; but this option is probably most readily available to the truly revengeful. Otherwise he must find a way to commit himself.

One may try to stake his reputation on fulfillment, in a manner that impresses the threatened person. One may even stake his reputation *with the threatened person himself,* on grounds that it would be worth the costs and pains to give a lesson to the latter if he fails to heed the threat. Or one may try to arrange a legal commitment, perhaps through contracting with a third party. Or if one can turn the whole business over to an agent whose salary (or business reputation) depends on carrying out the threat but who is unalterably relieved of any responsibility for the further costs, one may shift the incentive.

The commitment problem is nicely illustrated by the legal doctrine of the "last clear chance" which recognizes that, in the events that led up to an accident, there was some point at which the accident became inevitable as a result of prior actions, and that the abilities of the two parties to prevent it may not have expired at the same time. In bargaining, the commitment is a device to leave the last clear chance to decide the outcome with the other party, in a manner that he fully appreciates; it is to relinquish further initiative, having rigged the incentives so that the other party must choose in one's favor. If one driver speeds up so that he cannot stop, and the other realizes it, the latter has to yield. A legislative rider at the end of a session leaves the President the last clear chance to pass the bill. This doctrine helps to understand some of those cases in which bargaining "strength" inheres in what is weakness by other standards. When a person—or a country—has lost the power to help himself, or the power to avert mutual damage, the other interested party has no choice but to assume the cost or responsibility. "Coercive deficiency" is the term Arthur Smithies uses to describe the tactic of deliberately exhausting one's annual budgetary allowance so early in the year that the need for more funds is irresistibly urgent.

A related tactic is maneuvering into a *status quo* from which one can be dislodged only by an overt act, an act that precipitates mutual damage because the maneuvering party has relinquished the power to retreat. If one carries explosives visibly on his person, in a manner that makes destruction obviously inevitable for himself and for any assailant, he may deter assault much more than if he retained any control over the explosives. If one commits a token force of troops that would be unable to escape, the commitment to full resistance is increased. Walter Lippmann has used the analogy of the plate glass window that helps to protect a jewelry store: anyone can break it easily enough, but not without creating an uproar.

Similar techniques may be available to the one threatened. His best defense, of course, is to carry out the act before the threat is made; in that case there is neither incentive nor commitment for retaliation. If he cannot hasten the act itself, he may commit himself to it; if the person to be threatened is already committed, the one who would threaten cannot deter with his threat, he can only make certain the mutually disastrous consequences that he threatens. If the person to be threatened can arrange before the threat is made to share the risk with others (as suggested by the insurance solution to the right-of-way problem mentioned earlier) he may become so visibly unsusceptible to the threat as to dissuade the threatener. Or if by any other means he can either change or misrepresent his own incentives, to make it appear that he would gain in spite of threat fulfillment (or perhaps only that he thinks he would), the threatener may have to give up the threat as costly and fruitless; or if one can misrepresent himself as either unable to comprehend a threat, or too obstinate to heed it, he may deter the threat itself. Best of all may be *genuine* ignorance, obstinacy, or simple disbelief, since it may be more convincing to the prospective threatener; but of course if it fails to persuade him and he commits himself to the threat, both sides lose. Finally, both the threat and the commitment have to be communicated; if the threatened person can be unavailable for messages, or can destroy the communication channels, even though he does so in an obvious effort to avert threat, he may deter the threat itself. But the time to show disbelief or obstinacy is before the threat is made, that is, before the commitment is taken, not just before the threat is fulfilled; it does no good to be incredulous, or out of town, when the messenger arrives with the committed threat.

In threat situations, as in ordinary bargaining, commitments are not altogether clear; each party cannot exactly estimate the costs and values to the other side of the two related actions involved in the threat; the process of commitment may be a progressive one, the commitments acquiring their firmness by a sequence of actions. Communication is often neither entirely impossible nor entirely reliable; while certain evidence of one's commitment can be communicated directly, other evidence must travel by newspaper or hearsay, or be demonstrated by actions. In these cases the unhappy possibility of both acts occurring, as a result of simultaneous commitment, is increased. Furthermore, the recognition of this possibility of simultaneous commitment becomes itself a deterrent to the taking of commitments.

In case a threat is made and fails to deter, there is a second stage prior to fulfillment in which *both* parties have an interest in undoing the commitment. The purpose of the threat is gone, its deterrence value is zero, and only the commitment exists to motivate fulfillment. This feature has, of course, an analogy with stalemate in ordinary bargaining, stalemate resulting from both parties' getting committed to incompatible positions, or one party's mistakenly committing himself to a position that the other truly would not accept. If there appears a possibility of undoing the commitment, *both* parties have an interest in doing so. How to undo it is a matter on which their interests diverge, since different ways of undoing it lead to different outcomes. Furthermore, "undoing" does not mean neglecting a commitment regardless of reputation; "undoing," if the commitment of reputation was real, means disconnecting the threat from one's reputation, perhaps one's own reputation with the threatened person himself. It is therefore a subtle and tenuous situation in which, though both have an interest in undoing the commitment, they may be quite unable to collaborate in undoing it.

Special care may be needed in defining the threat, both the act that is threatened against and the counter act that is threatened. The difficulty arises from the fact, just noted, that once the former has been done the incentive to perform the later has disappeared. The credibility of the threat before the act depends on how visible to the threatened party is the inability of the threatening party to rationalize his way out of his commitment once it has failed its purpose. Any loopholes the threatening party leaves himself, if they are visible to the threatened party, weaken the visible commitment and hence reduce the credibility of the threat. (An example may be the ambiguous treatment of Quemoy in the Formosa Resolution and Treaty.)

It is essential, therefore, for maximum credibility, to leave as little room as possible for judgment or discretion in carrying out the threat. If one is committed to punish a certain type of behavior when it reaches certain limits, but the limits are not carefully and objectively defined, the party threatened will realize that when the time comes to decide whether the threat must be enforced or not, his interest and that of the threatening party will coincide in an attempt to avoid the mutually unpleasant consequences.

In order to make a threat precise, so that its terms are visible both to the threatened party and to any third parties whose reaction to the whole affair is of value to the adversaries, it may be necessary to introduce some arbitrary elements. The threat must involve overt acts rather than intentions; it must be attached to the visible deeds, not invisible ones; it may have to attach itself to certain ancillary actions that are of no consequence in themselves to the threatening party. It may, for example, have to put a penalty on the carrying of weapons rather than their use; on suspicious behavior rather than observed misdemeanors; on proximity to a crime rather than the crime itself. And, finally, the act of punishment must be one whose effect or influence is clearly discernible.

In order that one be able to pledge his reputation behind a threat, there must be continuity between the present and subsequent issues that will arise. This need for continuity suggests a means of making the original threat more effective; if it can be decomposed into a series of consecutive smaller threats, there is an opportunity to demonstrate on the first few transgressions that the threat will be carried out on the rest. Even the first few become more plausible, since there is a more obvious incentive to fulfill them as a "lesson."

This principle is perhaps most relevant to acts that are inherently a matter of degree. In foreign aid programs the overt act of terminating assistance may be so obviously painful to both sides as not to be taken seriously by the recipient, but if each small misuse of funds is to be accompanied by a small reduction in assistance, never so large as to leave the recipient helpless nor to provoke a diplomatic breach, the willingness to carry it out will receive more credulity; or if it does not at first, a few lessons may be persuasive without too much damage.

The threatening party may not, of course, be able to divide the act into steps. (Both the act to be deterred and the punishment must be divisible.) But the principle at least suggests the unwisdom of defining aggression, or transgression, in terms of some critical degree or amount that will be deemed intolerable. When the act to be deterred is inherently a sequence of steps whose cumulative effect is what matters, a threat geared to the increments may be more credible than one that must be carried out either all at once or not at all when some particular point has been reached. It may even be impossible to define a "critical point" with sufficient clarity to be persuasive.

To make the threatened acts divisible, the acts themselves may have to be modified. Parts of an act that cannot be decomposed may have to be left out; ancillary acts that go with the event, though of no interest in themselves, may be objects to which a threat can effectively be attached. For example, actions that are only preparatory to the main act, and by themselves do no damage, may be susceptible of chronological division and thus be effective objects of the threat. The man who would kick a dog should be threatened with modest punishment for each step toward the dog, even though his proximity is of no interest in itself.

Similar to decomposing a threat into a series is starting a threat with a punitive act that grows in severity with the passage of time. Where a threat of death by violence might not be credited, cutting off the food supply might bring submission. For moral or public relations purposes, this device may in fact leave the "last clear chance" to the other, whose demise is then blamed on his stubbornness if the threat fails. But in any case the threatener gets his overt act out of the way while it is still preliminary and minor, rather than letting it stand as a final, dreadful, and visible obstacle to his resolution. And if the suffering party is the only one in a position to know, from moment to moment, how near to catastrophe they have progressed, his is the last clear chance in a real sense. Furthermore, the threatener may be embarrassed by his adversary's collapse but not by his discomfort; and the device may therefore transform a dangerous once-for-all threat into a less costly continuous one. Tenants are less easily removed by threat of forcible eviction than by simply shutting off the utilities.

A piecemeal approach may also be used by the threatened person. If he cannot obviate the threat by hastening the entire act, he may hasten some initial stage that clearly commits him to eventual completion. Or, if his act is divisible while the threatener's retaliation comes only in the large economy size, performing it as a series of increments may deny the threatener the dramatic overt act that would trigger his response.

THE PROMISE

Among the legal privileges of corporations, two that are mentioned in textbooks are the right to sue and the "right" to be sued. Who wants to be sued! But the right to be sued is the power to make a promise: to borrow money, to enter a contract, to do business with someone who might be damaged. If suit does arise, the "right" seems a liability in retrospect; beforehand it was a prerequisite to doing business.

In brief, the right to be sued is the power to accept a commitment. In the commitments discussed up to this point, it was essential that one's adversary (or "partner," however we wish to describe him) not have the power to release one from the commitment; the commitment was, in effect, to some third party, real or fictitious. The promise is a commitment to the second party in the bargain and is required whenever the final action of one or of each is outside the other's control. It is required whenever an agreement leaves any incentive to cheat.

This need for promises is more than incidental; it has an institutional importance of its own. It is not always easy to make a convincing, self-binding, promise. Both the kidnapper who would like to release his prisoner, and the prisoner, may search desperately for a way to commit the latter against informing on his captor, without finding one. If the victim has committed an act whose disclosure could lead to blackmail, he may confess it; if not, he might commit one in the presence of his captor, to create the bond that will ensure his silence. But these extreme possibilities illustrate how difficult, as well as important, it may be to assume a promise. If the law will not enforce price agreements; or if the union is unable to obligate itself to a no-strike pledge; or if a contractor has no assets to pay damages if he loses a suit, and the law will not imprison debtors; or if there is no "audience" to which one can pledge his reputation; it may not be possible to strike a bargain, or at least the same bargain that would otherwise be struck.

Bargaining may have to concern itself with an "incentive" system as well as the division of gains. Oligopolists may lobby for a "fair-trade" law; or exchange shares of stocks. An agreement to stay out of each other's market may require an agreement to redesign the products to be unsuitable in each other's area. Two countries that wish to agree not to make military use of an island may have to destroy the usefulness of the island itself. (In effect, a "third-party commitment" has to be assumed when an effective "second-party commitment" cannot be devised.)

Fulfillment is not always observable. If one sells his vote in a secret election, or a government agrees to recommend an act to its parliament, or an employee agrees not to steal from inventory, or a teacher agrees to keep his political opinions out of class, or a country agrees to stimulate exports "as much as possible," there is no reliable way to observe or measure compliance. The observable outcome is subject to a number of influences, only one of which is covered by the agreement. The bargain may therefore have to be expressed in terms of something observable, even though what is observable is not the intended object of the bargain. One may have to pay the bribed voter if the election is won, not on how he voted; to pay a salesman a commission on sales, rather than on skill and effort; to reward policemen according to statistics on crime rather than on attention to duty; or to punish all employees for the transgressions of one. And, where performance is a matter of degree, the bargain may have to define arbitrary limits distinguishing performance from nonperformance; a specified loss of inventory treated as evidence of theft; a specified increase in exports considered an "adequate" effort; specified samples of performance taken as representative of total performance.

The tactic of decomposition applies to promises as well as to threats. What makes many agreements enforceable is only the recognition of future opportunities for agreement that will be eliminated if mutual trust is not created and maintained, and whose value outweighs the momentary gain from cheating in the present instance. Each party must be confident that the other will not jeopardize future opportunities by destroying trust at the outset. This confidence does not always exist; and one of the purposes of piecemeal bargains is to cultivate the necessary mutual expectations. Neither may be willing to trust the other's prudence (or the other's confidence in the first's prudence, and so forth) on a large issue. But, if a number of preparatory bargains can be struck on a small scale, each may be willing to risk a small investment to create a tradition of trust. The purpose is to let each party demonstrate that he appreciates the need for trust and that he knows the other does too. So, if a major issue has to be negotiated, it may be necessary to seek out and negotiate some minor items for "practice," to establish the necessary confidence in each other's awareness of the long-term value of good faith.

Even if the future will bring no recurrence, it may be possible to create the equivalence of continuity by dividing the bargaining issue into consecutive parts. If each party agrees to send a million dollars to the Red Cross on condition the other does, each may be tempted to cheat if the other contributes first, and each one's anticipation of the other's cheating will inhibit agreement. But if the contribution is divided into consecutive small contributions, each can try the other's good faith for a small price. Furthermore, since each can keep the other on short tether to the finish, no one ever need risk more than one small contribution at a time. Finally, this change in the incentive structure itself takes most of the risk out of the initial contribution; the value of established trust is made obviously visible to both.

Preparatory bargains serve another purpose. Bargaining can only occur when at least one party takes initiative in proposing a bargain. A deterrent to initiative is the information it yields, or may seem to yield, about one's eagerness. But if each has visible reason to expect the other to meet him half way, because of a history of successful bargaining, that very history provides protection against the inference of overeagerness.

COMMENT

Professor Schelling's essay is particularly valuable for the insights it develops concerning the importance of commitment in bargaining and the techniques by which it may be established. It also develops with illustrations not reproduced here the manner in which bargaining may be affected when each of two persons has a pair of alternatives from which to choose.

A few other negotiation tactics deserve discussion. It is not recommended that all the tactics discussed below be used. Some have an almost universal application; others may be useful for particular occasions; and still others should be identified primarily for the purpose of detection and avoidance.

B. Ascertaining the Other Party's Limits

In every negotiation it is desirable to learn what are the expectations, priorities, and limits which a bargaining opposite has established, and to do so without revealing one's own expectations, priorities, and limits. Such information is desirable because it permits one to make proposals close to the lower limits of acceptability to the bargaining opposite and then slide into the area of acceptability at minimum cost. A negotiator may learn that a particular matter is of great concern to the bargaining opposite, though of little value to the negotiator. He may then grant this opposite what is desired, obtaining bargaining leverage he might have given away if he had not discovered the priority assigned the matter by his opposite.

Some devices, such as the bland assertion, "You're the one trying to make the sale," or "I thought you came here to buy it," may put sufficient pressure on the bargaining opposite to reveal some of his bargaining structure. In dispute settlement, defendants frequently put the obligation of speaking first on plaintiffs by pointing out that they started the law suit and should know what they expect to obtain. In collective bargaining negotiations, management may suggest that it is the union and not management which is seeking a change in terms and conditions of employment. Ingenuity may suggest for various situations other reasons why it is "natural" to expect the other party to make the first disclosures. Thus if the subject of negotiation is multifaceted, one may make the first offer on one topic and then request the bargaining opposite to state terms for another, and perhaps more important, topic.

One may, of course, learn about the bargaining opposite's values and techniques by discussing matters with others with whom he has dealt. Upon occasion public records, such as the registry of deeds, may reveal through the tax stamps the prices paid and the system of financing used, including perhaps even the interest rate agreed upon in earlier comparable transactions. In dispute settlement, the opposing lawyer's reputation and record in litigation should be ascertainable.

A technique which may produce information for the occasion, but does little to enhance one's reputation, is the use of the negotiator without authority. Such a negotiator completely involves the bargaining opposite and negotiates to what would otherwise be a final agreement. Then, regretting his lack of authority, he reports to his principal for further instructions. The principal then decides whether to proceed with further negotiations through his negotiator or to take over negotiations personally.

C. THE FIRST REALISTIC OFFER

Obviously, if negotiations are to proceed one of the parties will have to make the first realistic offer. As Hermann and others have suggested, in dispute settlement it is probably best that the first offer one makes be a realistic offer. It is only a realistic offer that can create the uncertainty which induces the opposing side to accept it rather than face the possibility of a less desirable result in litigation. The first realistic offer establishes for the other side one of the offeror's limits, and thus gives credibility to a subsequent statement that there will be no further concessions. Such credibility may be lacking if there has been a series of steadily improving offers moving from the unrealistic into the realistic area without clear demarcation. Moreover, if one is dealing with a sophisticated bargaining opposite, a first offer which is realistic can produce professional respect that is advantageous for the remainder of the negotiation.

For similar reasons, a first offer which is realistic is probably to be desired in business transactions. The unrealistic offer may only convince the bargaining opposite that he is dealing with a neophyte, upon whom it is useless to spend more time. And the lack of procedures comparable to those available in litigation to educate the bargaining opposite in a business transaction makes it worthwhile to convince him that he is dealing with someone with whom it is desirable to do business.

D. AGENDA CONTROL AND THE FIRST DRAFT

What makes a good collective bargaining settlement depends upon what is in the total package rather than upon any single item. Thus a union may be willing to accept a lower wage increase if the contract contains provision for cost-of-living increases, improved health and welfare provisions, and a better retirement scheme. The same is true of many other agreements. Whether the price is acceptable may depend upon the period of time for payment and the rate of interest as well as the dollar figure. Agreements concerning future competition or employment of the seller may do much to make the sale of a business acceptable.

The reaching of agreement on the agenda of items to be negotiated is one of the most important stages of a negotiation. For example, an agenda which does not include improvements in pension or vacation benefits has already produced a substantial concession for the employer. If one of the parties is able to draw up the agenda of items to be discussed in negotiations he can be sure that all those items he desires have been included and many of those which his bargaining opposite might desire have been excluded. Of course, agenda control works only if it is thoroughly understood that additional items may not be added once negotiations on an accepted agenda have begun. This appears to be a rather pervasive ethic in established negotiation relationships.

One of the simplest ways to achieve agenda control is by presenting the first draft of an agreement. The bargaining agenda is usually set by the initial demand and the counterproposal. The person who elicits a response to his first draft may thus establish an agenda that is more favorable to him than one established explicitly by discussion of what the agenda should include. The real estate broker or the apartment house manager regularly practices agenda control through the use of printed forms which leave only a few items for negotiation. The typewritten first draft will probably receive closer scrutiny than most printed forms, but, if discussions can be made to center on it, the party offering it has succeeded in placing upon the other the burden of explaining why a new item should be added to the package under consideration. He has also placed upon the other the burden of explaining why any departure from the proposed language should be made, and each such departure is an obligation-inducing event justifying the proposer's demands in another area. Mutual agreement upon language drafted together would not produce such a feeling of obligation.

E. Agreement Upon Fundamentals

There is a much greater chance of success in business negotiations, whether a single-phase transaction or that of establishing an on-going relationship, if such an understanding can be reached upon the fundamentals of the transaction that each party can see and anticipate the benefits which will be derived from reaching complete agreement. If such an understanding is created, there will be an affirmative desire on both sides to work out solutions to less significant matters upon which there is a real difference in positions. Preliminary disagreements about minor or less important matters may create antagonisms or dislikes which interfere with the process of reaching agreement upon fundamental matters. Thus, one undertaking negotiations should know what he and his clients consider to be the matters of fundamental importance, and he should attempt to establish what matters the bargaining opposite considers important. Lawyers in particular need to guard against becoming prematurely involved in minutiae.

F. Recognizing the Bargaining Opposite's Concerns

Just as the negotiator must tend to his relationship with the person whom he represents, he should be aware of the bargaining opposite's problems in his relationship with those whom he represents. Thus, one should not challenge the expertise of his bargaining opposite, particularly in the presence of the opposing client. For example, in dispute settlement it is generally desirable to avoid an unqualified statement in the presence of the clients that the law is other than what the opposing attorney has just stated it to be. The response to such a challenge to professional qualifications may be a determination to prove the correctness of the statement through litigation; it is most unlikely to produce acknowledgment that he incorrectly stated the law. Whenever a negotiation confrontation appears to be building, a negotiator usually should be as attentive to preparing the escape route for his bargaining opposite as he is to mobilizing his attack forces.

The process of sublimation—the subconscious redirection of a drive or impulse from its original goal to one more socially acceptable or realistically attainable—is a well-known physic defense to a challenge to the ego. The negotiator who is determined to deny access to the original goal on the terms stated by a bargaining opposite should be alert to the possibility of suggesting an alternative goal which may be acceptable as a substitute. A trust fund for the education of children may be substituted for a desire for larger alimony payments; rental of a different building may be suggested in lieu of the originally desired location in a shopping center; the prospective purchaser who cannot afford waterfront property may accept a somewhat larger lot with beach rights at the community club.

Just as the negotiator may have difficulty convincing his client that his goals are unrealistic, he should be aware of the possibility that his bargaining opposite is experiencing similar difficulties. Possibly he can provide the bargaining opposite with materials, exhibits, or studies which the bargaining opposite will put to use in solving his problems with his client. Manifestations of respect and admiration for the bargaining opposite before his client may also assist him in dealing with the problem.

As mentioned above, concern for the physical welfare and comfort of a bargaining opposite has an obligation-inducing effect which may be put to advantage. Serious ethical problems may arise, however, when one attempts to deal with the personal concerns of the negotiator as opposed to concerns of the party he represents. Perhaps one is not troubled by proposing a settlement to an insurance adjuster near the end of the insurance company's operating year, relying upon the adjuster's desire to have a small number of unsettled claims and reduced reserves for liability at the time the statistics are compiled. Most certainly there is an ethical problem in a personal injury case in proposing a settlement to the plaintiff's attorney at the time when his quarterly income tax installment is due in the hope that his need for money will induce him to recommend to his client a settlement which he would otherwise consider inadequate.

G. Involving Other Parties

When the negotiation process appears to have come to a standstill, new movement may be brought about if it is possible to involve new parties. The case history of the Estate of Abigail Schnure, *supra* p. 25, is one in which the parties contesting the will broke from a course headed toward litigation by involving the representatives of the charity which was the beneficiary of the will. A subcontractor experiencing difficulties with a contractor may be able to find a solution to their problems if he involves the owner for whom the work is being performed. The defendant manufacturer in a products liability case may be able to produce a change in the bargaining structure by involving the retailer through whom the product was sold or the subcontractor who furnished a part. The bargaining potential of the situation is changed not only because of the introduction of new interests but also because new personalities may facilitate the negotiation process.

H. False Demands

Occasionally a negotiator will include in his opening statement a false demand—that is, a demand for an item which he really does not desire but which he presents for the purpose of being able to abandon it later in return for a concession which he really does desire. The gain in bargaining power from a successful assertion of a false demand is obvious. There is, however, a substantial danger in making false demands. The first is that the demand must be credible to be effective; one lacking credibility may set the negotiation process off to a start laden with suspicion. It is possible that the bargaining opposite will promptly agree to the false demand, thus imposing a sense of obligation to make a concession in return or to disclose the falseness of the original statement. Even if one decides against the use of false demands himself, he must be alert to the possibility that such a demand has been presented to him.

I. Threats, Bluff, and Irrationality

The use of threats in the bargaining process is limited to those situations in which the action threatened produces a leverage moving the other party toward agreement. They are situations in which pressures rather than persuasion or attractiveness are the primary forces producing agreement. Thus, threats made by a potential tenant may serve only to convince a landlord that he will be better off not to lease property to that tenant. Threats of strike by a union have a different power, as do threats of lockout or willingness to accept a strike.

The use of threats is complicated by the difficulty of convincing the bargaining opposite that one is not engaged merely in bluffing. As Schelling pointed out in his essay bargaining, *supra,* bargaining power can be gained if one has the power to bind oneself irrevocably. One cannot very well make Schelling's hypothetically enforceable agreement to forfeit a substantial sum of money if he changes position, and thus a negotiator must rely on other methods of communicating this firm resolve. As the note on the *General Electric* case suggested, the publicity which the employer gave to its position reinforced its statements that what was offered was "right" and would not be changed. The embarrassment which a change would entail served as a guarantee that General Electric meant what it said. One who develops a reputation of carrying through on threats will thereby gain credibility.

As poker players well know, an occasional well-performed bluff will do much to produce a winning record. The bluff is effective only if it is credible, and what is credible depends very much upon the particular circumstances. As in poker, the information available to the parties must be consistent with the possibility that the party bluffing is in a position to carry through and do that which he asserts he will do. The bluff which threatens conduct which is irrational on the information available will probably not succeed unless the person bluffing has persuaded the bargaining opposite that he does in fact have an irrational emotional commitment to his stated objective or the stated mode of obtaining it.

J. Publicity

As the case histories and materials have indicated, publicity, or the threat of publicity, may be a potent factor either in producing agreement or in preventing agreement. Which of these effects it will have depends upon the particular bargaining situation. It is not a factor to be ignored.

K. Good Guy–Bad Guy

The classic use of the good guy–bad guy routine is found in the performance of the salesman and sales manager on a used car lot. The "good guy" salesman undertakes to obtain price reductions and other concessions on a model chosen by his customer. The "bad guy" sales manager initially rejects all such suggestions, but finally strikes some sort of compromise with the "good guy." The customer accepts the terms of the compromise, grateful for the effective representation he has received from the "good guy." In fact, of course, the terms agreed upon are less advantageous than those which the customer might have arranged if he had not been misled into thinking that his interests were being protected.

The same technique may be used in other bargaining situations, though perhaps not so crudely. The vice-president in charge of production or the sales manager may be the good guy in negotiating a substantial production contract, and the treasurer and cost accountant may be the bad guys who insist upon oppressive terms. Perhaps the president then becomes the arbitrator of what appears to have been an internal dispute, and comes up with what are presented as the obvious fair terms for the contract.

Even if one does not believe that the bargaining opposite is attempting to utilize this old technique, the negotiator must guard against having his appraisal of the stance of negotiations controlled by what he observes of apparent disagreements between the persons on the other negotiating team.

L. Sleepers, Unexplained Provisions, and Mistakes

One way to obtain agreement—though not one recommended—is to use a standard form without undertaking to explain the significance of its various provisions to one who is not familiar with them. Indeed, the technique may be used even with typewritten proposals which the negotiator does not discuss or explain because he "assumes" their significance or effect is apparent. With a stretch of ethics to the breaking point, he may likewise use language or figures which he is prepared to explain apologetically were inserted by his secretary by mistake. Or perhaps his explanation may be that he is unfamiliar with the subject and relied upon the expertise of the person with whom he dealt to protect them both. Probably one who identifies the use of these techniques by the opposing party in negotiations would be well advised to break off negoiations. In any event, a negotiator must not be taken in by them.

NOTE

Bargaining tactics are subject to an excellent treatment, both analytical and illustrative, in Karrass, THE NEGOTIATING GAME (1970); Nierenberg, CREATIVE BUSINESS NEGOTIATING (1971); Nierenberg, THE ART OF NEGOTIATING (1968); Nierenberg, FUNDAMENTALS OF NEGOTIATING (1973); Stevens, STRATEGY AND COLLECTIVE BARGAINING NEGOTIATION (1963); J. Rubin and B. Brown, THE SOCIAL PSYCHOLOGY OF BARGAINING AND NEGOTIATION (1975); and H. Edwards and J. White, THE LAWYER AS A NEGOTIATOR 7-141 (1977).

Table of Cases

Cases presented in text or partial text are in italic type. Other cases—those discussed or merely cited—are in roman type. References are to pages.

Topical Index

263